Martin J. Kerney, Sisters of Mercy

A Catechism of Scripture History

Martin J. Kerney, Sisters of Mercy
A Catechism of Scripture History
ISBN/EAN: 9783337335533

Printed in Europe, USA, Canada, Australia, Japan

Cover: Foto ©Lupo / pixelio.de

More available books at **www.hansebooks.com**

A CATECHISM
OF
Scripture History,

COMPILED BY THE
SISTERS OF MERCY,
For the Use of Children attending their Schools

REVISED
BY M. J. KERNEY,
Author of Compendiums of Ancient and Modern History; First Class Book of History; Columbian Arithmetic, &c. &c.

18th *American from the last London Edition.*

BALTIMORE:
PUBLISHED BY JOHN MURPHY & CO.
182 BALTIMORE STREET,
PITTSBURG...GEORGE QUIGLEY.
Sold by Booksellers generally.
1867.

ENTERED, according to the Act of Congress, in the year eighteen hundred and fifty-four, by JOHN MURPHY & Co. in the Clerk's Office of the District Court of Maryland.

PREFACE.

The object of the following Catechism is to render children early acquainted with the truthful and interesting events recorded in the Sacred Scriptures; to familiarize them with the prophecies relating to the coming of the Messiah, and lead them to regard the Old Testament as a figure and a foreshadowing of the New.

In its style and arrangement, it is happily adapted to that class of learners for which it was designed. It was originally compiled for the use of the pupils attending the schools of the Sisters of Mercy, in the city of Limerick, Ireland. The first edition was published under the supervision of the Rev. Dr. O'Reilly, of Maynooth, and shortly after its appearance, it acquired an extensive circulation among the Catholic schools of England and Ireland. Its merits soon extended to this country, and in a short time it became extensively used in our Catholic institutions. Heretofore, however, our schools have been supplied from the English press, but in order to meet the increasing demand for the work, the publishers have deemed it expedient to issue an American edition.

Advantage has been taken of the present favorable opportunity, of having the work carefully revised and improved. Experience had shown that the *answers* were generally much too long for a work in the catechetical form, and consequently the task of committing them to memory was rendered unnecessarily difficult. To obviate this objection many of the answers have been divided and sub-divided by the introduction of additional questions, thus rendering the labor of preparing the lessons, much more easy for the pupil.

An Appendix has been added to the present edition, containing extracts from the Prophets, Scripture Texts, and short sketches of the lives of the Apostles and Evangelists. The Chronological Table, which has been carefully revised and considerably enlarged, fixes the dates of the most remarkable events recorded in the Sacred Writings.

These improvements, it is hoped, will add much to the merits of the work, and render the present edition still more valuable than those which have preceded it.

BALTIMORE, *July*, 1854.

TABLE OF CONTENTS.

CHAPTER.		Page.
I.	The Creation,	13
II.	Our first Parents in the Garden of Paradise,	14
III.	The Redeemer promised,	15
IV.	The Deluge—Noah and his family saved,	17
V.	Noah's Sacrifice,	19
VI.	The Tower of Babel,	20
VII.	History of Abraham to the Birth of Isaac,	22
VIII.	From the Birth of Isaac to the death of Abraham,	27
IX.	History of Jacob and Esau to the death of Isaac,	30
X.	History of Job,	34
XI.	Joseph sold by his brethren,	37
XII.	Joseph governor of Egypt,	39
XIII.	Jacob's Journey into Egypt and death of Joseph,	42
XIV.	Preservation of Moses,	44
XV.	The Burning Bush,	46
XVI.	The plagues of Egypt,	48
XVII.	The Paschal Lamb,	51
XVIII.	The crossing of the Red Sea,	52
XIX.	The Manna,	54
XX.	Water issues from the Rock,	57
XXI.	The Law given on Mount Sinai,	58
XXII.	The Tabernacle and the Ark of the Covenant,	61
XXIII.	Vestments of the priests, and the priestly office,	64
XXIV.	The order of encampment: the twelve spies,	65
XXV.	The priesthood confirmed to Aaron,	67
XXVI.	The Brazen Serpent.—Balaam the Soothsayer,	69
XXVII.	Josue appointed to succeed Moses.—Death of Moses,	72
XXVIII.	The crossing of the Jordan,	74
XXIX.	The taking of Jericho and Hai,	75
XXX.	The conquests of Josue—Division of the land among the tribes—Death of Josue,	77
XXXI.	History of the Judges, from Josue to Gedeon,	80
XXXII.	History of Gedeon and of Abimelech,	82
XXXIII.	History of the Judges from Thola to Samson,	85
XXXIV.	History of Ruth,	88
XXXV.	History of Heli and Samuel,	90
XXXVI.	Saul anointed King of Israel,	94
XXXVII.	Saul's conquests—Jonathan distinguishes himself,	96
XXXVIII.	David anointed King—his victory over Goliah,	98
XXXIX.	Saul's Jealousy—Death of Samuel,	100
XL.	Flight of David—Death of Saul,	104
XLI.	David acknowledged King,	105
XLII.	David's piety—His fall and repentance,	107

CHAPTER.		Page
XLIII.	David causes Solomon to be proclaimed King—His last instructions and death,	110
XLIV.	Solomon's Wisdom,	113
XLV.	The building of the Temple,	115
XLVI.	The dedication of the Temple—Death of Solomon,	118
XLVII.	Kings of Juda—Roboam, Abia, Asa,	120
XLVIII.	Contemporary Kings of Israel,	123
XLIX.	Kings of Juda, Josophat, Joram, Ochozias, and Joas,	125
L.	Contemporary Kings of Israel,	127
LI.	The Prophets—Elias,	128
LII.	Eliseus,	131
LIII.	Kings of Juda, Amasias and Azarias,	134
LIV.	Contemporary Kings of Israel,	135
LV.	The Prophet Jonas,	136
LVI.	Kings of Juda—Joathan, Achaz, Ezechias,	137
LVII.	Contemporary Kings of Israel to the Assyrian Captivity,	138
LVIII.	Prophets,	140
LIX.	History of Tobias—his virtues and afflictions,	141
LX.	The young Tobias is conducted by an angel; his marriage and return to his father,	143
LXI.	Death of Tobias,	145
LXII.	Kings of Juda, after the Assyrian Captivity—Continuation of the reign of Ezechias—Manasses,	147
LXIII.	Manasses,	148
LXIV.	History of Judith—Siege of Bethulia,	148
LXV.	The siege raised by the fortitude of Judith—Death of Holofernes,	151
LXVI.	Kings of Juda, from Manasses to the eleventh year of Sedecias, when the remnant of the people were carried captive to Babylon,	153
LXVII.	The Prophet Jeremiah,	156
LXVIII.	The Prophet Ezechiel,	157
LXIX.	The Prophet Daniel in the Court of Nebuchodonosor,	159
LXX.	Preservation of the Hebrews when cast into the fiery furnace,	161
LXXI.	Bel and the Dragon,	162
LXXII.	Baltassar's Feast,	165
LXXIII.	Prophecies of the capture of Babylon,	167
LXXIV.	Daniel in the Lion's Den,	169
LXXV.	Temple of Jerusalem rebuilt,	170
LXXVI.	History of Esther,	172
LXXVII.	Edict of Artaxerxes to rebuild the walls of Jerusalem—Nehemias appointed governor,	177
LXXVIII.	Civil disturbance—Foreign invasion,	179
LXXIX.	Martyrdom of Eleazer and of the Seven Machabees,	183

CHAPTER.	Page.
LXXX. History of the Asamonean family—Mathathias,	185
LXXXI. Mathathias is succeed in the government by his son Judas Machabeus,	188
LXXXII. Judas Machabeus succeeded by his brothers Jonathan and Simon,	191
LXXXIII. Simon succeeded by his son John Hyrcanus—Conclusion of the History,	194

CONTENTS OF NEW TESTAMENT.

CHAPTER.	Page.
I. The Incarnation of our Divine Lord—Visit of the Blessed Virgin to St. Elizabeth,	196
II. The birth of St. John the Baptist,	199
III. The birth of our Divine Lord,	200
IV. Our Saviour's birth made known to the Gentiles by a star,	203
V. The Purification of the Blessed Virgin, and the Preservation of our Divine Lord,	204
VI. The Massacre of the Holy Innocents—Flight of our Divine Lord into Egypt, and his return,	206
VII. The Baptism of our Divine Lord—The preaching and martyrdom of St. John the Baptist,	207
VIII. Our Divine Lord's Fast and Temptation in the Desert—The opening of his Mission,	211
IX. The call of the Apostles, and Christ's Miracle,	212
X. The Centurion's servant—The widow's son of Naim,	215
XI. Sermon on the Mount,	216
XII. On Prayer,	218
XIII. On perseverance in Prayer,	220
XIV. Our Lord instructs his Apostles—He casts the buyers and sellers out of the Temple,	223
XV. Christ instructs the Samaritan woman—He heals the Ruler's son,	225
XVI. Miracle at the pond of Probatica, and cure of the man blind from his birth,	228
XVII. Miracle performed on the woman who had been sick eighteen years—Cure of the man afflicted with dropsy,	230
XVIII. Parables of the Sower and of the Cockle,	232
XIX. The storm at sea,	234
XX. The daughter of Jairus raised to life,	235
XXI. Multiplication of the loaves and fishes—St. Peter upon the waters,	237
XXII. St. Peter's confession of Christ—Transfiguration of our Lord,	238
XXIII. Instructions on zeal, humility, and on the necessity of giving good example,	240
XXIV. On fraternal correction and forgiveness of injuries	242

CONTENTS.

CHAPTER.		Page
XXV.	On charity, and on the evil of setting the heart on riches,	244
XXVI.	Parable of the rich man and Lazarus,	246
XXVII.	Parable of the barren fig tree, and of the Laborers in the Vineyard,	247
XXVIII.	Parable of the Vineyard let out to Husbandmen,	249
XXIX.	Parable of the Marriage Feast and of the Ten Virgins,	251
XXX.	Parable of the lost sheep, and of the Prodigal Son,	253
XXXI.	Parable of the Ten Talents,	255
XXXII.	Miraculous cure of the ten lepers—Lazarus raised to life,	257
XXXIII.	St. Mary Magdalen's forgiveness pronounced by our Lord,	261
XXXIV.	On the signs that are to precede the end of the world,	264
XXXV.	Our Lord foretells his approaching Passion—His reply when called on for a sign similar to the Manna,	265
XXXVI.	Our Lord directs his Apostles to prepare the Pasch—He institutes the Blessed Sacrament,	268
XXXVII.	Our Lord's agony in the Garden—The treachery of Judas—St. Peter's denial,	271
XXXVIII.	Christ before the High Priest and Council—The despair of Judas,	274
XXXIX.	Christ is delivered to Pilate, who condemns him to be crucified,	275
XL.	Christ's last words and death,	277
XLI.	Our Lord's Burial and Resurrection,	280
XLII.	Apparition of our Divine Lord to St. Mary Magdalen and his Apostles on the day of his Resurrection,	282
XLIII.	Other Apparitions of our Divine Lord—He gives charge of the flock to St. Peter—His Ascension into Heaven,	285
XLIV.	Short account of the Books of Holy Scripture,	288
XLV.	The Descent of the Holy Ghost,	290
XLVI.	Manners of the first Christians, and miracles performed by the Apostles,	291
XLVII.	Martyrdom of St. Stephen—Ordination of the Seven Deacons—Mission of St. Philip,	294
XLVIII.	Conversion of St. Paul—Baptism of Cornelius,	296
XLIX.	Miraculous deliverance of St. Peter from prison—Preaching of St. Paul,	298
L.	Council at Jerusalem—Travels and labors of St. Paul,	301
LI.	St. Paul's return to Jerusalem—His persecution by the Jews—He appeals to Cæsar, and is sent to Rome,	303

CHAPTER.	Page.
LII. St. Paul's Epistles to the Romans, Corinthians, and Galatians,	306
LIII. St. Paul's Epistles to the Ephesians, Philippians, Colossians, and Thessalonians,	310
LIV. St. Paul's Epistles to Timothy, Titus, Philemon, and the Hebrews,	312
LV. Epistle of St. James,	313
LVI. St. Peter's two Epistles,	314
LVII. St. John's three Epistles—Epistle of St. Jude—Apocalypse,	315
Appendix—Extracts from the Prophets,	317
Scripture Texts,	332
Short sketches of the Lives of the Apostles and Evangelists, taken from Ecclesiastical History,	336
Chronological Table of the Principal Events in Sacred History,	342

Catechism of Scripture History.

FIRST AGE OF THE WORLD.

From the Creation to the Deluge, A. M. 1 to 1656.

CHAPTER I.

THE CREATION.

What do you know of the history of the creation?
From the Sacred Scriptures we learn that, God created heaven and earth; the earth was void and empty, and darkness was on the face of the deep; and the Spirit of God said: "Be light made," and light was made; and he divided the light from the darkness and called the light day, and the darkness night.

On the second day what did God do?
On the second day God made the firmament and called it heaven, dividing the waters that were under it from those that were above it.

What did God do on the third day?
On the third day God commanded the waters on the earth to be gathered together, and to let the dry land appear: the gathering together of the waters he called seas, the earth he commanded to bring forth fruit trees and herbs.

On the fourth and fifth day what did God do?
On the fourth day God made lights in the firmament of heaven; a greater light to rule the day and a lesser light to rule the night; and the stars. On the fifth day God created the fish of the sea and the fowls of the air.

On the sixth and seventh day what did he do?
On the sixth day God created beasts, cattle and creeping things; and last of all man, to whom he gave dominion over the earth and all it contained. The seventh day God blessed and sanctified, for on it he rested from all his work.

Of what did God make man?
He made his body of the slime of the earth, and his soul, which he breathed into him, he created out of nothing.

To whose image did God make man?
To his own image. "To the image of God he created him." (Gen. i. 27.)

In what is man like to God?
In his soul.

In what is the soul like to God?
In being a spirit and immortal, and in being capable of knowing and loving God.

Why did God give us souls capable of knowing and loving him?
That we might attain the end for which he made us, that is, to know and serve him here on earth, and hereafter to see and enjoy him for ever in heaven.

CHAPTER II.

OUR FIRST PARENTS IN THE GARDEN OF PARADISE.

What was the name of the first man?
Adam.

Where did God place Adam?
In the garden of Paradise.

What was the name of the first woman?
Eve.

Of what did God make Eve?
Of one of the ribs of Adam, which he took from him whilst he slept.

Where is it supposed that the Garden of Eden was situated?
In Asia, between the rivers Euphrates and Tigris.
Who gave names to all animals on earth?
Adam, before whom God caused them all to pass in review.
What command did God give to Adam on placing him in Paradise?
That he should not eat the fruit of the tree of the knowledge of good and evil under penalty of death.
Why was that command given?
To make Adam, though vested with authority over the earth, sensible of God's supreme dominion over him, and of his dependence on God, and as a trial of obedience.
Did our first parents disobey the command of God?
Yes, Eve weakly yielded to the temptation of the devil, who in the form of a serpent persuaded her that God would not put his threat in execution, and that by eating the forbidden fruit she would become more wise, on which "She did eat, and gave to Adam, and he also did eat." (Gen. ii. 6.)
What is this sin of our first parents called?
Original sin; this we inherit from them, and every one coming into the world is infected with it.
What punishment did God inflict on them?
He drove them out of Paradise, stripped them of original justice, and condemned them to death with their posterity.

CHAPTER III.

THE REDEEMER PROMISED

Did God give Adam and Eve any consolation in their affliction?
Yes, in the promise of a Redeemer to come

When was that promise fulfilled?
About 4,000 years afterwards.

What was the name of the first son of Adam and Eve?
Cain, who was the first murderer, having killed his brother Abel.

Why did he commit so great a crime?
Through envy and jealousy on account of his brother's superior piety and merit: and because Abel's offering was more acceptable to God than his own.

What punishment did God inflict on Cain?
He cursed him, and pronounced him a fugitive and vagabond on the face of the earth, which he decreed should not yield Cain fruit on his tilling it.

Where did Cain dwell after his sentence was pronounced?
To the east of Eden, whither he was constrained to fly; where he in some time built a city which he called after his son Enoch.

What was the name of the son whom God gave to Adam and Eve in place of Abel?
Seth, who was born A. M. 130; he was just and like unto Abel.

Did any remarkable person descend from Seth?
Yes, Enoch, a just and holy man, who, at the age of 365 years, was taken from among men without dying, and translated to some place of rest and happiness, whence, as the holy Fathers gather from the Apocalypse, chap. xi., he and Elias will come before the last day to oppose antichrist, and having suffered martyrdom, and been again restored to life, will ascend gloriously into heaven.

Who was Mathusalem?
The son of Enoch, and remarkable for being the oldest man that ever lived, having attained the age of 969 years. He was grandfather to Noah.

How many years from the Creation of the world to the Deluge?
About 1656 years.

Names and ages of the Patriarchs of the first age?

	A. M.		
	BORN.	DIED.	AGED.
Adam,		930	930
Seth,	130	1042	912
Enos,	235	1140	905
Cainan,	325	1235	910
Malaleel,	395	1290	895
Jared,	460	1422	962
Enoch,	622	987	365 translated to heaven
Mathusalem,	687	1656	969
Lamech,	874	1651	777
Noah,	1056	2006	950

SECOND AGE OF THE WORLD.

From the Deluge to the Vocation of Abraham, A. M. 1656 to 2023.

CHAPTER IV

THE DELUGE.—NOAH AND HIS FAMILY SAVED.

What was the Deluge?
A great inundation that covered the whole earth with water to the height of fifteen cubits above the tops of the mountains.

For what reason was the Deluge sent?
In punishment of sin.

How was so great an inundation produced?
The fountains of the deep were broken up, the flood-

gates of heaven opened, and rain fell in torrents for forty successive days and nights.

Were any saved from the Deluge?
Yes, Noah and his wife, his three sons, and their wives; eight persons in all.

Were any animals preserved?
Yes; all kinds of birds, beasts, and creeping things; of birds and clean beasts seven and seven, male and female; of unclean animals two and two; with food suited to each.

How were they preserved?
In the Ark, which Noah built by the command of God.

Describe the Ark?
It was like a great ship, except that instead of a flat deck on the top; it had a sloping roof, which saved it from being sunk by the torrents of rain, and was pitched within and without. It was three hundred cubits long, fifty broad, and thirty high, having lower, middle, and third stories; it had one window and a door, which God secured on the outside as soon as Noah and all with him had entered.

How long was the Ark in being built?
One hundred years.

How old was Noah when he entered the Ark?
Six hundred years.

How long was Noah in the Ark when the waters began to abate?
One hundred and fifty days.

In what month and where did the Ark rest?
In the seventh month, on one of the mountains of Armenia, generally supposed to be Mount Ararat.

In what month did the tops of the mountains appear?
On the first of the tenth month.

How did Noah ascertain that the waters had subsided?

He first sent out a raven, and then a dove: the raven did not return, but the dove finding no place to rest her foot, returned to the Ark. After seven days he sent her out again, and she came to him in the evening, bringing an olive branch with green leaves in her mouth, which he joyfully received as a proof that the waters were dried up.

How long was Noah in the Ark from the time he entered till the time he came out?
About twelve months.

CHAPTER V.

NOAH'S SACRIFICE.

What was Noah's first act on quitting the Ark?
He built an altar and offered up holocausts to God of all cattle and fowl that were clean.

How did God testify his approval of Noah's piety and gratitude?
By promising that he would not again curse the earth or destroy it as he had done.

What sign did God give of his covenant?
The rainbow.

Of what should the rainbow remind us?
Of the infinite mercy and forbearance of God, who, though often outraged, is ever mindful of the covenant he made.

What should we learn from the fate of those who were drowned?
To avoid sin, which was the cause of their punishment; and to lead holy lives, that when death comes we may not be unprepared to meet it.

Of what do the Holy Fathers consider the Ark a figure?
Of the Holy Catholic Church, which, like the Ark has triumphantly risen above floods and storms, and

which carries secure within her pale all people, tribes and tongues.

What change did God make in man's diet after the Deluge?
He permitted the use of animal food, "save flesh with the blood in it."

Name the three sons of Noah?
Sem, Cham, and Japheth.

Why did Noah bless Sem and Japheth, and not Cham?
Because on one occasion Noah having drank wine, of the intoxicating effects of which he appears not to have been aware, was found uncovered by Cham, who, instead of concealing his aged father's weakness, published it to his two brothers; these with more regard for filial piety, immediately threw a cloak over him.

Who was Cham's son?
Canaan, who was cursed by Noah for his father's want of filial respect.

What should children learn from this?
To pay that honor and respect to their parents which God commands, and carefully to avoid exposing them to ridicule or contempt for any private failings they may discover in them.

CHAPTER VI.
THE TOWER OF BABEL.

In what did the descendants of Cham distinguish themselves, when people became numerous after the Deluge?
In building great cities, and establishing themselves in great possessions.

Name their principal possessions?
Babylon and Nineve, both built by Nimrod; the land which was named after Canaan was divided between some of his sons.

Why was the Tower of Babel commenced?
When the people became numerous and were about to disperse, they proposed to build a tower the top of which should reach to heaven, as a lasting monument of their greatness; and it is supposed that they designed it as a place of security from the effects of any future deluge.

Why was the tower called Babel?
Babel signifies confusion; for God, to counteract the project of the builders, confounded their language so that they could not understand each other.

Whom did Almighty God select as his faithful servant, with whom to establish his Covenant?
Abraham, a just and holy man, descended from Sem, and a native of Ur, a city of the Chaldees, where he dwelt until Thare, his father, removed his family to Haran, a city of Mesopotamia, in which place, after a residence of some years, he died; and Abraham, at the age of seventy-five years received a command from God to leave his country, and his father's house, and go to the land which he would show him.

When did Abraham receive this command?
About 367 years after the Deluge.

Names and ages of the Patriarchs of the second age

A. M.

	BORN.	DIED.	AGED.
Sem,	1556	2158	600
Arphaxad,	1658	1996	338
Sale,	1693	2126	433
Heber,	1723	2187	464
Phaleg,	1757	1996	239
Rehu,	1787	2026	239
Sarug,	1819	2049	230
Nachor,	1849	1997	148
Thare,	1878	2083	205

THIRD AGE OF THE WORLD.

From the Vocation of Abraham to the Deliverance of the Jews from Egypt. A. M. 2023 to 2453.

CHAPTER VII.

HISTORY OF ABRAHAM TO THE BIRTH OF ISAAC.

Did Abraham obey the command of God without delay?
Yes, taking Sarah his wife, Lot, his brother's son, and all the substance they had acquired in Haran, he left his father's house, and set out on his journey.

What promise did God make to Abraham when he gave him the above-mentioned command?
"I will make of thee a great nation, and I will bless thee, and magnify thy name, and thou shalt be blessed. I will bless them that bless thee, and curse them that curse thee, and in thee shall all the kindred of the earth be blessed." (Gen. xii. 1, 2, 3.)

How was the latter part of the promise fulfilled?
By the birth of the Redeemer, who was descended from him.

To what country did God direct Abraham's steps?
To the land of Canaan, where at Sichem he appeared to him, and promised the land to his descendants.

When was the promise fulfilled?
About 477 years after, when Josue having conquered it, divided it among the twelve tribes, the descendants of Abraham.

What did Abraham at Sichem?
He built an altar to God, which was his practice wherever he settled; whence we should learn to give the first and principal place in all our actions to God.

Whither did Abraham go from Sichem?
To the east of Bethel, near Hai, where he also built

an altar; and thence continued his journey to the south; but on account of a famine was obliged to go on to Egypt where he encountered many dangers from which he was delivered by God in reward of his faith and obedience.

Where did Abraham dwell when he returned from Egypt?
In the place where he had dwelt before, between Bethel and Hai; and on the site of the altar he had formerly erected, he built another, and called upon the name of the Lord.

Why did Lot separate from Abraham?
Because a contest arose between their herdsmen, the land being too narrow to contain their increased flocks and herds.

Where did Lot choose to dwell?
In Sodom, the plains about which being watered by the Jordan were well calculated for feeding his flocks.

What did God say to Abraham after Lot separated from him?
He renewed the promise that his posterity should be numerous, and desired him to walk through the land, for it should all be his; Abraham accordingly removed and dwelt by the vale of Mambre, in Hebron where he built an altar.

What befel Lot in Sodom?
He was taken prisoner, and his property carried away by the armies of four confederate kings, who made war against the king of Sodom.

How was he restored to liberty?
By Abraham, who being informed of what befel him, armed 318 of his servants, pursued and defeated the enemy, restored Lot to liberty, and recovered all the spoils.

How did the king of Sodom act when Abraham returned after the victory?
He congratulated him, and begged him to accept of

all the property he had recovered, but to give him back the people.

Did Abraham accept the reward?
No, he disinterestedly refused to take anything as a recompense for himself or his servants; but he permitted his confederates Aner, Eschol, and Mambre who accompanied him, to take their shares.

What other distinguished person came to congratulate Abraham on that occasion?
Melchisedech, the king of Salem, "Who brought forth bread and wine, for he was priest of the Most High God and blessed him." (Gen. xiv. 18.)

What did Abraham give to Melchisedech?
The tithes of all.

What did the sacrifice offered by Melchisedech prefigure?
That wonderful sacrifice which Jesus Christ, the priest for ever, according to the order of Melchisedech instituted, and ordained to be offered in his church to the end of time.

What vision had Abraham after the deliverance of Lot?
The Lord renewed his former promise to him, but foretold him that his posterity should be strangers, and in bondage in a land not their own for four hundred years, after which they should come out with great wealth, and possess the land of promise.

Did Abraham believe the Word of God?
Yes, but as the fulfilment of the promise was deferred, Sarah appears to have doubted that she was to be a mother, and therefore desired Abraham to take her Egyptian maid, named Agar, to wife, that she might have the happiness of seeing an heir to their great possessions.

What was the name of Agar's son?
Ismael.

How did Agar act towards Sarah before the birth of Ismael?
Very disrespectfully, of which Sarah complained to Abraham, who desired her to act as she thought best: she punished Agar who ran away, but being admonished by an angel, returned and humbled herself to her mistress.

How long after the birth of Ismael did God more expressly renew his covenant with Abraham?
Thirteen years, when he changed his name from Abram to Abraham; and his wife's from Sarai to Sarah; instituted the right of Circumcision, and promised that Sarah should bring forth a son that time the next year, who should be called Isaac, with whom and his posterity he would establish a perpetual covenant.

Was the promise of Isaac's birth confirmed in any extraordinary manner?
Yes; by the angels who were entertained by Abraham on their way to destroy Sodom.

For what reason were the angels sent to destroy Sodom?
On account of the grievous sins of the inhabitants.

How did Abraham act when he understood that Sodom was to be destroyed?
He humbly begged that the devoted city would be spared for the sake of the just that might be in it; and at length obtained a promise that it would not be destroyed if even ten just could be found; but Sodom had them not.

Were any rescued from Sodom?
Yes; Lot, Abraham's nephew, with his wife and two daughters.

What directions did the angels give Lot and his family when leading them out of Sodom?
To fly to the mountain and not to look back.

Did any of his family disobey the direction?
Yes, his wife, who, on looking behind her, was turned into a statue of salt; her fate should be a warning to all to obey the commands of God, even in the most trifling particulars.

In what manner were Sodom and the adjoining cities destroyed?
By fire and brimstone, which God rained on them, and by which he consumed not only the inhabitants, but the fruits and produce of the land.

What allusion did our Lord make to the destruction of Sodom, when reproaching those cities, in which he performed most of his miracles, for not doing penance?
"If in Tyre and Sidon had been wrought the miracles that have been wrought in you, they had long ago done penance in sackcloth and ashes...... If in Sodom had been wrought the miracles that have been wrought in you, perhaps it had remained unto this day; but I say unto you that it shall be more tolerable for the land of Sodom in the day of judgment than for you." (Mat. xi. 21, 24.)

Whither did Abraham remove soon after the destruction of Sodom?
To Gerara, which is situated between Cades and Sur in the south of Palestine.

What happened on his arrival at Gerara?
Abimilech, the king, admiring Sarah's beauty, and supposing her to be Abraham's sister, for she had concealed the truth lest he might be put to death on her account, proposed marrying her; from this perplexity God delivered them by admonishing Abimilech in a vision, who immediately relinquished his design, made Abraham many rich presents, and formed a league of friendship with him.

How old were Abraham and Sarah when Isaac was born?

Abraham was one hundred, and Sarah ninety, years old.

CHAPTER VIII.

From the Birth of Isaac to the Death of Abraham, A. M. 2048 to 2123.

ABRAHAM ABOUT TO SACRIFICE HIS SON.

What did Sarah require Abraham to do when Isaac was weaned?
To send away Ismael and his mother, as she would not suffer Ismael to be heir with her son Isaac.

How did Abraham act?
Though grieved to part with his son he complied with Sarah's demand, being ordered by God to do so; and sent Agar and Ismael away, giving them some provisions for a journey, and leaving the event to God.

What became of them?
They wandered in the wilderness of Bersabee until the provisions were spent, when Agar, dreading to see her child die, placed him under a tree and retired to a distance; but God sent an angel who comforted her, and showed her a well of water with which she refreshed the boy. They afterwards removed to the wilderness of Pharan; Ismael married an Egyptian and had twelve sons, from whom the wandering Arabs claim descent.

What trial did God make of Abraham's faith when Isaac was grown up?
He desired him to take Isaac and offer him as a holocaust on one of the mountains in the land of vision.

Did Abraham hesitate or remonstrate?
No, the same night in which he received the com-

mand he arose, and taking with him two servants and his son Isaac, he cut wood for the holocaust, and set out on his journey to execute the will of God.

Why is the command that God gave Abraham to sacrifice his son considered a trial of faith?
Because not doubting the promise God had made him, "That in Isaac he should become father of a great nation, he prepared to sacrifice him, accounting that God is able to raise up even from the dead." (Heb. xi. 19.)

What directions did Abraham give his servants when he approached the place appointed by God for the sacrifice?
To remain where they were whilst he and Isaac sacrificed; then laying wood for the holocaust on his son, and, carrying fire and a sword himself, they both proceeded.

Of whom do the holy fathers consider Isaac a figure whilst carrying the wood for the holocaust?
Of our Lord Jesus Christ carrying his cross.

What did Isaac say to his father as they went towards the place appointed for sacrifice?
"Father, behold fire and wood, where is the victim for the holocaust?"

What did Abraham reply?
"God will provide himself a victim for a holocaust, my son."

What did Abraham when he reached the appointed place?
He built an altar, and laid the wood on it, then having bound Isaac he laid him on the altar on the pile of wood, and took the sword in his hand to sacrifice him.

Did he sacrifice him?
No: God by an angel commanded him not to do so, declaring at the same time his approbation of Abra-

ham's readiness to fulfil the command which had been imposed on him as a trial.

What did Abraham offer as a holocaust instead of his son?
A Ram, which he saw behind him, held fast by the horns amongst briars.

What did the angel say after the sacrifice was offered?
He renewed the covenant that God had made with Abraham, and confirmed it with an oath. (Gen. xxii. 16, 18.)

How old was Sarah when she died?
One hundred and twenty-seven years. She died at Hebron, and was buried in a double cave in a field in the vicinity, which Abraham purchased of Ephron, the Hethite, for four hundred sicles of silver.

What commission did Abraham give his principal servant about three years after Sarah's death, when Isaac was forty years of age?
"To go to Haram of Mesopotamia, and choose a wife for Isaac of his own kindred." (Gen. xxiv.)

How did the servant act?
He took ten of his master's camels, and set out on his journey with suitable presents. Drawing near the city, he made the camels lie down near a well, whence the inhabitants used to draw water, and begged that God would give him as a sign by which he might know her whom he designed for Isaac's wife, that she should reply when asked for some water, "Drink, and I will also give drink to the camels."

What happened when he had ended his prayer?
He had scarcely ended his prayer, when Rebecca, grand-daughter to Nachor, Abraham's brother, came to the well to draw water, and on being asked for a drink of water, answered in the way specified by the servant, who presented her with ornaments, and

prostrate before God, thanked him for his infinite goodness.

What followed?
On the invitation of Laban, Rebecca's brother, he went into their house, made known his commission, with the favor God had just done him, and asked Rebecca's father and brother to permit her to accompany him as his master's wife. They replied, that the will of God being manifested they could not act contrary to it, and Rebecca having consented, was married to Isaac.

Did Abraham marry after Sarah's death?
Yes, and had several children, but they had no share in the inheritance with Isaac, for he was the child of promise to whom Abraham gave all his possessions; but to the others he gave gifts before his death, and sent them to the east of the promised land.

How long did Abraham survive Sarah?
Thirty-eight years, having lived to see his twin grand-children, Jacob and Esau, and attained the age of 175 years. His sons, Isaac and Ismael, buried him in the same cave with Sarah.

CHAPTER IX.

HISTORY OF JACOB AND ESAU.

Describe Jacob and Esau?
Jacob was of domestic habits, and his mother's favorite; Esau, was a skilful hunter, and loved by his father. He was remarkable for his skin being red and hairy.

How did Jacob, who was born after Esau, obtain the right of primogeniture?
By means of Esau's gluttony and want of faith, who sold his birthright to Jacob for a mess of pottage, preferring a present gratification to a future reward.

How was the birthright afterwards confirmed to Jacob?
Isaac having desired Esau to procure him meats by hunting, such as he knew he liked, that he might bless him before his death. Rebecca, who had been present, told Jacob what his father said, and when Esau had gone out, she prepared meat such as she knew Isaac liked, dressed Jacob in Esau's clothes, covered his hands and feet with kid skins, (in order to deceive Isaac, who was old and blind,) and desired him to personate his brother. He did so, and had scarcely gone out after having received his father's blessing, when Esau returned.

What did Esau when he discovered that Jacob had supplanted him and got the right of primogeniture confirmed to himself?
He cried aloud in the bitterness of grief, begging his father to bless him also, who, being moved at his son's affliction, blessed him, and though he could not recall the prophetic blessing that established Jacob his superior and lord, yet he foretold him, "that the time would come when he would shake off and loose his yoke from his neck." (Gen. xxvii. 40.)

When was this prophecy fulfilled?
When Herod, the Idumean, ascended the throne of Juda

How did Rebecca act when she perceived Esau' resentment, and understood that he would be revenged of Jacob at his father's death?
With Isaac's concurrence, who renewed his blessing before he set out, she sent him to her brother Laban, in order to give Esau's anger time to abate, and that he might marry one of her own kindred; for Esau had given his father and herself dissatisfaction by marrying women of Canaan.

What vision had Jacob on his journey?
In his sleep he saw a ladder standing on the earth

the top of which reached heaven, with angels ascending and descending by it, and the Lord appeared leaning on the top, who confirmed the covenant made with Abraham and Isaac, and promised to be with him in all his ways.

What did Jacob say when he awoke?
"Indeed, the Lord is in this place, and I knew it not. How terrible is this place, this is no other than the house of God and gate of heaven." (Gen xxviii. 17.) He then vowed to serve God, and to offer him tithes of all that he would bestow on him.

Whom did Jacob marry?
Lia and Rachel, the daughters of Laban.

How did Laban treat him?
At first with kindness, but afterwards harshly and unjustly, obliging him to serve longer than he had agreed for, and endeavoring to cheat him of his wages.

How long did Jacob serve Laban?
Twenty years; fourteen for Lia and Rachel, the remaining six for a portion of the flocks. (Gen. xxxi. 41.)

Why did Jacob leave Laban
Because Laban and his sons envied him on account of the wealth he had acquired; and also because God encouraged him to return to his native country by promising to be with him.

How did Laban act when he discovered that Jacob had left him?
He pursued him, but was warned by God in a vision not even to speak harshly to Jacob; accordingly, when he overtook him he made a friendly treaty with him, and took leave of his daughters and grandchildren.

What means did Jacob adopt to conciliate his brother Esau?
He sent him rich presents, and, when he met him humbled himself before him.

After what manner did Jacob pray when he reached the Jordan?
He humbled himself profoundly, acknowledged his unworthiness of the least of God's mercies, and of the blessings bestowed on him. He called to mind his former crossing of the Jordan when fleeing from his brother he had nothing but his staff, and compared it with his present return, surrounded, as he then was, by two companies, and possessing immense wealth, for which he was indebted to God, and concluded by earnestly praying, that he who desired him to return to his native country, would protect him according to his promise, and deliver him from the effects of his brother's anger.

What occurred to Jacob when all but himself had crossed the Jordan?
An angel wrestled with him, who, not being able to overcome him, touched the sinew of his thigh, which made him lame, but as Jacob refused to let him go until he blessed him, he did so, and changed his name from Jacob to Israel.

How did Esau receive his brother's presents?
He was at first unwilling to accept them, but being overcome by Jacob's importunity, at length kindly did so.

Where did Jacob dwell after his return from Haran?
First at Socoth, then near Salem, and afterwards at Bethel, where he built an altar by the special direction of God, in memory of his appearing to him in that place when he fled from Esau. (Gen. xxxv. i. 7.)

What did Almighty God say to Jacob after he had sacrificed at Bethel?
He blessed him, confirmed the covenant he had made with Abraham and Isaac, and repeated what the angel who wrestled with him had said that he should be called Israel.

Whither did Jacob go after this?
To Bethlehem, where Rachel died and was buried, after having given birth to Benjamin.

What did Jacob after Rachel's death?
He erected a pillar over her tomb, and removed to Mambre, near Hebron, where Isaac, his father, still dwelt.

How many sons had Jacob?
Twelve: Reuben, Simeon, Levi, Juda, Issachor, Zabulon, Dan, Nephtali, Gad, Aser, Joseph, and Benjamin.

How old was Isaac when he died?
One hundred and eighty years. He was buried by his sons, Jacob and Esau, in the family burial-place which Abraham had purchased.

What did Esau after his father's death?
He took his family with all the property he had acquired in the land of Canaan to Seir, the country about which was called after him Idumea or Edom, which signifies red, and was a name given him from the color of the pottage for which he sold his birthright. (Gen. xxv. 30.)

Was Esau prosperous in his undertakings?
Yes, he became very rich and powerful; his sons were styled dukes, and many kings of his race reigned in Edom before there was a king in Israel.

CHAPTER X.

HISTORY OF JOB.

Who was Job?
It is supposed that holy Job, whose invincible patience is proverbial in all nations, was of the race of Esau, and the same with Jobab king of Edom, mentioned by Moses, to whom some ascribe the history of this holy man.

Where did he live and what is said of his charity?

He lived in the land of Hus, was possessed of great wealth, and had seven sons and three daughters. He was charitable to the poor, learned, humble, upright, and pious, and so fearful lest his children should fail in any part of the homage and duty they owed to God, that he every day offered holocausts for each.

Of what did Satan accuse him?
Satan envying his great merit, accused him to God of being faithful to him only on account of the abundant blessings he bestowed on him, and asserted that his fidelity would not be proof against adversity, which he would evince if permitted to tempt him

To what did God consent?
God knowing his servant's fidelity, consented, as far as regarded Job's possessions, but strictly enjoined Satan not to injure his person. Thus restricted, Satan thought, by overwhelming him at once with the loss of all he possessed and held dearest on earth, to surprise him into murmuring against God; but as his piety was not based on the temporal favors he had received, it was not lessened by his being deprived of them.

What did he exclaim, when informed of the misfortunes which had befallen him?
When one messenger after another came breathless to inform him that his camels and oxen were carried away by robbers, his servants slain, his flocks killed by lightning, and all his children crushed by the fall of a house; though he rent his garments and shaved his head, he fell prostrate on the ground, and worshipping God, said, "Naked came I into the world, and naked shall I leave it, the Lord gave and the Lord hath taken away, as it has pleased the Lord, so is it done, blessed be the name of the Lord."

Of what did Satan a second time accuse Job?
When Satan found that he had not prevailed, and

that God regarded Job with increased complacency, he again accused him, representing that it was comparatively easy for him to part with his possessions, but that he would surely rebel if afflicted with sickness.

What did God permit?
God then permitted Satan to afflict his person with the reservation that he should not deprive him of life; for the power of the enemy is not equal to his malice, and extends no farther than God is pleased to permit. Having obtained the desired permission, Satan struck Job with a grievous ulcer from the top of the head to the sole of the foot.

What is now said of him?
Reduced now to the most pitiable state of distress, without possessions, without house, without children, abandoned by his friends, reproached by his wife, he sat on a dung-hill, and through necessity used a potsherd to remove the corrupt matter from the ulcers with which he was covered.

What did he answer when his wife exhorted him to ask God to deprive him of life?
When his wife, through immoderate grief and impatience, exhorted him to provoke God to deprive him of his life, he rebuked her, saying, "If we received good things from the hand of God, why should we not receive evil," thus patiently submitting to the trial that God was pleased to permit, he consoled himself with the testimony of a good conscience, and the firm belief and hope of a glorious resurrection.

What is said of three of his friends?
Three of his friends who lived at a distance, hearing of his affliction, came to comfort him; but by their erroneous and rash judgment, they increased, rather than alleviated his sufferings, foolishly thinking and obstinately persevering in the opinion that the great miseries that befel Job were sent by God

in punishment of some secret sin, and by urging him
to repent of what he was not guilty, they put him to
the necessity of defending himself against their unjust accusations.

What did God undertake?
But God himself undertook the defence of his servant, and at his intercession only pardoned his three
friends who had judged him rashly, delivered him
from the power of Satan, who could no longer urge
anything against him; and rewarded him even in
this life for his patience and piety, by giving double
what he had been deprived of, turning the hearts of
his relations and friends with increased affection
towards him, and giving him other and fairer children than the former, whose children and children's
children he lived to see.

CHAPTER XI.

JOSEPH SOLD BY HIS BRETHREN.   A. M. 2198.

Which of his sons did Jacob love most?
Joseph, who was the first-born of Rachel, and the
son of his old age, being born when he was ninety.

Why did his brethren hate him?
Because his father loved him more than all the rest
and because he related to them dreams which por
tended his future superiority.

Relate his dreams?
In the first, he dreamed that he and his brethren
were binding sheaves in a field, and that his sheaf
arose, and, as it were, stood, whilst theirs bowed down
before it; in the second, he dreamed that he saw the
sun, moon and eleven stars worshipping him.

How did his brethren interpret these dreams?
His brothers interpret these dreams to mean that
they would be subject to him, for which they envied
him.

How did his brethren treat him when sent by his father to them whilst at a considerable distance with the flocks?

They determined to kill him, thinking it a favorable opportunity to make his dreams come to nothing, but on the interposition of Reuben, threw him into a pit, and a little after, when Reuben was absent, sold him to Ismaelite merchants, who were travelling to Egypt.

How old was Joseph at this time?

About sixteen.

How did Joseph's brethren conceal their treatment of him from their father?

They dipped his coat in the blood of a kid, and sent it to him, thus leading him to suppose that Joseph was devoured by some wild beast.

How did the merchants treat Joseph?

They sold him to Potiphar, an officer in the court of Pharaoh, king of Egypt.

What befell him there?

He was cast into prison on a false accusation.

What occurred whilst he was in prison?

The chief butler and chief baker having been likewise imprisoned had each a dream, and applied for its interpretation to Joseph. He foretold that the baker would be put to death, and the butler restored to favor. He entreated the butler to remember him when so restored. This he promised, but forgot.

What caused Joseph's release from prison?

About two years after the chief butler's release. Pharaoh had mysterious dreams, and anxiously sought their interpretation of his wise men, but they were unable to satisfy him. The butler then remembered Joseph, and mentioned to the king what had occurred to him in prison; on which Joseph was immediately sent for, and interpreted the dreams with such wisdom that Pharaoh gave him his own ring, and appointed him governor over all Egypt.

Relate Pharaoh's dreams?
He dreamed that he stood on the bank of the river, out of which came up seven very beautiful and fat kine, after which, seven others ill-favored and lean came up and devoured the former. Again Pharaoh dreamed that he saw seven full and fair ears of corn come up upon one stalk, and then seven others that were thin and blasted, which devoured all the beauty of the former.

How did Joseph interpret them?
Joseph said, God hath shown to Pharaoh what he is about to do, the seven beautiful kine, and the seven full ears are seven years of plenty, and the seven lean kine, and the seven thin ears that were blasted, are seven years of famine to come, which will be so great that the plenty of the former years will be forgotten; the fulfilment of the thing is at hand as denoted by one dream succeeding the other to the same effect.

What advice did Joseph give Pharaoh?
To appoint a wise governor over the land, who would gather into barns a fifth of the produce of the land during the years of plenty, as a provision against the famine that would ensue.

Who was the governor appointed by Pharaoh?
Joseph himself, whose appointment met with general approbation.

CHAPTER XII.

JOSEPH GOVERNOR OF EGYPT.

How old was Joseph when he was appointed governor of Egypt?
Thirty years: at the same time at Pharaoh's desire he married Asenath, daughter to Potiphar, priest of Heliopolis.

What were the names of Joseph's two sons?
Ephraim and Manasses, who were born during the years of plenty.

Did the famine extend to other countries as well as to Egypt?
Yes, Canaan also felt the effects of it. All were obliged to have recourse to Joseph in Egypt. Amongst the rest, his ten elder brothers, who were sent by their father to buy corn.

How did Joseph act when he saw his brethren bowing down before him?
Seeing that they did not recognise him, he pretended to think them spies, that he might the more easily make inquiries for his father and young brother Benjamin. To secure the pleasure of seeing the latter, he kept Simeon as a hostage, and declared that they should not see himself again unless they brought Benjamin; yet he had their sacks filled with corn, and the money put back into each.

Was Israel willing to let Benjamin go back with his brethren?
No, he at first decidedly refused, and it was only the dread of perishing of famine with all his family, that made him at length yield, and entrust the boy to the care of Juda, who promised to be responsible for him.

How did Joseph receive his brethren when they returned with Benjamin?
He made a feast for them, and, to their surprise, helped them according to seniority, but gave the largest share to Benjamin.

What directions did Joseph give the steward of his house when his brethren were about to return?
To fill each one's sack with corn, and to put the money as before into the top of each, and his silver cup in addition into the sack of the youngest

How did Joseph act when they had gone a little distance on their journey?
He sent the steward after them to accuse them of having stolen his cup.
What did they do?
Shocked at such an accusation, and conscious of their innocence, they desired him to search, declaring that e with whom it would be found should die, and the rest serve as bondmen: the cup being found in Benjamin's sack they rent their garments, returned to the town, fell prostrate before Joseph, and acknowledged themselves his bondmen.
What did Joseph answer?
He answered: "Not so, he alone with whom the cup was found shall be my bondman: go you away free to your father." Juda, encouraged by this clemency, earnestly entreated that Benjamin might be permitted to return to his father, and that he would be allowed to serve as bondman in his stead, and so eloquently and pathetically urged his petition, that Joseph could no longer defer making himself known.
What did Joseph say when he saw the consternation of his brethren on discovering that the mighty Governor of Egypt was the brother whom they had sold for twenty pieces of silver?
"Come nearer to me, be not afraid, nor troubled at selling me into these countries, for God sent me before you into Egypt for your preservation; not by your counsel was I sent hither but by the will of God, who hath made me as it were a father to Pharaoh, and lord of his whole house, and governor in all the land of Egypt: tell my father of all my glory, and of all you have seen, and make haste and bring him to me, for five years of famine yet remain; and I will feed him, and all that belongs to him." Then

falling on the neck of his brother Benjamin he wept and kissed all his brethren.

How did Pharaoh act when told that Joseph's brethren had come?
He desired Joseph to send for his father and kindred, promising them the riches of Egypt; and to facilitate their travelling he desired him to send waggons for the women and children.

How did Israel receive the intelligence that his son Joseph still lived?
At first he did not believe it, but when he saw the waggons and presents which were sent, he rejoiced, and eager to see his son, immediately prepared for his journey.

CHAPTER XIII.

JACOB'S JOURNEY TO EGYPT.—DEATH OF JOSEPH.

What vision had Israel on the way?
After sacrificing at Bersabee God called him and said, "I am the most mighty God of thy father; fear not, go down into Egypt, for I will make a great nation of thee there. I will go down with thee thither, and will bring thee back again from thence; Joseph also shall put his hands on thy eyes.

What is the meaning of Bersabee?
It means *the well of the oath,* because Abraham who dug it, made there a league with Abimilech, confirmed it with an oath, and paid him for a right to the well.

How many of Israel's family entered Egypt?
Seventy, including Joseph and his two sons.

Where did Joseph meet his father?
At Gessen, which was intended by Joseph for his father and family, and confirmed to them by Pharaoh on their arrival.

Why did Joseph select the land of Gessen for his father and brethren?
Because it was fertile, and well calculated for feeding their flocks, and also that they might be separated from the rest of Egypt, for they were shepherds, and the Egyptians held all shepherds in abomination.

How long did Jacob live after he went into Egypt?
Seventeen years. He died at the age of 147, after blessing his sons who surrounded him.

What request did he make of Joseph?
That he would bury him in the double cave in which Abraham, Sarah, Isaac, Rebecca and Lia, were buried. (Gen. xlvii. 30: xlix. 31.)

To which of his sons did Israel give the principal blessings?
To Juda and Joseph. To the former, he said, Juda, thee shall thy brethren praise; thy hands shall be on the necks of thy enemies; the sons of thy father shall bow down to thee. The sceptre shall not be taken away from Juda, nor a ruler from his posterity, till he come that is to be sent, and he shall be the expectation of nations. To Joseph, he assigned a double portion, blessed and adopted his two sons, preferring Ephraim the younger, to Menasses the elder.

Were not the sovereign power and double portion the birthright of Reuben, Israel's eldest son?
Yes, but he forfeited them by his sins.

Did Joseph execute all his father's commands?
Yes, he had his remains embalmed after the manner of the Egyptians, and when the seventy days of mourning were over, conveyed them with great pomp into the land of Canaan.

What did Joseph's brethren after their father was interred?
They earnestly besought his forgiveness, for they greatly feared, that no longer restrained by respect

for his father's presence, he would be revenged on them for the injury they had done him.

How did Joseph reply to their petition?
He wept, and told them not to fear, for that God had turned the evil they designed into good, by making him an instrument to save many. Thus he kindly comforted them, and he renewed his promise to feed them and their children.

What ought we learn from Joseph's conduct to his brethren?
Perfect forgiveness of injuries; and to deal towards enemies with kindness whenever an occasion offers.

What did Joseph foretell his brethren a little before his death?
That God would visit them after his death, and put them in possession of the land which he promised to Abraham, Isaac and Jacob.

What promise did Joseph exact of his brethren on that occasion?
That they would carry his bones with them when going to take possession of the promised land.

How old was Joseph when he died?
One hundred and ten years, having been eighty years governor of Egypt.

CHAPTER XIV.

PRESERVATION OF MOSES. A. M. 2373.

How were the Israelites treated after Joseph's death?
With great severity and cruelty by a new king, another Pharaoh, who grew jealous of them on account of their power and numbers; and attempted to destroy them by imposing on them such heavy burthens as he hoped would ruin their health.

Were they weakened by the harsh treatment they received?
No; God strengthened them in proportion to the oppression of the Egyptians.

What means did Pharaoh adopt when he perceived that his design of lessening their numbers was counteracted?
He first gave private directions to the midwives to kill all the male children as soon as they were born; but finding they did not obey, he gave public orders that all the male children should be thrown into the river.

How was Moses preserved?
His mother, who had concealed him for three months, finding she could do so no longer put him in a basket made of bulrushes, which she cemented to keep out the water, laid it in the sedges by the bank of the river, and sent his sister to watch the result. Pharaoh's daughter coming a little after to bathe, saw the basket and desired one of her maids to bring it to her: seeing an infant crying within, she was moved with compassion, and desired the child's sister to procure her a nurse, the girl went for her mother, to whom Pharaoh's daughter entrusted the child, whom she then adopted as her son and called him Moses.

Who were the parents of Moses?
Amram and Jochabed, both descended from Levi. Amram was the eldest son of Caath, the second son of Levi.

Where did Moses spend his youth until the fortieth year of his age?
In the Court of Pharaoh, where he was treated as the son of Pharaoh's daughter, and instructed in all the learning of the Egyptians. (Acts vii. 22.)

Why did he renounce his title and deny himself to be the son of Pharaoh's daughter?
St. Paul says, "He chose to be afflicted with the

people of God, rather than have the pleasure of sin for a time, esteeming the reproach of Christ greater riches than the treasure of the Egyptians." (Heb. xi. 25.)

Why did he leave Egypt?
He fled to avoid Pharaoh's anger excited by his having killed an Egyptian, whom he saw striking a Hebrew.

Whither did he fly?
To Madian, where he married Sephora, daughter of Jethro, priest of the place, and had two sons born to him, Gersam and Eliezer.

CHAPTER XV.

THE BURNING BUSH. A. M. 2413.

How long did Moses dwell in Madian?
Forty years, (Acts vii. 30,) when having driven his father-in-law's flocks into the desert as far as Mount Horeb, the Lord appeared to him in a flame of fire out of the midst of a bush, which, though burning, was not consumed. On his approaching to observe the wonder more closely, the Lord called to him out of the bush, and commissioned him to go to Pharaoh, and bring the children of Israel out of Egypt.

What did Moses reply?
"Who am I, that I should bring forth the children of Israel out of Egypt?" and "What shall I say to the children of Israel, if when I tell them that the God of their fathers sent me, they should ask me his name?

What did God reply to Moses?
"I Am who Am. You shall say to the children of Israel: He who Is hath sent me to you."

What particular directions did God give him?
To collect the ancients of Israel, and inform them

that God would bring them out of the affliction of Egypt to give them the land which he promised their forefathers, and having told them so, to go with them to Pharaoh, and beg permission to obey the call of God, and go three days' journey into the desert to sacrifice to him.

What did Almighty God foretell to Moses?
That the ancients would believe him, and that Pharaoh would at first refuse to allow the children of Israel to go, but afterwards on experiencing the divine vengeance would permit them. God also said that they should not come forth empty, but that on their coming away, they should ask raiment and vessels of gold and silver of the Egyptians, and that he would incline them to give liberally.

Was Moses still fearful of undertaking the mission?
Yes, he feared they would not believe that God had appeared to him, so the Lord to encourage him by a miracle, commanded him to cast the rod he held in his hand on the ground, upon which it was changed into a serpent, and being desired to take it by the tail it became a rod again. The Lord then desired him to put his hand into his bosom, on which it became covered with leprosy; he was directed again to put his hand into his bosom, when the leprosy disappeared.

What then did the Lord say?
"If they will not believe the former sign," said the Lord, "they will believe the latter, but if they will not believe either, take water out of the river, and pour it out, when it shall be turned into blood."

Did Moses still hesitate?
Yes, he represented his want of eloquence and slowness of speech, which increased after the Lord had spoken to him.

What answer did the Lord make to his objection?

"Who made man's mouth? Did not I? Go, therefore, and I will be in thy mouth and will teach thee what thou shall speak."

Did Moses make any further objection?
Yes, deeming himself unworthy and incapable of so great a work, he said, "I beseech the Lord send whom thou will send."

Was the Lord displeased at the perseverance of Moses?
He was; yet, to meet his weakness, told him that his brother Aaron, who was eloquent, would come to meet him, and speak to the people for him, and that he would be with them both. The Lord desired him to take the rod in his hand, and work signs with it in the presence of Pharaoh, and to go fearlessly, as all who sought his life were dead.

Did Moses then consent?
Yes, taking his wife and two sons, he went into Egypt, having on the way met Aaron, who came to him by the command of God.

CHAPTER XVI.

THE PLAGUES OF EGYPT. A. M. 2453

What did Pharaoh say when Moses and Aaron begged him to allow the Israelites to go into the desert to sacrifice to the Lord?
That he knew not the Lord whom they adored, and would not suffer them to go; and that it was a spirit of idleness prompted their petition. He then commanded the taskmasters to be more rigorous than ever, to provide no straw, and yet to exact as much work as before.

Did Moses and Aaron renew their petition to Pharaoh?
Yes, and by the command of God, wrought a miracle

to convince him that they were sent by divine authority.

What miracle did they work?
Aaron cast the rod on the ground, and it immediately turned into a serpent. Pharaoh called his magicians, who cast down their rods, which also became serpents, but Aaron's rod devoured theirs.

By what means did Moses and Aaron obtain Pharaoh's consent to lead the Israelites out of Egypt?
By bringing on him and his people ten successive plagues.

What was the first plague?
The first was a change of all the water throughout Egypt into blood, which was effected by Aaron stretching the rod, at the command of Moses, over the river.

What was the second plague?
The second was the production of an innumerable swarm of frogs.

What was the third plague?
The third was a change of the dust over the land into sciniphs, a kind of small flying insect that tormented man and beast, at seeing which, the magicians declared to Pharaoh that it was the work of God; they had imitated the other plagues, but failed in this.

What was the fourth plague?
The fourth was a grievous swarm of flies, which was so great an annoyance, that Pharaoh relented a little in his obduracy, and offered to permit the Israelites to sacrifice in Egypt.

Did Moses object to that?
Yes; "It cannot be," he said, "for we shall sacrifice the abominations of the Egyptians to the Lord our God, now, if we kill those things which the Egyptians worship, in their presence, they will stone us: we will go three days' journey into the wilderness.

and will sacrifice to the Lord our God, as he hath commanded us."

Did Pharaoh consent to their going into the wilderness?
He pretended to do so until the plague was removed at the prayer of Moses, he then retracted and refused to allow them.

Describe the fifth, sixth and seventh plagues?
The fifth was a grievous disease of which multitudes of cattle died. The sixth afflicted man and beast with boils and swelling blains, on account of which the magicians could not stand before Moses. The seventh was a dreadful storm of hail, thunder, and lightning, which destroyed the trees and early crops, and killed all the men and beasts that were in the fields.

Did Pharaoh then consent to let the Hebrews go?
At first he did, having been terrified at the awful storm; but when, at the prayer of Moses, it ceased, he refused to allow them.

Describe the eighth and ninth plagues?
The eighth was a multitude of locusts that devoured the herbs and trees which escaped the hail. The ninth was a horrible darkness, so thick that it might be felt, which covered Egypt for three days, except the land of Gessen, for the Israelites were exempt from all the plagues.

Describe the tenth and last plague?
At midnight, on the fourteenth of the month Nisan, which the Israelites thenceforward counted the first month of the year, the destroying angel entered Egypt, and slew the first-born throughout the land, from the first-born of Pharaoh, to the first-born of the humblest captive; and the first-born of all beasts

How were the Israelites preserved from this visitation?
By the blood of the Paschal Lamb sprinkled on the

upper and side door-posts of their houses, in commemoration of which an annual feast was enjoined, and thenceforward observed by the Israelites.

CHAPTER XVII.

THE PASCHAL LAMB.

What do you mean by the Paschal Lamb?
A lamb, a male of a year old, which each family, by the command of God, sacrificed on the fourteenth of the month in the evening, and having signed the door-posts with its blood, roasted the flesh, and ate it hastily with unleavened bread and wild lettuce, standing all the time with shoes on their feet, staves in their hands, and girded like travellers ready for a journey. They were forbidden to break a bone, or leave any part until morning.

Of what was the Paschal Lamb a figure?
Of the Blessed Eucharist, and of the Passion of our Lord.

What did Pharaoh and his people, when a cry was raised through the land at midnight, that there was death in every house?
They arose, urged Moses and all the Israelites to depart immediately with their flocks, herds, and all that belonged to them; and gave them all that they asked of gold, silver, and raiment to a very great amount.

How many were the children of Israel at that time?
Six hundred thousand men, who marched armed out of Egypt that same night, besides women and children; and notwithstanding the precipitation with which the Egyptians obliged them to go they carried Joseph's bones with them.

How long did the Hebrews sojourn in Egypt?
Four hundred and thirty years, which time is com-

puted from Abraham's first going there the year after his call.

Names and ages of the Patriarchs of the third age.

A. M.

	BORN.	DIED.	AGED.
Abraham,	1948	2123	175
Isaac,	2048	2228	180
Jacob,	2108	2255	147
Levi,	——	——	137
Moses,	——	——	——

Amram, the father of Moses, was grandson of Levi, who had lived thirty-three years with Isaac, and Isaac had lived one hundred and eight years with Sem; Sem surviving the Deluge five hundred years, and Isaac being born three hundred and ninety-two years after that event. Thus it appears that what Moses recorded in his sacred history was still fresh in the memory of men.

FOURTH AGE OF THE WORLD.

From the Deliverance of the Jews out of Egypt to the Foundation of the Temple, A. M. 2453 to 2972.

CHAPTER XVIII.

THE CROSSING OF THE RED SEA.

What command did God give the Israelites on leading them out of Egypt?
To keep the feast of unleavened bread and the Phase annually, as a perpetual memorial of their deliverance from Egypt; and that on their arrival in the promised land they should consecrate to him their first-born sons, and the first-born of every beast

In what manner did God conduct the Israelites?
By an angel who went before them in a pillar of
cloud by day, and in one of fire by night: he led
them through the desert by the Red Sea, lest, if they
were marched through the land of the Philistines
which was nearer, they might repent, and return into
Egypt, if they met with serious opposition.

Did Pharaoh regret having allowed them to go?
Yes; and collecting his army, with six hundred
chariots, he pursued and overtook them when encamped in front of the Red Sea, having Phihahiroth
on one side, Beelsephon on the other, and the Egyptian army in the rear.

*What did the Israelites when they saw how they
were hemmed in?*
Being exceedingly terrified, they murmured against
Moses, and reproached him with having brought them
out of Egypt to perish in the wilderness.

What did Moses then?
He desired them not to fear, but to stand and see
the wonders which God would work in their favor:
immediately the angel who went before them, with
the cloud, moved to the rear and stood between them
and the Egyptians, while Moses, by the command of
God, stretched the rod over the sea, which dividing
left a dry passage, through which they walked, the
water standing on each side, like a wall.

What did the Egyptians do?
The Egyptians followed close, but when the Israelites reached the opposite side, Moses, by the command of God, again stretched the rod over the sea,
which returned to its former place, overwhelming
Pharaoh and all his host.

*What part of the Red Sea is it supposed they
crossed?*
The north-western gulf, near the Isthmus of Suez.

What did Moses and all the people on reaching the opposite shore?
They with one accord sang a canticle of thanksgiving to God.

Did the Israelites soon after murmur against Moses?
Yes; having marched three days through the wilderness without finding water, they murmured when they reached Mara, the water whereof was bitter.

How did Moses act?
He prayed to God, who directed him to a tree, the wood of which rendered the water sweet when thrown into it.

Where did the children of Israel next encamp?
At Elim, where there were twelve fountains of water and seventy palm trees.

Whither did the children of Israel next journey?
To the desert of Sin, between Elim and Mount Sinai, which they reached on the fifteenth of the second month after their departure from Egypt.

CHAPTER XIX.

THE MANNA

How did they act on reaching the desert of Sin?
They murmured against Moses and Aaron, because they had no bread, saying it were better they had died in Egypt, where they had abundance, than be brought there to perish of want.

What did Moses and Aaron say?
'In the evening, you shall know that the Lord hath brought you forth out of the land of Egypt, and in the morning you shall see the glory of the Lord, for he hath heard your murmuring against him; but as for us, what are we that you mutter against us. In the evening, the Lord will give you flesh to eat, and in the morning bread to the full."

How was this promise fulfilled?
In the evening, a great number of quails covered the camp; and in the morning, a dewlike frost lay round about it, which they gathered and made it into cakes by the direction of Moses, the taste being like bread tempered with oil. (Numbers xi. 8.)

What did the Israelites say to one another when they saw it?
"Manha," which signifies "What is this?" to which Moses replied, "This is the bread which the Lord hath given you to eat."

What directions did Moses give concerning the manna?
To gather a gomer for each person before sunrise, (for it melted by the heat of the sun,) and a double quantity on the sixth day, as no manna fell on the Sabbath.

What should we learn from these injunctions concerning the manna?
To overcome sloth by rising early, to anticipate the sun in the service of God, and not to be too solicitous about the necessaries of life, nor anxious to hoard up a quantity of superfluities for the future.

What was the consequence when some kept manna until next day, contrary to the directions of Moses?
It putrified and became full of worms; yet when there was a gomer of it placed in the tabernacle by the command of God, it remained for ages as a memorial of the manner in which he had fed his people in the desert.

What was the consequence when more or less was gathered than was prescribed?
On measuring it, it was found that he who had gathered more had not more, nor he less who had gathered less; but all had sufficient.

What allusion did our Lord make to the manna, when teaching in the synagogue at Capharnaum?

"Amen, amen, I say unto you he that believeth in me hath everlasting life; I am the bread of life. Your fathers did eat manna in the desert and are dead. This is the bread which cometh down from heaven, that if any man eat of it he may not die. I am the living bread which came down from heaven If any man eat of this bread he shall live for ever, and the bread that I will give is my flesh for the life of the world."

What did the Jews say?
The Jews, therefore, strove among themselves, saying, "How can this man give us his flesh to eat?" Then Jesus said to them, "Amen, amen, I say unto you, except you eat the flesh of the Son of Man, and drink his blood, you shall not have life in you He that eateth my flesh, and drinketh my blood, hath everlasting life, and I will raise him up in the last day, for my flesh is meat indeed, and my blood is drink indeed; he that eateth my flesh and drinketh my blood abideth in me, and I in him. As the living Father hath sent me, and I live by the Father, so he that eateth me the same also shall live by me. This is the bread that came down from heaven. Not as your fathers did eat manna, and are dead. He that eateth this bread shall live for ever." (John vi. 47—59.)

How long were the Israelites fed with manna?
Forty years: it did not cease until they eat of the corn of the promised land.

Did they ever murmur at having nothing but manna to eat?
Yes; saying their souls loathed that very light food; on which God sent a multitude of quails into the camp, of which the people eat so ravenously that an immense number of them died. (Num. xi. 33.)

CHAPTER XX.

WATER ISSUES FROM THE ROCK.

How were the people supplied with water when in the desert of Raphidim?
By a plentiful stream which issued from the rock Horeb on its being struck (at the command of God) by Moses, with the rod which had been the instrument of so many miracles.

When the people were in want of water at Cades in the desert of Sin, how did they act?
They seditiously assembled murmuring against Moses and Aaron, and violently reproaching them with having brought them into the desert to perish. Moses and Aaron, prostrate before God, besought him to take pity on the people: he directed them to assemble the multitude, and taking the rod, to strike the rock in their presence, which would immediately yield an abundant supply of water. They did as God commanded, but Moses, striking the rock twice, seemed to doubt of the event, for which Almighty God told him and Aaron that they should not lead the people into the promised land.

Which was the first nation that made war on the Israelites?
The Amalekites, over whom they gained a complete victory by the prayer of Moses, who remained on a hill at a little distance, holding the rod of God in his hand. Aaron and Hur, observing that the Amalekites overcame, when Moses, through weariness, let his hands down a little, stayed them up until they were totally defeated. (Exod. xvii.)

What advice did Jethro, the father-in-law of Moses, give him, when he saw that he was overpowered by too much business in judging all the causes of the people?

To choose just men from among them as rulers under him to judge the people in minor things, and to have matters of consequence only referred to him. (Exod. viii.)

Did Moses follow this advice?
He did, with great humility and meekness; and a little after, referred the matter to God. The Lord desired him to select seventy ancients of the people as assistants, to whom he imparted a share of Moses' spirit and gift of prophesy. (Num. xi. 25.)

What did Moses reply to Josue, when he asked him to forbid Eldad and Medad to prophesy?
"Why hast thou emulation for me, O that all the people might prophesy, and that the Lord would give them his Spirit."

CHAPTER XXI.

THE LAW GIVEN ON MOUNT SINAI.

At what period after their deliverance from Egypt did the Israelites receive the commandments?
In the third month. (Exod. xix. 1.)

What circumstances accompanied the giving of them?
God having announced to Moses his intention of giving the people a law, desired him to have them in readiness to receive it on the third day, at which time he accordingly descended in fire on Mount Sinai, accompanied with thunder, lightning, and sound of trumpet; and pronounced the ten commandments in the hearing of all the people, who were so terrified at the awful sublimity of the scene, and at hearing the voice of God, that they kept at a distance, saying to Moses, "Speak thou to us, and we will hear, let not the Lord speak to us lest we die."

What did Moses then do?
Moses encouraged them, telling them not to fear, as God had come only that the dread of him might be in their hearts to deter them from sin; they continued at a distance, while he went to the dark cloud wherein God was, and there received from him a collection of wise and holy laws for the regulation of the religious and civil duties of his people, with two tables of stone, on which the ten commandments were written by the finger of God. (Exod. xix., Deut. v.)

How long did Moses spend in that secret interview with God?
Forty days and forty nights, during which he tasted no food.

How did the people act in his absence?
They assembled round Aaron for permission to have an idol like other nations, and he weakly yielding to their impious demand, desired them to bring him the gold ornaments belonging to their wives and daughters, which he moulded into the form of a calf.

How did Moses find them when he came down from the Mount?
They were engaged rejoicing before it, and singing, "These are thy gods, O Israel, that brought thee out of the land of Egypt," when Moses came down from the Mount with the tables of the law of God in his hands.

What did Moses when he found them so engaged?
With grief and anger he threw down the tables, which were broken in the fall; and laying hold of the calf he burned and beat it to powder, which he put into water and made the children of Israel drink. Then severely reprehending Aaron for suffering such a scandal, he called on all who still retained a sense of their duty to God, to join themselves to him: he was immediately obeyed by the

whole tribe of Levi, whom he commanded to unsheath their swords, and march right through the camp and back again, putting all whom they met to death.

How many were executed that day?
About twenty-three thousand. The whole body of the Israelites had grievously sinned; and a part were punished as they deserved, that the rest might repent and live.

What did Moses after punishing the people?
Prostrate before God, he earnestly implored his forgiveness for the people, or else to blot him out of the book of life. God mercifully pardoned them at his entreaty.

Did God renew the commandments?
Yes; Moses by the divine command hewed two tables of stone like the former, and took them up to Mount Sinai, where God wrote on them the same words as before.

How long did Moses spend in this second interview?
The same length of time as in the first. On descending from the Mount, his face shone so brightly from the intercourse he had with God, that Aaron and the people were afraid to approach him.

How did Moses act when told the cause of their fear?
He covered his face with a veil, which he wore ever after unless when he went into the Tabernacle. (Exod. xxxiv. 33.)

What may we learn from this conduct of Moses?
To condescend to the weakness of others as far as duty will permit, and carefully to avoid the display of any extraordinary favor.

CHAPTER XXII.

THE TABERNACLE AND THE ARK OF THE COVENANT.

What was the first work proposed by Moses to the people when he came down from the Mount?
To make the Ark of the Covenant and the Tabernacle, according to the directions he had received from God.

How were the materials provided for them?
Moses invited all to make offerings for the work, and desired those who were instructed in the workmanship required, to come forward and assist, particularly Beseleel of the tribe of Juda, and Ooliab of the tribe of Dan, whom God had specially named and inspired. The people contributed their richest stuffs, plate, ornaments and perfumes so generously, that in a short time they had more than was necessary, and Moses had to make proclamation that they should bring no more.

Describe the Ark of the Covenant?
It was made of setim wood, and measured two cubits and a half in length, one and a half in height, and the same in breadth. It was overlaid within and without with the purest gold; the top, called the oracle or propitiatory, because from it God was pleased to give his orders, was made entirely of gold; on either end was a gold cherub, whose wings spread over the propitiatory, and towards one another.

What encircled the Ark?
The Ark was encircled by a crown of gold, in which were four rings, two at each side, through which bars of setim wood overlaid with gold were put, for the purpose of carrying it. In the Ark were deposited the tables of the law, a golden pot of manna, and the rod of Aaron that had blossomed. (Heb. ix 5.)

Describe the Tabernacle?
It was made of setim wood overlaid with gold, and measured thirty cubits in length, nine in breadth, and ten in height. At the entrance which looked towards the east were five pillars covered with gold, supporting a richly embroidered hanging: the roof was covered with dyed skins fastened together with loops and buckles of brass, the inside was divided into two parts by four pillars of setim covered with gold, which were set in silver sockets, and supported a veil of exquisite workmanship.

What was the Holy of Holies?
The apartment enclosed by the veil was called the Holy of Holies, in which the Ark was placed, the part outside the veil was called the sanctuary, and contained the golden altar of incense, the table of show-bread, and the seven-branched candlestick which bore the lamps that according to the command of God were to be kept constantly burning.

Was there any enclosure to the Tabernacle?
Yes; it was placed in the centre of a court one hundred cubits long, and fifty broad, formed by hangings of fine linen, supported by pillars of brass, overlaid with silver, five cubits high. At the entrance of the court was an embroidered hanging of violet, purple, scarlet, and fine linen twenty cubits in length, and supported by four pillars of the same height and workmanship as the rest.

Where were the altar of holocausts and the laver for the priests to wash themselves placed?
Within the court, in front of the tabernacle, the laver being between the tabernacle and the altar of holocausts.

At what time after the deliverance of the children of Israel from Egypt was the Tabernacle erected?
On the first day of the second year; and when consecrated, and all things perfectly arranged in it, it

was covered by the cloud, and the glory of the Lord filled it.

How did the Israelites know when to journey and when to rest?

"If at any time the cloud removed from the tabernacle they went forward by their troops. If it hung over they remained in the same place. For the cloud of the Lord hung over the tabernacle by day, and a fire by night, in the sight of all the children of Israel throughout all their mansions. (Exod. xl. 34.)

What tribe did God appoint to take charge of the tabernacle and all things appertaining to the divine service?

The tribe of Levi, whom God took in place of the first-born of the children of Israel. Whilst journeying towards the land of promise, the principal duty of the Levites was to watch round the tabernacle; to carry it, the ark, and all belonging to the divine service: and to set up the tabernacle when they were to encamp.

What offering did the Israelites make at the dedication of the tabernacle and altar?

Six wagons and twelve oxen, which Moses, by the command of God, gave the Levites for the service of the tabernacle. Besides, the prince of each tribe beginning with Juda gave each a silver dish and bowl, the one weighing one hundred and thirty, the other seventy sicles, full of flour tempered with oil for sacrifice, a gold mortar weighing ten sicles, full of incense: an ox, a ram, and a lamb of a year old for peace offerings. (Num. vii.)

CHAPTER XXIII.

VESTMENTS OF THE PRIESTS AND PRIESTLY OFFICE.

Whom did God select from the tribe of Levi to minister to him as priests?
Aaron and his sons. (Exod. xxviii.)

Were the priests distinguished by dress from the rest?
Yes, vestments were made for them by the command of God, some of which were common to all the priests and some peculiar to the High Priest.

Describe the vestments worn by the High Priest?
Besides the white linen garment common to all the priests, he wore a violet tunic which reached to his feet, confined by an embroidered girdle at the waist; the lower part of the skirt was ornamented all round with embroidered pomegranates and little gold bells placed alternately.

What was worn over this?
Over this was the Ephod, a vestment embroidered in the richest manner having an onyx stone on each shoulder, (where it was joined,) with the names of six tribes engraved on each.

What was worn on the breast?
On the breast was the Rational, embroidered like the Ephod, and fastened to it, having in it twelve precious stones, with the name of a tribe engraved on each. In the Rational, also, were two words, "Urim and Thummin," which signify "Doctrine and Truth." The High Priest likewise wore a mitre, on which the words "Holy to the Lord" were engraved on a plate of gold over the forehead.

What was the office of the High Priest?
To burn sweet incense morning and evening on the altar of incense, and at the same time to dress the lamps on the seven-branched candlestick, and to offer

sacrifice for his own sins and those of the people once a year.

Was there any remarkable solemnity observed on occasion of this yearly sacrifice offered by the High Priest for his own sins and those of the people?
Yes, many striking ceremonies were performed, and on this occasion alone did the High Priest enter the Holy of Holies.

How did God testify his acceptance of the first holocaust offered by Aaron after he was consecrated High Priest?
By sending fire from heaven, which consumed it.

How were Nadab and Abiu, the sons of Aaron, punished for offering strange fire in their censers?
They were struck dead by fire from the Lord; and by the command of Moses, were cast without the camp, vested as they were in their priestly attire, and their father and brethren forbid to mourn for them.

What place was appointed for the Israelites to offer sacrifice in?
Before the door of the Tabernacle only, and by the hand of the priest. (Lev. xvii.)

CHAPTER XXIV.

THE ORDER OF ENCAMPMENT.—THE TWELVE SPIES.

In what order did the Israelites encamp?
The camp of Juda, consisting of 186,400, including the tribes of Issacher and Zabulon, on the east; the camp of Reuben, consisting of 151,450, including the tribes of Simeon and Gad, on the south; the Levites were in the centre, surrounding the Tabernacle, except at the east end, which was occupied by the priests; the camp of Ephraim, consisting of 108,100, including the tribes of Manasses and Benjamin, on the west; and on the north was the camp of Dan,

consisting of 157,600, including the tribes of Aser and Nephtali. (Num. ii.)

Who were appointed by God to give the signal to march when the cloud was raised from the Tabernacle?
The priests, who were to sound silver trumpets, made by the command of God for that purpose. (Num. x. 8.)

How long after the Israelites left Egypt did they get the signal to march, in order to take possession of the promised land?
A year and nearly two months. On the 20th of the second month, the second year, the signal was given (Num. x. 11.)

How long did they continue the march?
Three days; when, murmuring at the fatigue, they displeased God so much that he sent fire into the camp, which killed several.

How was the burning put a stop to?
By the prayer of Moses.

How was Mary, the sister of Moses, punished for murmuring against him?
She was reproved by God and struck with leprosy, but was healed at the prayer of Moses, after being excluded seven days from the camp.

Whither did they journey after Mary was recalled?
To the desert of Pharan, whence Moses, by the command of God, sent twelve men, one from each tribe, to view the land of Canaan.

How did the twelve spies act?
They spent forty days viewing the land, and on their return praised its fertility, and produced as specimens of its fruits, a vine branch with a cluster of grapes which required two men to carry, and some pomegranates and figs; but (with the exception of Caleb and Josue) gave such a terrific description of the inhabitants of the country and the strength of its

cities, that the people murmured, some praying that they might die in the wilderness, and others proposing to appoint a captain to lead them back to Egypt. (Num. xiv. 4.)

What did Almighty God then threaten?
To consume them with pestilence; yet at the prayer of Moses he forgave them, but condemned them to wander in the desert for forty years, declaring that none of them, save Caleb and Josue should enter the land, and that their children whom they said would fall a prey to their enemies should take possession of it. (Num. xiv. 31.)

How were the ten spies who excited the people to sedition punished?
By sudden death.

In what direction did God command Moses to lead the people then?
Back again into the wilderness by the Red Sea.

Did any of them repent of not having gone to take possession of the land?
Yes, and they attempted to do so then, but were defeated with great slaughter because God was not with them, as they acted against his will made known to them by Moses.

How was the man that was found gathering sticks on the Sabbath day punished?
He was stoned to death outside the camp by the command of God. A similar punishment was inflicted a short time before on another who had blasphemed the name of God. (Num. xv. 36; Lev. xxiv. 14.)

CHAPTER XXV

THE PRIESTHOOD CONFIRMED TO AARON.

What do you know of the schism of Core and his adherents?
Core, a Levite. Dathan and Abiron, of the tribe of

Reuben, with 250 leading men, assembled seditiously, and called Moses and Aaron to account for assuming authority over the people of God. Moses astonished at the charge fell prostrate on the ground, then addressing himself to Core and the schismatic Levites represented to them the honor God had done them in selecting their tribe for the service of the Tabernacle, which ought to satisfy them without arrogating to themselves the priesthood.

What did Moses then do?
He then sent for Dathan and Abiron, but they contemptuously refused to appear and remained in their tents, on which he told Core to attend the next day with his 250 adherents, each man holding a censer to offer incense to God, that Aaron also would be present with his censer, and God would prove before all whom he had chosen.

What followed?
Next day they assembled, and when the 250 offered incense, a fire from God consumed them, and the earth opening under the tents of Core, Dathan and Abiron, swallowed them with all that belonged to them except the sons of Core, who were miraculously preserved from death on this occasion. (Num xxvi. 11.)

What did God command concerning the censers that were used by the schismatics?
That Eleazer, the son of Aaron, should beat them into plates and fasten them to the altar as a perpetual admonition to the children of Israel, and a memorial that Aaron and his sons only were chosen by God as priests. (Num. xxvi. 11.)

What accusation did the Israelites bring against Moses and Aaron next day?
That they were guilty of the death of those who were killed the day before.

How did God punish the seditious?

He sent fire on them, which killed 14,700 before the flames were checked.

How was the burning stopped?
By Aaron offering incense, and praying between the living and the dead.

In what manner did God confirm the priesthood to Aaron and his sons?
He commanded Moses to assemble the children of Israel, to take of the prince of each tribe a rod, marked with his name, and to place them in the Tabernacle, saying that the rod of him whom he had chosen should blossom. The next day, all being again assembled, Moses went into the Tabernacle and brought out the rods, when Aaron's was found covered with leaves, blossoms, and fruit. (Almonds.) (Num. xvii.)

What did God command Moses to do with Aaron's rod?
To lay it up in the Tabernacle as a memorial to the rebellious children of Israel.

Where did Mary the sister of Moses die?
At Cades, in the desert of Sin, where she was buried.

Where did Aaron die?
On Mount Hor, on the borders of the land of Edom, in the fortieth year after coming out of Egypt, and the hundred and twenty-third of his age. Moses accompanied him and his son Eleazer to the top of the mountain, stripped him of his vestments by the command of God, and clothed Eleazer with them, whom he presented to the people instead of Aaron. for whom they mourned thirty-days.

CHAPTER XXVI.

THE BRAZEN SERPENT.—BALAAM THE SOOTHSAYER.

In what direction did the Israelites march after the death of Aaron?

By the way that led to the Red Sea, in order to compass the land of Edom, being refused by the inhabitants permission to pass through.

Did they murmur on their journey?
Yes, for which God sent fiery serpents among them that bit and killed a great many.

How were they relieved from them?
By the prayer of Moses, who, upon their acknowledging their fault besought God for them, and was directed by him to make a brazen serpent and set it up for a sign, by looking on which they that were bitten were healed.

Of what was the brazen serpent a figure?
Of Jesus Christ on the Cross, (John iii. 14, 15,) the true restorer of our health, on whom we should fix our eyes when attacked by the infernal serpent.

What opposition did the Israelites meet with when they drew near the land of promise at the close of the forty years?
The Edomites and Amorites refused them permission to pass through their land. Sehon, king of the Amorites, and Og, king of Basan, attacked them, but were defeated; and Balac, king of Moab, seeing that human power could not withstand them, sent Balaam, a famous soothsayer, to curse them, but he was unable to do so, and instead of curses pronounced blessings on the chosen people of God.

Who was Og?
He was the last of the giants. His iron bed is said to have measured nine cubits in length and four in breadth.

Did any extraordinary circumstance occur whilst Balaam was on his way to the King of Moab with the intention of cursing the Israelites?
The ass on which he rode spoke, and expostulated with him because he beat her severely for twice turning out of the way, and at length throwing her-

self down, in order to avoid an angel who stood with a drawn sword ready to kill him, but whom Balaam did not perceive until the ass spoke; then prostrating himself, he acknowledged his fault, and even offered to return, but the angel permitted him to go on; at the same time charging him to speak only what he should command. (Num. xxii.)

Repeat that part of the prophecy which Balaam was constrained to utter relative to the coming of the Messiah?
"I shall see him, but not now; I shall behold him but not near. A star shall rise out of Jacob and a sceptre shall spring up from Israel." (Num. xxiv. 17.)

What advice did the impious Balaam give Balac to withdraw the blessing and protection of God from the Israelites?
To ensnare them into idolatry to which they were but too prone (Num. xxxi. 16;) in this he unhappily succeeded by the assistance of some of his subjects.

How were the Israelites and Moabites punished on that occasion?
Twenty-four thousand Israelites were struck dead by God, when he was appeased by the zeal of Phineas son of Eleazer, the High Priest, under whose command Moses placed twelve thousand chosen men; one thousand from each tribe, who attacked the Moabites and utterly exterminated them.

To what tribes did Moses give the conquered land of Moab and other lands east of the Jordan?
To the tribes of Reuben, Gad, and the half tribe of Manasses, on condition of their assisting their brethren in the conquest of the promised land.

To what number did the children of Israel amount at that time?
Six hundred and one thousand seven hundred and thirty, among whom the tribe of Levi was not num

bered, because the Levites were specially devoted to the service of God, and were not to receive any portion of the land, tithes being allotted to them, and forty-eight cities with suburbs, six of which to be cities of refuge, three on the east of the Jordan and three in the land of Canaan.

What command did Moses give the Israelites on the part of God when they were about to enter the promised land?
To make no league with the inhabitants, but utterly to exterminate them, to break their pillars and statues, and to cut down their groves. (Deut. vii. 2—5.)

CHAPTER XXVII.

JOSUE APPOINTED TO SUCCEED MOSES—DEATH OF MOSES.

Whom did God appoint to lead the people across the Jordan into the land of promise?
Josue, the faithful minister of Moses, who served in the Tabernacle from his youth, and was one of those sent to view the promised land. (Num. xvii. 18.)

Why did not Moses lead them in, as he so earnestly wished? (Deut. iii. 25.)
Because he displeased Almighty God at Cades, in the desert of Sin, by striking the rock twice, thereby manifesting a weakness of faith.

What did Moses, when he perceived that God would not permit him to enter the promised land, but only to view it at a distance?
He presented Josue to the people, and informed them of the will of God; reminded them of all that God had done for them; exhorted them to be faithful to him; recapitulated all his former instructions; added others, regulating their conduct when they would be in possession of the promised land, and finally gave them his blessing.

Relate some of the instructions given by Moses on that occasion?

He dwelt at length on their duty to God, warned them against idolatry, and against offering to God anything maimed or lame. He decreed that in case of controversies arising, they should be referred to the priests and the judge, from whom there should be no appeal; and that all who would not abide by their decision should be put to death. He inculcated kindness towards all, (except those whom God commanded them to eradicate,) and desired them not to injure the trees or other produce of their enemies' land.

What did Moses say in prophesying the coming of our Lord?

"The Lord thy God will raise up to thee a prophet of thy nation, and of thy brethren like unto me: him thou shalt hear." (Deut. xviii. 15.) And again, in blessing the tribes, he said to Levi: "Thy perfection and thy doctrine be to thy holy man, whom thou hast proved in the temptation, and judged at the waters of contradiction; who hath said to his father and to his mother, I do not know you, and to his brethren, I know you not." (Deut. xxiii. 8.)

To what place did Moses go, by the command of God, to view the promised land?

To the top of Phasga, on Mount Nebo, which is in the land of Moab, opposite Jericho, and there he died, according to the appointment of God.

How old was Moses when he died?

One hundred and twenty years. His health was unimpaired, and his sight undimmed. He was buried in the valley opposite the temple of Phogor, near Mount Nebo, but the exact spot is not known. (Deut. xxxiv. 6.)

CHAPTER XXVIII.

From the entrance of the Israelites into the Land of Promise to the Foundation of the Temple. A. M. 2493.

THE CROSSING OF THE JORDAN.

What directions did Josue give when the thirty days' mourning for Moses had expired?
That the people should be ready to cross the Jordan on the third day.

Did they readily obey Josue?
Yes; and the Rubenites, Gadites, and half tribe of Manasses, prepared to cross the Jordan with their brethren to assist them, according to promise, in the conquest of the land.

How did they cross the Jordan?
In the same manner that their fathers crossed the Red Sea: God exerted in their behalf, on entering the land of promise, the same miraculous power he displayed at the coming out of Egypt.

Describe the passage of the Jordan?
By the command of God, Josue directed the priests to move forward carrying the Ark, and keeping 2000 cubits in advance of the people who were ordered not to approach nearer. As soon as the priests touched the water it immediately divided, leaving a dry passage into which they entered; having reached the middle of the river they stood until all the people passed; and when all were over, as soon as the priests carrying the Ark came on the bank, the river returned to its accustomed channel.

What monument did Josue cause to be made of this miracle?
While the priests carrying the Ark were in the middle of the bed of the river, he directed twelve men,

one from every tribe to take each a stone from the spot where the priests stood and place them in the midst of the camp in the plains of Jericho (Galgal,) putting twelve others in their place.

When did the children of Israel cross the Jordan after this manner?
On the tenth of the first month, the forty-first year after their deliverance from Egypt. (Jos. iv. 19.)

How long did they remain encamped at Galgal before besieging any place?
Ten days, during which they kept the phase, and eat bread of the corn of the land, after which the manna ceased.

CHAPTER XXIX.

THE TAKING OF JERICHO AND HAI.

Which was the first place they took?
Jericho.

Relate the manner of taking it?
By the Divine command, Josue directed the priests to sound the seven trumpets of the Jubilee, and with the Ark, accompanied by the entire army, to march in procession once a day, for six days, round the walls of Jericho, and on the seventh day to march seven times round, and shout at a given signal. These directions they punctually observed, and as they simultaneously shouted, the walls of Jericho fell, and they took possession.

What reflection do the holy Fathers make on this miracle?
That Jericho, with its high walls and strong fortifications, thrown down by the sound of the trumpets, may be considered emblematic of the pride and greatness of this world, overthrown by the trumpet of the gospel; for God makes use of the foolish things of

this world to confound the wise, and the weak things to confound the strong.

Did the Israelites spare any of the inhabitants of Jericho?
Rahab and her family only, because she saved the lives of the spies whom Josue sent to view the place; all the rest they put to death, and killed all the cattle, having been commanded to destroy every thing but gold, silver, brass, or iron vessels, which should be reserved for Divine service.

What town did the Israelites attack next?
Hai. They were so elated with their success at Jericho, that they persuaded Josue to send only 3,000 men against it, thinking they had nothing to do but take possession: they, however, met with opposition, and fled, losing in their flight thirty-six of their number.

Was their flight owing to the fewness of their number?
No; but the anger of God was kindled against all, in consequence of the sin of one. Josue, ignorant of this, humbly prostrate before the Ark, his garments rent and dust on his head, expostulated with Almighty God for forsaking his people, and then learned from him that one had sinned, who should be sought for, by lot, next day and burned, with all belonging to him.

On whom did the lot fall?
The lot fell on Achan, of the family of Zare and tribe of Juda, who had appropriated to himself of the spoils of Jericho a scarlet robe, two hundred sicles of silver, and a gold rule of fifty sicles, which he kept concealed in his tent. Having confessed his guilt, he was executed, as God had directed.

Was Hai then taken?
Yes; God being appeased, delivered it to them, and permitted them to divide the spoils.

Did he deliver Hai to them in the same manner as Jericho?
No; but as if training them to battle, he directed an ambush to be laid behind, and a number of chosen men to attack in front, and after a little time to retreat, as if flying, to entice the enemy to pursue. When all the warriors had rushed out of Hai and Bothel, those who were in ambush entered, and set the towns on fire, while their brethren turned on their pursuers and exterminated them.

What did Josue after the destruction of Hai?
He built an altar of unhewn stones on Mount Hebal, as Moses had commanded, and offered on it holocausts and peace offerings, then to fulfil every direction of Moses, he wrote the law on stone, and divided the people, placing one half by Mount Hebal, the other by Mount Garizim, with the ark in the midst, and blessing them, read aloud the benedictions they should receive if faithful to God, and the curse that awaited them if unfaithful. (Jos. viii. 30.)

CHAPTER XXX.

THE CONQUESTS OF JOSUE.—DIVISION OF THE LAND AMONG THE TRIBES.—DEATH OF JOSUE.

What resolution did the princes of the land take?
To unite, and make war on the Israelites.

Were there any who did not enter into the league?
Yes, the Gabaonites, who foreseeing that it would be vain to contend with the people of God, had recourse to stratagem to induce them to enter into a friendly league with them. They sent ambassadors dressed in old clothes, who carried bread that was dry and hard, to make the Israelites think they had travelled a great distance, thus deceiving Josue and the ancients who entered into a compact with them?

How did it happen that Josue was deceived?
Because he did not consult God, but depended on his own judgment.

How did Josue act when he afterwards discovered that the Gabaonites had deceived him?
He spared their lives, as he had promised, but appointed them servants to the Israelites.

What did Adonisedec, king of Jerusalem, when he heard that the Gabaonites had leagued with Israel?
He assembled the neighboring kings in order to besiege Gabaon.

What did the Gabaonites then?
They sent to Josue for help, who immediately went to their assistance, and suddenly overthrew the confederates?

What miraculous events occurred during that battle?
The sun and moon stood still, at the command of Josue, "God obeyed the voice of man," and also fought for him, casting hailstones on the enemy, by which many more were killed than by the swords of the Israelites. (Jos. x. 13.)

How do you understand the expression, "The sun and moon stood still?"
In the same manner as we still say, "The sun rises in the east and sets in the west." Hence the fact here related is not at variance with the common opinion of modern astronomers, that the motion which regulates day and night is that of the earth, not of the sun or moon. The standing still of the earth is not less a miracle than that of the sun or moon would be, and the latter form of expression is alone intelligible.

What effect should such evidences of the omnipotence of God produce in us?
They should enliven our faith and animate our hope in him who is ever ready to grant the prayer of his

faithful servants, sometimes even suspending the laws of the universe for that purpose.

Was Josue successful in all his undertakings?
Yes; so that in five years after crossing the Jordan, the land rested from war, and was divided by lot among the nine tribes and half as commanded by God, Josue being assisted in the division by Eleazer, the priest, and a prince from each tribe. (Num. xxxiv. 17.; Jos. xi. 23, and xiv. 1.)

What particular portion was assigned to Caleb?
The fields and villages about Hebron, which he claimed in virtue of a promise made by Moses forty-five years before on his return from viewing the land. (Jos. xiv. and xxi. 12.)

How did Josue act towards the warriors of the two tribes and half who had assisted in conquering the land?
He dismissed them with rich presents to their families and possessions east of the Jordan.

What did the princes of the two tribes and half, on reaching their possessions?
They built a high altar as a testimony that they and the tribes that crossed the Jordan were of one family and faith. (Jos. xxii. 34.)

To what limits did Almighty God tell Josue he extended the eastern boundary of the Israelites' possessions?
To the river Euphrates, as he before promised Moses. (Deut. i. 7; Jos. 1, 4.)

What did Josue when he was grown old and saw his death approaching?
He assembled the ancients, princes, and judges, with the people, and represented to them the many favors God had done them in subduing the surrounding nations, and dividing the entire country among them by lot; and as for those nations that still remained unsubdued, he would also enable them to

conquer them, and continue his blessings and favors to them if they remained faithful, but would certainly drive them out of the land of promise, if they turned to the worship of false gods.

What did the people answer?
"God forbid that we should leave the Lord and serve strange gods; the Lord our God brought us and our fathers out of the land of Egypt, out of the house of bondage, and did very great signs in our sight, and preserved us in all the way by which we journeyed, and among all the people through whom we passed; and he hath cast out all the nations, the Amorrhite, the inhabitants of the land into which we are come; therefore we will serve the Lord, for he is our God."

How old was Josue when he died?
A hundred and ten years, having governed the people twenty-five years after the death of Moses. (Josephus Ant. c. i., and Pet., par. ii. 83.)

What other illustrious person died about the same time?
Eleazer, the son of Aaron. He was buried at Gabaoth, in Mount Ephraim, the possession of Phineas, his son.

CHAPTER XXXI.

HISTORY OF THE JUDGES, FROM JOSUE TO GEDEON.

Whom did God appoint to conduct the Israelites to battle after the death of Josue?
Caleb, prince of the tribe of Juda, who had formerly gone with Josue to view the land, and like him, was victorious over its inhabitants. He took many cities, among the rest Jerusalem, which he burned. This city was rebuilt, in consequence of the Benjamites, to whose lot it fell, having entered into a league with the Jebusites, who dwelt in it. (Jud. i.

2, 8, 21); but, nevertheless, during his time and that of the ancients who were with him, the Israelites did not fall into idolatry. (Jos. xxiv. 31.)

Did any of the other tribes follow the example of Benjamin, in making leagues with the Canaanites?
Yes, the greater number, for which God sent an angel to reproach them with their disobedience; on which they expressed contrition, and offered sacrifices. They did not, however, correct their fault, and, in consequence, fell into idolatry, as had been foretold them, and into very great temporal calamities.

Which were the principal temporal calamities they suffered?
Civil war, in which about 100,000 lost their lives, the tribe of Benjamin being nearly exterminated; together with several grievous oppressions and harassings by the neighboring nations.

Who was the first foreign potentate that God delivered them to after the death of Josue?
Chusam Rasathaim, King of Mesopotamia, who oppressed them greatly; but on their repentance, God raised them a deliverer, in the person of Othoniel, son-in-law to Caleb, who conquered their oppressors and preserved peace during the remainder of his life. He judged Israel forty years.

How long after Josue's death was Othoniel appointed?
About fifteen years, (according to the computation of Bossuet and Petavius.)

Did the Israelites remain faithful after the death of Othoniel?
No; they again abandoned the service of God, who delivered them into the power of the Moabites, but on their repentance raised Aod, and after him Samgar, who defeated their enemies and judged for eighty years.

For what were these two judges remarkable?
Aod for using the left hand as well as the right, and for killing Eglon, King of Moab. Samgar for slaying six hundred Philistines with a plough-share.

Did the Israelites again transgress?
Yes, and God delivered them into the power of Jabin, King of Canaan, who with his general, Sisara, grievously oppressed them.

Whom did God raise to deliver them, when called on?
Deborah, a prophetess, who judged Israel forty years. Sending for Barac, a valiant man of the tribe of Nephtali, she told him that God appointed him to lead an army to Mount Thabor, where he would deliver to him Sisara, with the warriors and chariots in which he trusted; on which Barac accepted the charge, but required that she should go with him.

Did Deborah consent?
Yes, but told him that the victory should not be attributed to him, as Sisara would be slain by a woman; which happened as she foretold; God struck Sisara with such fear at the sight of Barac, that, although in the midst of his great army, with 900 chariots armed with scythes, he fled and took refuge in the tent of a man named Haber, whose wife drove a nail into his head whilst he slept. His army in the meantime was utterly destroyed by Barac

CHAPTER XXXII.

HISTORY OF GEDEON AND OF ABIMILECH.

Did the Israelites again offend God?
Yes, for which he delivered them into the power of the Madianites, who treated them very cruelly, laying waste their fields and obliging them to fly to the mountains, to seek shelter in dens and caves.

Whom did God raise to rescue them when they returned to him?
Gedeon, who was of an obscure family of the tribe of Manasses, but valiant and pious. He was employed in cleansing wheat, when an angel appeared to him and told him to go and conquer the Madianites.

What sign did the angel give that the appointment was from God?
He waited until Gedeon prepared a sacrifice, consisting of a boiled kid and unleavened bread, and having desired him to lay it on a rock and pour the broth of the kid on it, he touched it with the rod he held in his hand, upon which fire arose from the rock and consumed it.

What command did Gedeon receive from God on the night of that day?
To destroy the altar of Baal, which was in the neighborhood, and cut down the grove that surrounded it; to offer two holocausts to God, one on the rock whereon he had sacrificed the kid, the other on a pile of the wood that was dedicated to Baal.

What did the townspeople next day, when they discovered what Gedeon had done?
They demanded him of his father, to put him to death; but he refused to give him up, saying, "Let Baal revenge himself if he be able;" on which Gedeon was surnamed Jerobaal.

What did Gedeon when he understood that the armies of Madian, Amelec, and other eastern nations had crossed the Jordan, to pillage the Israelites and destroy their harvests, as they had been in the habit of doing?
He assembled an army of 32,000 men from the neighboring tribes, and besought God to give him as a sign of victory, that the fleece he laid on the ground might be saturated with dew, whilst the ground about

it remained dry. The next morning, finding that his prayer was granted, he begged, as a further proof, that the fleece might be dry and the ground wet; which being also granted, he with confidence led out the army against the oppressors of his country.

What did Almighty God say to Gedeon when he led out the army?
" The people that are with thee are many, and Madian shall not be delivered into their hands, lest Israel should glory against me, and say, I was delivered by my own strength." He then desired Gedeon to make a proclamation that all who were timorous should return; in consequence of which only 10,000 remained.

Did God consider them still too numerous?
Yes, and gave Gedeon a sign by which he should know those whom he designed to accompany him to battle.

What was the sign?
That when they approached the water, those only should go who raised it to their mouths in the hollow of their hands, whilst all who drank kneeling at the stream should return.

How many were thus chosen?
Three hundred.

What stratagem did Gedeon make use of to conquer the Madianites?
He divided his men into three companies, and dispersed them round the enemies' camp, giving each a trumpet and a pitcher with a lighted lamp inside. At midnight, on a sign from Gedeon, they broke the pitchers simultaneously, and holding the lamps in their hands, shouted: "The sword of the Lord and of Gedeon."

What followed?
Sounding the trumpets, they so terrified the Madian-

ites that they killed one another, and the survivors in their flight were cut off by the Israelites, to whom Gedeon sent a message to pursue them; but the 300 continued sounding the trumpets until the enemy was completely routed.

How long did Gedeon judge Israel?
Forty years. After his death, the Israelites, forgetful of the great services he had rendered them, permitted his illegitimate son, Abimelech, to make himself king, and put Gedeon's seventy sons to death, the youngest, only, named Joatham, escaped by being concealed.

How long did Abimelech survive the murder of his brethren and enjoy his ill-gotten dignity?
Three years, which he passed in strife with the very people who had assisted him in his injustice and iniquity, at the end of which time he was killed.

CHAPTER XXXIII.

HISTORY OF THE JUDGES FROM THOLA TO SAMSON.

Who succeeded Abimelech?
His uncle Thola, who judged Israel twenty-three years, and was succeeded by Jair, who governed twenty-two years; he had thirty sons, who were princes of thirty cities.

After his death what happened?
After his death the Israelites again strayed from the service of God, and were guilty of idolatry, for which they were delivered into the power of the Philistines and Ammonites, until, humbled by their misfortunes, they again implored relief from God.

What answer did God give them on that occasion?
"Did not the Egyptians and the Amorrhites, the children of Ammon and the Philistines, the Sidonians also and Amelec, and Canaan, oppress you, and you cried to me, and I delivered you out of their

hands, and yet you have forsaken me, and have worshipped strange Gods, therefore I will deliver you no more: go and call upon the gods which you have chosen, let them deliver you in the time of distress." (Jud. x. 11.)

What did the Israelites then say?
"We have sinned;. do thou unto us whatsoever pleaseth thee, only deliver us this time;" and having said so, they cast away all their idols and turned to the service of God, who, being touched with their miseries, raised Jephte, a valiant man of Galaad, to deliver them.

What did Jephte do, when called to lead the army of Israel?
He first endeavored, by treaty, to induce the enemy to suspend hostilities, but failing in that, prepared for battle, and vowed to offer as a holocaust to God the first who would come out of his house to meet him on his return from the victory.

Who was the first that came to meet and congratulate him?
His only daughter, who seeing the grief and consternation of her father, and understanding from him the cause, encouraged and exhorted him to fulfil the vow he had made, only begging a respite of two months. (Jud. xi. 39.)

In what manner did Jephte fulfil his vow?
Interpreters of holy Scripture differ in opinion on the subject; some suppose that he consecrated her to God by a vow of perpetual virginity, others that he offered her a holocaust to God.[*]

How long did Jephte judge Israel?

---

[*] This is the more common opinion. Supposing him to have done so, we must say either that what he did was wrong, although, perhaps, excusable in him on the ground of ignorance; or that it was justified by a special inspiration of God, who, being the supreme Lord of all, could, of course, authorize such an action.

Six years, during which an unhappy sedition was raised by the tribe of Ephraim; Jephte had at length to take arms, and forty-two thousand Ephraimites fell in the contest. (Jud. xii. 16.)

How long were the Israelites in possession of the promised land at this time?
About three hundred years. (Jud xi. 26.)

Who succeeded Jephte?
Abesan, of Bethlehem, who judged Israel seven years, and was succeeded by Ahialon, who judged ten years, to whom succeeded Abdon, who governed eight years, after whose death the Israelites again fell into idolatry, and were delivered into the power of the Philistines.

After they were sufficiently punished, whom did God raise to relieve and judge them?
Samson, of the tribe of Dan, who was consecrated to God from his birth, and was remarkable for his great strength; he judged Israel twenty years. (Jud. xv. 20.)

Relate some of the exploits of Samson?
On one occasion, though unarmed, he killed a furious lion, which he seized and tore to pieces. Being insulted by the Philistines, the oppressors of his people, he caught three hundred foxes and tied lighted torches to their tails, and let them loose among the corn and vineyards of the Philistines. On another occasion being surrounded by an army of Philistines, he seized the jaw-bone of an ass, and slew a thousand of the enemy and routed the remainder.

How was Samson miraculously supplied with drink when weary and faint with combating the Philistines?
God opened a great tooth in the jaw of the ass (which he had used as his weapon,) and water issued forth, with which he refreshed himself.

How did Samson fall into the power of the Philistines?
He suffered himself to be deceived by a woman named Dalila, who after some fruitless attempts to discover wherein his great strength lay, at length induced him to tell her that being consecrated to God from his birth, his hair had never been cut, and that if it were shaved he would be weak like other men. She immediately gave notice to the princes of the Philistines, and sending for a barber, had his head shaved whilst he slept; on which his strength left him, the Philistines made him prisoner and pulled out his eyes.

Can you relate the particulars of his death?
As his hair grew his strength returned; and being conducted by the Philistines into a great hall where they were holding a feast, Samson laying hold of two pillars upon which the building rested, and prayed to God, saying: "Let me die with the Philistines," then shaking the pillars, the house fell, and Samson was buried in the ruins with three thousand of the enemy.

CHAPTER XXXIV.

HISTORY OF RUTH.

What is related of Elimelech?
During a famine in part of Palestine in the time of the judges, Elimelech, a native of Bethlehem, retired with his wife and two sons into the land of Moab, where he soon after died; after his death his sons married women of the country, but at the end of ten years died without children, and their mother, Neomi, in deep affliction, prepared to return home.

What did Neomi persuade her daughters-in-law?
Her two daughters-in-law expressed a wish to accompany her, but she endeavored to dissuade them, representing to them that it would be better for

them to remain with their relations in their own country than go to a strange land with her, from whom they could expect nothing.

What did one of them declare?
One of them, whose name was Ruth, would not leave her, declaring that death alone should part them. "Whithersoever thou shalt go," said she, "I wil go, where thou shall dwell, I also will dwell, th people shall be my people, and thy God my God."

What is said of her faith and piety?
Her faith and filial piety were rewarded, for when Neomi saw that Ruth was determined to accompany her, she no longer offered any opposition, and both returned to Bethlehem in the beginning of the barley harvest.

What is related of her?
As they were very poor, Ruth asked her mother-in-law's permission to go into the fields to glean. Providence directed her to the field of a rich man named Booz, a near relation of her deceased husband, who, noticing her assiduity, inquired of his overseer concerning her, and hearing an account of her dutiful behavior to her mother-in-law, directed that every civility and kindness should be shown her, desired the reapers to let some corn fall purposely that she might not feel embarrassed in taking it, and invited her to eat at meal-times with them.

Did Ruth accept the invitation?
Yes; she gratefully accepted the invitation, and in the evening related to her mother-in-law all that had passed, and gave her part of her dinner which she had reserved for her: Neomi prayed for blessings on their benefactor, and when she understood that it was Booz, told Ruth that he being nearly related, ought, according to the Mosaic law, to be her husband, and desired her to claim the affinity; she obeyed her mother-in-law: Booz acknowledged her

claim, and promised to marry her, if another, who was more nearly related, should refuse.

The next day, what did Booz do?
The next day, Booz, in the presence of ten respectable witnesses explained Ruth's claim to his kinsman: "Neomi," said he, "the widow of Elimelech, is willing to sell a certain field that belonged to the deceased, if thou art willing to take it by right of kindred, buy and possess it; but if not, say so, that I may know what I have to do;" he answered "I will buy the field;" "then," said Booz, "you must also marry Ruth, the Moabitess, who was wife to the deceased."

The man having declined, what followed?
The man having declined doing so, as he was married, yielded his right of kindred to Booz, who immediately married Ruth, with the good wishes and blessings of all present, for they were interested in her, and admired her for her virtue and piety. Neomi's happiness was complete when Ruth presented her a son to be a comfort to her in her old age: she called him Obed, he was father to Issai, and grandfather to David. In the history of Ruth, the holy Fathers admired the liberal goodness of God in rewarding her piety with the highest dignity on earth, that of being ranked in the genealogy of the Messiah.

CHAPTER XXXV.
HISTORY OF HELI AND SAMUEL.

Who judged Israel after Samson?
Heli, the High Priest, for forty years. (1 Kings iv. 18.)

Who was Heli?
He was High Priest and ministered to God in Silo where the ark rested from the time that the Israelites entered the promised land

How many sons had he, and what is said of them?
He had two sons, Ophni and Phineas, who scandalized the people by their crimes, and deterred them from sacrificing to God by their extortions. When they were complained to him, instead of punishing them as they deserved, he contented himself with advising them; whereupon Almighty God sent a prophet to foretell him the sudden death of his two sons, and the removal of the priesthood from his family, in which there should not be an old man from that time forward.

What is said of the prophesy relating to his sons?
The prophesy relating to his sons was fulfilled soon after, for in a battle with the Philistines, the Israelites seeing that they were likely to be defeated, sent for the ark, that its presence might ensure the victory; but the event proved contrary to their expectations, they were defeated, the two sons of Heli killed, and the ark taken, on hearing which, Heli fell from his seat, and broke his neck, being then ninety-eight years old. (1 Kings iv. 15.)

When was the other part of the prophesy fulfilled?
The other part of the prophesy relating to the removal of the High Priesthood from his family, was not fulfilled until the reign of Solomon, when Abiather, the last of his race that held that dignity, was banished for treasonable practices. (3 Kings ii. 27.)

What illustrious person was consecrated to God in the time of Heli?
The prophet Samuel, who was the fruit of his mother's prayers, and consecrated by her to God from his birth. When very young, his parents Elcana and Anna presented him in the House of the Lord in Silo, and left him in Heli's care.

Of what tribe was he?
He was of the tribe of Levi, and family of Caath, which was the principal among the Levites, and to which

the guard of the sanctuary was entrusted. (Num. iii. 28.)

What occurred to Samuel when he was about twelve years old?
As he slept in the place where the ark was kept, he was called three different times. Each time he arose, and went to Heli, thinking it was he who called him. The third time, Heli understanding it to be the voice of God, told Samuel to say, when next he heard it, "Speak, Lord, thy servant heareth."

When called again, what did Samuel do?
Accordingly, when God called again, Samuel answered as he was directed, and God repeated to him what he had before foretold to Heli by the mouth of the prophet, of the punishments that awaited him on account of not chastising his sons

What did the Philistines do with the ark when they got possession of it?
They placed it in the temple of Dagon, but the idol could not stand in the presence of the ark of the Lord, and fell on its face. Being replaced, it was found the next day also fallen on the ground before the ark, its head and hands broken off.

How long did the Philistines keep the ark?
Seven months; during which time they were obliged to send it from place to place, everywhere it rested the people being struck with plagues. At length they consulted their wise men, who advised them to send it back, and with it as a propitiation a little box containing golden representations of the plagues with which they were afflicted.

In what manner did these wise men order the ark to be sent back?
On a new cart, having yoked to it two cows that had calves which were to be allowed to go whatever way they pleased; and according to the direction they

took, the people were to consider the plagues as coming from God or happening by chance.

What direction did the cows take?
That which led to Bethsames, the nearest Levitical town, which was the way specified by the wise men as the proof that their punishment came from God.

How did the Bethsamites act on seeing the ark?
They rejoiced exceedingly, and breaking up the cart, laid the cows on it a holocaust to the Lord, (the Levites having previously taken down the ark and little box;) but the people, unmindful of the prohibition under pain of death, of looking with curiosity on holy things, approached nearer than was permitted and 50,000 of them were struck dead for their irreverence.

What did the Bethsamites then do?
They informed the inhabitants of Cariathiarim of the arrival of the ark, and begged them to send for it. They did so immediately, and carried it to the house of Abinidab, in Gabaa, near Cariathiarim, whose son Eleazer was sanctified to keep it.

What effect did the presence of the ark then produce?
It became the source of blessings to all around, and of undisturbed peace to Israel for twenty years, when on occasion of a religious festival held at Maspath by the prophet Samuel, the Philistines attacked them, but God fought for his people by sending a dreadful thunder-storm on the enemy, which so encouraged the Israelites that they completely routed them.

Who was the last judge in Israel?
The prophet Samuel, who was always deservedly held in the highest estimation.

CHAPTER XXXVI.

SAUL ANOINTED KING OF ISRAEL.

What led to the Israelites demanding a king?
Samuel, being grown old, entrusted a share of his authority to his two sons, who abused it by taking bribes and judging unjustly, which gave the Israelites, who longed to be like other nations, a pretext for demanding a king to judge them and lead them to battle. (1 Kings viii. 20.)

Did Samuel immediately comply with their demand?
No; he was grieved at it, and consulted God, who answered that it was himself, and not Samuel, whom they rejected, and told him to represent to them the great power a king would have, and how he would oppress them; but that if they still persisted in their demand, he should yield to them.

Did they persist in their demand?
Yes; and Samuel anointed Saul, the son of Cis, of the tribe of Benjamin, their first king. (1 Kings x. 1.)

What circumstances led to the anointing of Saul?
Being sent to seek his father's asses, which had strayed away, he spent three days in a fruitless search, and then, by his servant's advice, went to consult the prophet Samuel concerning them.

On his approach, what is said of Samuel?
On his approach, Samuel understood that he was the person whom God decreed to be king; he accordingly invited him to his house, treated him with distinction, told him that his father's asses were found, and in the morning, before they parted, anointed him king, assuring him that he should deliver the people from the enemies who surrounded and harassed them.

What did Samuel do after that?
He assembled the people to draw lots for the sovereignty, and the lot fell on Saul, who, not being present, was sought for, and presented by Samuel to them as their king, desiring them to observe the majestic appearance of him whom God gave to reign over them, for Saul was much taller than any of them; and in this also God condescended to their weakness, who were always attracted by externals.

How did they receive their first king?
The generality cried out, "God save the king;" but some malcontents commenced saying, "Shall this fellow be able to save us?" But Saul graciously dissembled, as though he did not hear, and acted with great forbearance towards them.

In what enterprise did Saul first engage after his exaltation?
In an expedition against the Ammonites, who attacked the town of Jabes Galaad, and refused to enter into a treaty with the inhabitants, but on condition of their submitting to have their right eyes plucked out.

What did the besieged implore, and what did Saul do?
The besieged implored a respite of seven days, and consented to what the Ammonites required, if within that time they could not procure help. They then sent messengers to Saul, who, on hearing the melancholy account, peremptorily assembled an army, and gave the Ammonites a signal defeat. (1 Kings xi 11.)

What did Saul after that victory?
He went with Samuel to Galgal to offer sacrifices of thanksgiving, and to be more solemnly acknowledged king.

What reproach did Samuel make the people on that occasion?

That they had rejected God, who was himself their king, and who when called on had always raised up a leader from among them to deliver them from their enemies; yet he promised that God would still protect them if they continued faithful, but declared that they and their king should perish, if they kept not their faith with God. (1 Kings xii 25.)

CHAPTER XXXVII.

SAUL'S CONQUEST—JONATHAN DISTINGUISHES HIMSELF

What enemies were next encountered by Saul?
The Philistines, whose garrison in Gabaa (Saul's residence) being attacked by Jonathan, they assembled in great numbers and encamped in Macmas with 30,000 chariots and 6,000 horsemen.

What number had Saul with him at that time?
Two thousand chosen men, whom he had selected after the battle with the Ammonites. On that occasion he formed a standing army of three thousand, two thousand of whom he appointed to attend himself, and one thousand to attend his son Jonathan.

What place of rendezvous did Saul appoint for the Israelites before encountering the Philistines?
Galgal, whither he immediately repaired, and there aited the arrival of the prophet Samuel, who was ,o have offered sacrifice before the battle, but as the prophet delayed to come, the people slipped away until only six hundred remained with Saul.

What did Saul then do?
Saul, impatient at the delay, and fearful of being attacked by the Philistines, usurped an office to which God had not appointed him, and offered the holocaust himself, foolishly thinking that God would be rendered propitious by the victims being sacrificed to him, though not offered in accordance with

the law; but the holocaust was scarcely consumed when Samuel arrived, and, understanding what had been done, severely reprimanded Saul, and told him that God would not continue the kingdom to his family.

Were the six hundred who remained with Saul well armed?
No; they had neither sword nor spear, and even their implements of husbandry were blunt, for the Philistines had taken particular care that they should not have a smith among them. (1 King xiii. 19.) Saul and Jonathan alone had arms.

How were the Philistines defeated?
Jonathan, relying on the power of God, and considering that he could defeat an army by means of few as well as many, entered the camp of the Philistines attended only by his armor-bearer, and having killed a great many, created such confusion that in their terror they killed one another. The tumult being observed by the Israelites, they regained courage, and pursued the enemy until evening, when fatigue obliged them to desist. (1 Kings xiv. 6.)

What rash vow did Saul make during the battle?
That none should taste food until evening.

Did any one break the vow?
Yes, Jonathan not having been aware of his father's vow, and being faint and weary, took in passing a little wild honey.

How was it discovered?
At night, when the people had refreshed themselves, Saul proposed to renew the battle and utterly exterminate the Philistines before morning. They all readily consented; but Achias, the High Priest, advised him to consult God. He did so; but receiving no answer, understood that God was offended, and immediately drew lots to discover by whom.

On whom did the lot fall?

The lot fell on Jonathan, who acknowledged having tasted the honey; but when his father would have put him to death, the people would not suffer it, and Saul had to desist from the pursuit of the Philistines who returned to their homes.

Was peace established after this battle?
No, Saul had almost continued wars during his reign but by the help of God was always victorious.

Whom did Saul encounter after defeating the Philistines?
The Amalekites, whom the prophet Samuel, on the part of God, commanded him to destroy with all that belonged to them.

Was Saul guilty of any act of disobedience in this war?
Yes, he spared Agag, king of the Amalekites, and reserved the fairest of the flocks, under pretence of keeping them for sacrifice.

What did Samuel say to Saul when he understood how he had acted?
That God preferred obedience to sacrifice; and that as Saul rejected the command of God, so God rejected him from being king of Israel, and would confer that dignity on another.

What became of Agag?
He was hewed in pieces by Samuel before the ark in Galgal, and in presence of all the people who were assembled to celebrate the triumph; after which, Samuel returned home, greatly grieved for the sin of Saul. (1 Kings xv. 32.)

CHAPTER XXXVIII.

DAVID ANOINTED KING—HIS VICTORY OVER GOLIAH.

What command did God give Samuel whilst he mourned for Saul?
To go to Bethlehem, on the plea of offering sacrifice,

and anoint as king one of the sons of Issai, of the tribe of Juda. (1 Kings xvi. 1.)

Which of the sons of Issai did Samuel anoint?
David, the youngest, who was employed at the time of the prophet's visit in keeping his father's sheep in the fields, and was not brought forward until Samuel had seen his seven brothers successively. Understanding that God had not chosen any of them, he asked Issai had he no other son, and being informed that he had, ordered him to be sent for, and immediately on his coming in the prophet was desired by God to arise and anoint him. Then the Spirit of God, forsaking Saul, came on David. (1 Kings xvi. 13.)

What affliction befel Saul immediately?
An evil spirit troubled him, which his officers perceiving, advised him to send for a good performer on the harp, to soothe him in the frantic fits to which he had become subject. David being recommended, was sent for, and succeeded in calming the king, with whom he became so great a favorite that he made him his armor-bearer.

What was David's character?
He was meek, humble, patient, and forgiving; prudent, pious, and valiant; and was an excellent musician.

Relate as much as you know of David's victory over Goliah?
The Philistines assembled in great numbers to attack the Israelites, who, on their part, under the conduct of Saul, prepared to make a vigorous resistance. As the two armies lay encamped opposite each other, a Philistine, named Goliah, of gigantic size, came into the midst, scornfully defying the Israelites to produce a man who could terminate the war by engaging in single combat with him.

How long did Goliah repeat the challenge?

For forty days he daily repeated his challenge twice, but no one had courage to accept it, though Saul had promised to enrich and make the victorious champion his son-in-law.

Who accepted the challenge?
David, who had been sent by his father with provisions to his brethren who were in the camp, and saw Goliah and heard his challenge.

What did Saul do?
Saul, on hearing it, expostulated with him, representing to him that he was only a boy and the Philistine a warrior from his youth; but David alleged that he had already killed a bear and a lion that had attacked his father's flocks, and that he who had preserved him in those dangers would deliver him from the proud idolator who had dared to curse the army of the living God.

On seeing him advance, what did Goliah?
Goliah, seeing him advance, reviled him, despising his youth and weapons, for he had only a shepherd's sling, while he himself was cased in armor, and had a shield, sword, and spear proportioned to his enormous bulk. David replied: "You come to me, trusting in your armor, but I come to you in the name of the Lord of Hosts;" and putting a stone in his sling, struck the giant in the forehead, who instantly falling, David ran up and cut off his head with his own sword, upon seeing which the Philistines fled. (1 Kings xvii. 52.)

CHAPTER XXXIX.

SAUL'S JEALOUSY.—DEATH OF SAMUEL.

How was Saul affected by the fame that David acquired?
He was filled with such envy and hatred that he sought occasion to kill him. (1 Kings xviii. 8.)

How did Jonathan feel towards David?
He loved him as a brother, and cemented with him
a friendship which ended only with his life.
What appointment did Saul give David?
He made him captain over a thousand, at the same
time admonishing him to be valiant, and that he
would, according to promise, give him his eldest
daughter in marriage. This he said, in the hope
that David by endeavoring to distinguish himself in
battle would be killed.
*Did Saul give David his eldest daughter as he
had promised?*
No; at the time appointed for the marriage he gave
her to another; but being informed that his younger
daughter Michol was attached to David, he said he
would give her to him, but yet, not without the further condition that he should kill a hundred Philistines. Not having as yet avowed himself David's
enemy, he used these means to rid himself of him;
but the event disappointed his envious calculations,
for David having killed two hundred, Saul was
obliged to fulfil his promise, and Michol became
David's wife.
Did Saul become more reconciled to David then?
No; he still pursued him with unrelenting animosity, and made many attempts on his life, from
which David, being guarded by an ever-watchful
Providence, escaped. On one occasion he was saved
by the contrivance of Michol, who deceived the king's
messengers; on another, by a timely warning of
Jonathan.
At another time, how was David saved?
Another time, Saul in person pursued him, and had
him and his few followers surrounded by his troops,
when a sudden inroad of the Philistines obliged him
to withdraw, and so David escaped.
Did any suffer from Saul's vengeance for having

shown kindness to David when he fled to save his life?

Yes, eighty-five priests, together with their families, were put to death by his orders, and all that belonged to them destroyed, because Achimilech, the High Priest, had given bread, and the sword of Goliah to David, though at that time he was not aware of David's flight from Saul. (1 Kings xxi.)

Did any of the priests dwelling in Nobe escape on that occasion?

Abiather only, who was son to Achimilech, the great grandson of Heli. He took the ephod, and fled for protection to David, who, acknowledging himself the cause of all the miseries that befel the priest and his family, promised to protect him.

Did David require the ministry of the High Priest whilst he was endeavoring to elude Saul?

Yes, on one occasion he consulted God through him as to whether he should attack the Philistines who were then besieging a town, named Ceila. God replied to do so, promising victory. A little after, on the report that Saul intended to attack Ceila where he then dwelt, and being apprehensive that the inhabitants would deliver him up, he had again recourse to God, who answered, "They will deliver thee up." (1 Kings xxiii. 32.) So David fled and escaped. Also when robbers attacked Sicoleg, David's residence, and carried off all that belonged to him and his followers in their absence, he consulted God to know what he should do, who directed him to pursue them, and promised that he should recover what was taken. (1 Kings xxx. 8.)

To whom did God usually give oracles?

To the judge, High Priest, or king.

How used the oracle to be given?

When counsel was implored in presence of the ark,

Note.—The loaves of proposition, for he had no other.

the oracle or voice proceeded from between the cherubim on the propitiatory. When the ark was not present, the oracle proceeded from the Rational on the High Priest's vestment, on which were the words Urim and Thummin. God sometimes gave answers without either, by prophets.

Mention some of the instances of magnanimity and piety exhibited by David whilst pursued by Saul with deadly hatred?
At one time Saul accidentally went unattended into a cave where David lay concealed with his followers, who urged him to cut off his enemy at once, as he was then in his power, but David would not raise his hand against the Lord's anointed, nor suffer him to be injured by any one, and merely cut off a piece of the king's robe, which, when Saul had gone a little way, he called after him and showed, remonstrating with him at the same time for his unjust hatred.

Can you relate any thing further?
On another occasion he and one of his followers named Abisai penetrated into Saul's camp, and even into the royal tent whilst Saul and his attendants slept, and again he would not suffer Abisai to kill him, but contented himself with taking the king's spear which was at his head, of which he made n other use than to produce it as a proof of his loyalty for when he had gone a little distance he called out to Saul, told what he had done, again remonstrated with him, and desired one of his servants to come for the spear.

What do the holy Fathers say of David's conduct on these occasions?
That it is a reproach to those Christians who retain resentment, and fancy that they may push it to what lengths they please, to see David who had not had the example, nor been taught by the word of an incarnate God, so far surpass them in charity and

forgiveness of injuries: he preferred remaining continually exposed to death from the unjust persecution of a tyrant, rather than free himself by raising his hand against the anointed of the Lord.

What great person died whilst David was still pursued by Saul?
The prophet Samuel to the great grief of the entire nation. (1 Kings xxv. 1.)

CHAPTER XL.

FLIGHT OF DAVID.—DEATH OF SAUL.

To whom did David flee when he found that he could no longer prudently remain in the kingdom?
To Achis, king of the Philistines, who received him courteously, and gave him the town of Siceleg, where he and his followers dwelt four months.

What happened about the end of that time?
The Philistines going to war with Israel, Achis was anxious that David and his followers should accompany him; but on the eve of the battle, the lords of the Philistines objected so strongly that Achis was obliged to send them back.

On returning to Siceleg, what is related?
On returning to Siceleg, they discovered that the Amalekites had burned the houses, and carried the women and children away, on which David having consulted God through Abiather, the priest, immediately pursued the enemy, vanquished them, and took possession of the spoil they had collected during their robbing expedition, which he divided equally between those who had assisted him in the combat, and those who through fatigue remained behind. (1 Kings xxx. 24.)

How did Saul act previously to the threatened attack of the Philistines?
Dismayed at their appearance, he consulted God as

to the result of the approaching battle, but received no answer. To discover what God would not reveal, he had recourse to sorcery, and going to a witch who lived at Endor, desired her to call to him the prophet Samuel, lately deceased. The witch used her incantations, and it pleased God to permit the prophet to appear.

What did Samuel say to Saul?
He asked him why he troubled him, and sought information from any one, as God had departed from him on account of the disobedience for which he had been before reproved, adding, that the Philistines would be victorious next day, and he with his sons numbered among the dead.

Was the result of the battle such as Samuel predicted?
Yes, the Israelites were totally routed, and Saul, his son Jonathan, and two other sons were killed on Mount Gelboe, where the battle was fought.

In what manner did Saul die?
Being grievously wounded, and fearing to fall into the hands of the Philistines, he threw himself on his own sword. (1 Kings xxxi. 4.)

How long did Saul reign?
Forty years. (Acts xiii. 21.)

How did David receive the news of Saul's death?
With sincere grief; and he caused the man who brought the intelligence to be put to death, because he said he had killed Saul, hoping to ingratiate himself with David.

CHAPTER XLI.

DAVID ACKNOWLEDGED KING.

What did David, when the time of mourning for Saul and Jonathan had expired?
He consulted God as to how he should act, who de-

sired him to go to Hebron, where, on his arrival, he was acknowledged king by the tribe of Juda. (2 Kings ii. 4.)

How old was David when he was anointed king in Hebron?
Thirty years. (2 Kings v. 4.)

How long did David reign in Hebron before all Israel acknowledged him?
Seven years and six months, during which time there was a contest between him and Isboseth, a son of Saul, who was made king by Abner, general of Saul's army. (2 Kings v. 5.)

How was the contest terminated?
By the death of Isboseth and Abner; the former was murdered in his bed by two of his captains, and the latter treacherously killed by Joab, general of David's army, under pretence of revenging his brother Asael, who was slain in battle by Abner.

Did David resent these murders?
Yes, he caused the murderers of Isboseth to be put to death, but had to be content with mourning for Abner, and disavowing all knowledge or share in his death, because Joab and his family were too powerful for him, as he himself complained, and besides the murder was clothed with some show of justice. (2 Kings iii. 39, iv. 12.)

Why was Joab made general of David's army?
In consequence of a promise which David had made when he attempted to take Jerusalem, the stronghold of the Jebusites, that he who would first effect an entrance should obtain the command of the army. Joab succeeded in the attempt, and was made general. (1 Par. xi. 6.)

What was Joab's character?
He was a loyal subject and an excellent general, but imperious and rude, even to the king; jealous in his disposition, and treacherous to those he considered

rivals. He slew Abner at the time that general came over to David's interests, and stabbed Amasa, because David on one occasion gave him the command of the troops; he afterwards killed Absalom, David's son, contrary to the express command of his father, who desired the rebel's life to be spared.

What place did David choose for his residence when acknowledged king by all Israel?
The castle of Sion, in Jerusalem, from which he had previously driven the Jebusites, and having built round it, called the place the City of David.

How did the Philistines act when they heard that David was made king?
They assembled their forces against him, but he, having consulted God, who promised him victory, attacked them vigorously and gave them a signal overthrow.

CHAPTER XLII.

DAVID'S PIETY.—HIS FALL AND REPENTANCE.

What was David's first care when he found himself established in the kingdom?
To promote the glory of God and establish Divine worship with due honor, for which purpose he convened the princes of the tribes, and all the chief officers, with the priests and Levites, to translate the ark from Cariathiarim, (where it still remained since the Philistines returned it,) to the royal city. (1 Par. xiii. 1.)

Why did not David convey the ark at that time to Jerusalem, as he intended?
When he had accompanied it part of the way, with great pomp and rejoicing, he was so terrified at the fate of Oza, son of Aminidab, who was struck dead for having rashly taken hold of the ark when it ap-

peared in danger of falling, that he had it carried into the house of a Levite, named Obededom. (2 Kings vi. 11.)

How long did the ark remain in the house of Obededom?
Three months, during which time God so manifestly blessed him and all his family, that David, with great joy and every mark of veneration, had it removed to the tabernacle prepared for it on Mount Sion. On this occasion he took care to have it carried by the Levites, according to the appointment of God. (1 Par. xv. 2.)

What did Michol when she saw David, divested of his royal robes, dancing before the ark?
She reproached him with being like a buffoon, and forgetful of his royal dignity.

What did David say?
He meekly and religiously replied that he would humble himself more and more in presence of God, who had chosen him preferably to her father and her father's house.

What ought we learn from David's example in this?
Not to be deterred by the raillery of the world from the performance of our religious duties, but, with meek Christian fortitude, manifest by our works what we inwardly believe.

What design did David form when he got a respite from war?
To build a Temple to God, as it grieved him to think that the ark of the Covenant rested in a tabernacle covered with skins, whilst he dwelt in a palace of cedar. (2 Kings vii.)

Did the prophet Nathan approve his design?
Yes, and at the moment encouraged him to put it into execution; but at night God desired him to inform David that the work should be reserved for his

son and successor, Solomon, who would enjoy perfect peace throughout his reign, and therefore be better qualified to build the Temple than he, who had been engaged in so many wars. (1 Par. xxii. 9; xxviii. 6.)

Did David acquiesce in the Divine decree?
He did, and much as he desired to build the Temple, he contented himself with providing materials, leaving the accomplishment of the work to him whom God had chosen and devoted himself to promote the happiness of his people, whom he relieved from a tribute which they had formerly incurred to some of the neighboring states. (2 Kings viii. 1—15.

Did David, when at the height of prosperity, remember his former friendship to Jonathan?
Yes; having discovered that Miphiboseth, a son of Jonathan, lived, he sent for him, had him to eat at his own table, gave him all that belonged to Saul, and appointed Siba, with his family (formerly servants to the late king) to serve him.

What circumstance led to David's war with the Ammonites?
Daas, the king, died, and David, desirous of testifying gratitude for favors received from him, sent ambassadors to Hanon, his son, to comfort him. That young king, suffering himself to be persuaded that the ambassadors were spies, had their heads and beards shaved, and half their clothes off, which so incensed David, that he sent Joab against him, and went himself against his allies, to whom he gave a signal overthrow.

What special mark of loyalty and fidelity did Joab give in the course of the war with the Ammonites?
Having closely beseiged Rabbath, the royal city, which contained great treasures, and brought it to the point of surrendering, he sent word to David to

come and take it, lest, if he delayed, the glory would be given to himself. (2 Kings xii. 27.)

What grievous sins did David commit during this war?
The horrid crimes of murder and adultery.

By what parable did the Prophet Nathan reprehend these crimes?
"A rich and a poor man dwelt in one city; the former had great numbers of sheep and oxen; the latter had only one little lamb. A visitor coming to the rich man, he would not serve him out of his abundance, but took the poor man's lamb and dressed it for him."

At this, what did David say?
At this David, with indignation, said, "He shall restore fourfold, and shall die." Nathan replied, "Thou art the man;" then pointing out to him his sins, added threats of the Divine justice. David, with bitter grief, confessed his iniquity, which the Prophet said was pardoned, but for which, nevertheless, he should be severely punished. (2 Kings xii.)

CHAPTER XLIII.

DAVID CAUSES SOLOMON TO BE PROCLAIMED KING.—HIS LAST INSTRUCTIONS AND DEATH.

How did David pass the remaining twenty years of his life?
In wars, and civil dissensions, his son Absolom headed a rebellion, and drove him from the throne, to which he was scarcely restored when Siba, a Benjamite, raised another, and withdrew all but the tribe of Juda from their allegiance; after which, the kingdom not being long established in peace, he yielded to vanity in numbering the people, which so displeased God that he sent a plague, of which seventy thousand died within three days.

What return did Joab give of the number of the people?
That there were 470,000 fighting men of Juda and 1,100,000 of Israel, exclusive of Levi and Benjamin, whom Joab did not number, having unwillingly executed the king's orders. (1 Par. xxi.)

How did David act when he saw the people punished for his sin?
Prostrate before God, in a penitential garb, he humbly implored him to turn his wrath from the people on him who alone was guilty; on which God, who is ever ready to grant more than he is asked, commanded the destroying angel to stop.

Where did the destroying angel stop?
Over the thrashing floor of Ornan or Arenna, the Jebusite, on Mount Moria, in Jerusalem, where David, by command of the prophet Gad, erected an altar and offered sacrifice, of which God testified his acceptance by sending fire from heaven, which consumed it. (1 Par. xxi.) It was on this site that the temple was afterwards built. (2 Par. iii. 1.)

What did David a little before his death?
He assembled the princes and ancients, and presenting his son Solomon, announced that God had chosen him for his successor, and appointed him to build the temple, for which he himself had to the utmost of his ability amassed materials of the richest description, but from his having been engaged in war was not permitted by God to erect it.

What did he then do?
He then exhorted them to assist Solomon, who was very young, (only eighteen,) in the great work, and invited them all to contribute to it. They joyfully complied, and promised allegiance to Solomon.

Repeat part of David's thanksgiving on that occasion?
" Thine, O Lord, is magnificence, and power, and

glory, and victory; and to thee is praise, for all that is in heaven and in earth is thine. Thine is the kingdom, O Lord, and thou art above all princes. Thine are riches, and thine is glory, thou hast dominion over all, in thy hand is power and might, in thy hand greatness and the empire of all things. Now, therefore, our God, we give thanks to thee, and we praise thy glorious name. Who am I, and what is my people, that we should be able to promise thee all these things? All things are thine, and we have given thee what we received of thy hand. (1 Par. xxix.)

How did Adonias, David's eldest son, act, when he perceived that his father drew near his death?
He attracted Joab, Abiather, and other persons in power, to his interest, and having made a great feast, to which he invited all his brethren, except Solomon, caused himself to be proclaimed king by his guests. (3 Kings 1.)

How were the designs of Adonias frustrated?
The prophet Nathan being informed of what was done, went to Bethsabee, Solomon's mother, and desired her to go immediately to the king, and remind him of the promise he had made in favor of her son. She did so, and had scarcely ended, when Nathan entered, supported her words, and related what had just occurred; on which David desired him to go instantly with Sadoc, the priest, anoint, and proclaim Solomon king, and place him on the throne that very day. (3 Kings i. 34.)

What did David do when his directions relative to Solomon were executed?
He returned thanks to God for beholding the successor whom he had chosen, filling the throne; gave instructions to Solomon relative to the building of the temple, and the regulation of divine worship, and exhorted him to be faithful to God. (3 Kings i. 48.)

What distribution did David make of the Levites?
He divided the family of Aaron into twenty-four courses, consisting of chief men whose turn to minister in the priestly office was decided by lot, and under whom he placed 24,000 Levites to perform other duties in the house of God. He also appointed 6,000 overseers and judges, 4,000 porters, and 4,000 musicians. (1 Par. xxiii.)

What arrangements did David make for the army?
He required 24,000 from each tribe to attend in turn, one month each. (1 Par. xxvii.)

How old was David when he died?
About seventy years. He was thirty when he began his reign in Hebron, where he reigned seven years and a half, and thirty-three over all Israel, in Jerusalem. (3 Kings ii. 11.)

Where was David buried?
In that part of Jerusalem called the city of David, which thenceforward became the burying place of the kings of Juda. (2 Kings v. 9., and 3 Kings ii. 10.)

How did Adonias act when he heard that Solomon was proclaimed king?
He fled to the altar for sanctuary, but Solomon forgave him, and permitted him to return to his house.

CHAPTER XLIV.

SOLOMON'S WISDOM.

Did Adonias renew his pretensions to the throne after the death of his father?
Yes, for which Solomon condemned him to death, together with Joab, who was in his interest, and banished Abiather, thus fulfilling the prophecy pronounced against Heli's race, (1 Kings ii. 32,) for the High Priesthood immediately passed into another branch, and Sadoc was appointed to succeed

Whom did Solomon make general in place of Joab?
Banais, one of the most valiant among the thirty renowned warriors who adhered to David during the persecution he underwent from Saul.

Whom did Solomon marry?
The daughter of Pharaoh, king of Egypt, about a year after his father's death.

For what was Solomon particularly renowned?
For his wisdom, and in the beginning of his reign for his sincere piety, and exact observance of his father's precepts.

How did Solomon acquire the great degree of wisdom he possessed?
On one occasion, when he had celebrated a religious festival with great splendor, and sacrificed a thousand victims, God appeared to him at night, and desired him to ask what gift he pleased. Through a sense of lively gratitude for all that God had done for him and his father, and conscious of his youth and inexperience, he asked for wisdom to govern the people over whom God had placed him, which request was so pleasing to God that he granted it, and with it all temporal blessings.

Relate what you remember of a remarkable decision of his?
Two women, whose children were born within three days of each other, came before the king. One charged the other with having accidentally smothered her own child at night, and then stolen her living child, leaving the dead one in its place. The other denied the charge, and claimed the living child as hers.

As there was no witness in the case, what did Solomon do?
As there was no witness, and each being positive, Solomon called for a sword, and ordered the living

child to be divided, and half given to each; the mother of the child hearing this decision, cried out, "I beseech thee, my Lord, give her the child alive, and do not kill it;" while the other said, "Let it belong to neither, but divide it." Solomon then ordered the child to be given to the former, whose feelings evinced that she was really the mother.

To what did Solomon particularly direct his attention after his father's death?
To the building of the Temple, for which he entered into a contract with Hiram, king of Tyre, who agreed for the annual tribute of 20,000 measures of wheat, and twenty measures of the purest oil, to supply him with skilful workmen and timber.

FIFTH AGE OF THE WORLD.

From the foundation of the Temple, to the return from the Babylonian captivity in the reign of Cyrus, A. M. 2972 to 546.

CHAPTER XLV.

THE BUILDING OF THE TEMPLE.

When did Solomon begin to build the Temple?
In the second month of the fourth year of his reign, and the 480th from the coming of Israel out of Egypt into the land of promise. (Deut. i. and Deut. iv., 3 Kings vi.)

Describe the Temple?
It was built of ready cut stone, (for the sound of no tool was permitted,) was sixty cubits long, twenty

Note.—The fourth year of his reign, computed from the time of his being associated with his father in the kingdom, the first of his reign alone. He began the building in the second month after his father's death.

wide, and thirty high. The inner part, called the "Holy of Holies," was twenty cubits square, being the full breadth of the Temple, and a third of its length, separated from the remainder of the Temple, called the sanctuary, by a richly carved and gilt cedar partition, against which hung an exquisitely embroidered veil.

How was the interior of the Temple ornamented?
The interior of the Temple was highly ornamental with carving and gilding; and the floor was of the most precious marble. In front was the porch, twenty cubits in length, ten cubits deep, and one hundred and twenty high, in which were two pillars of great size and beauty, one at each side of the entrance. At the distance of five cubits from the Temple was a wall the height of the Temple, and surrounding it on three sides; the space between was divided into three stories of chambers for the use of the priests, and to store the treasures of the Temple. (2 Par. iii., and 3 Kings vi.)

Describe the Holy of Holies?
It was entirely lined with gold, and over that part in which the ark of the Covenant was placed, were two cherubims covered with gold, with extended wings, and of such size that a wing of each reached the opposite wall, whilst the other two joined in the centre.

Who was permitted to enter the Holy of Holies?
The High Priest only, and he but once a year, when having performed the legal rites, he entered with incense and the blood of victims; and from the time he went in, until he came out, no one was permitted to enter the sanctuary. (Exod. xxx., Lev. xvi., Heb. ix.)

Of what was the entrance of the High Priest into the Holy of Holies a figure?
Of the sacrifice of our Lord Jesus Christ, the obla-

tion of whose precious blood was prefigured by the repeated offerings of the blood of victims, and who opened for us a new and living way through the veil, that is his flesh, into the Holy of Holies. (Heb. ix and x. 19.)

Of what was the offering of incense emblematic?
Of fervent prayer, according to these words of the Psalmist, "Let my prayer be directed as incense in thy sight;" and of St. John, "And the smoke of the incense of the prayers of the saints ascended up before God from the hand of the angel." Psm. cxl., Rev. viii.)

What was in the Sanctuary, that is, that part of the Temple outside the veil of the Holy of Holies?
The golden altar of incense, ten tables for the loaves of proposition, ten golden candlesticks, with censers and vessels for perfumes. (2. Par. iv.)

Where was the altar of holocausts placed?
In the Court before the Temple: at each side stood five brazen lavers in which the victims were washed before sacrifice, and one to the right for the use of the priests only, which from its great size was called the molten sea; it was of circular form, five cubits high and ten wide, and was supported by twelve brazen oxen, three of which looked towards the north, three towards the south, three towards the east, and three towards the west.

What do the holy Fathers remark of the constant purifications prescribed by the old law to those who ministered in the Temple?
That the great external purity of the Jews, though an actual ordinance, was symbolic of the purity of heart and soul which Christians should bring to the altar of God.

In how many years from its foundation was the Temple finished?
In seven

CHAPTER XLVI.

THE DEDICATION OF THE TEMPLE.—DEATH OF SOLOMON.

What did Solomon when the Temple was finished and furnished with every requisite?
He assembled the princes of tribes, the ancients, and the heads of families to assist at the dedication, and the solemn translation of the ark from the Tabernacle made by David, to the place destined for its reception in the Holy of Holies. (2 Par. v. 7.)

Did God testify his acceptance of the homage paid him on the day of the dedication of the Temple by any remarkable sign?
Yes; when the priests came out from the Sanctuary, after placing the ark in the Holy of Holies, and all with one accord had chanted: "Give glory to the Lord for he is good, for his mercy endureth for ever," the Temple was filled with a cloud, so that the priests could not stand to minister, for the glory of the Lord had filled the house.

What did Solomon then do?
Then Solomon returning humble and grateful thanks to God, earnestly besought him to bless the people, and to be ever mindful of all the petitions they would make in that house, and finally, foreseeing their banishment, he prayed God to hear them, when with contrite hearts they should pray turned towards it.

What sign did Almighty God give that he heard Solomon's prayer?
He sent fire from heaven which consumed the holocausts. Solomon kept the feast of the dedication seven days, during which 22,000 oxen and 120,000 sheep were sacrificed.

What vision had Solomon after this?
The Lord appeared to him, told him that he had heard his prayer, and had chosen the house he built for a place of sacrifice; that his eyes would be on it, and his ears attentive to the prayers made in it; and that if Solomon continued faithful, he would exalt him, as he had promised David his father; but that if he forsook his service for that of idols, he would cast him, his people, and the Temple, far from him. (2 Par. vii.)

What other buildings besides the Temple did Solomon erect?
A magnificent palace for himself and another for his queen, besides rebuilding several towns and fortifying others.

What were the characteristics of Solomon's reign?
Universal peace, and great abundance, not only of the necessaries of life, but even of luxuries, gold and silver being in such quantity that they were scarcely valued.

What was the daily provision for Solomon's house?
Thirty measures of fine flour, sixty measures of meal, thirty oxen, one hundred sheep, besides venison and fatted fowls.

How many chariots and horses had Solomon?
One thousand four hundred chariots, forty thousand chariot horses, and twelve thousand for the saddle.

What distinguished person visited Solomon?
The Queen of Saba, who, full of admiration at his wisdom, learning, and piety, pronounced the servants blest who were always in his presence. (1 Par. ix.)

What did our Lord say in allusion to the visit of the Queen of Saba, when his miracles and doctrines were contradicted by the Pharisees?
"The queen of the south shall rise in judgment with

the men of this generation, and shall condemn them, because she came from the ends of the earth to hear the wisdom of Solomon, and behold more than Solomon here." (Luke xi.)

Did Solomon always continue faithful to God?
No; towards the close of his life he married idolatrous wives, and to please them built altars to their idols, to which he himself offered incense.

What punishment did God decree for so great a sin?
That his kingdom should be divided; the greater part given to his servant Jeroboam, and the smaller to his son, and even that for David's sake alone, for whose sake also he deferred the execution of his threat until Solomon's death. (3 Kings xi.)

Who was Jeroboam?
He was a valiant and an ingenious man, whom Solomon placed over the tributes of all the house of Joseph, but when he heard of Ahias' prophecy, that Jeroboam should reign over ten tribes, he sought to take his life, so that Jeroboam, to avoid the king's wrath, fled into Egypt.

How long did Solomon reign?
Forty years from the time he was associated with his father, thirty-seven alone.

CHAPTER XLVII.

KINGS OF JUDA.—ROBOAM, ABIA, ASA.

Who succeeded Solomon?
His son Roboam.

What petition did the people make to Roboam soon after his accession?
That he would lighten the burden with which his father oppressed them.

What answer did Roboam give them?

"My father made your yoke heavy, but I will add to it. My father beat you with whips, but I will beat you with scorpions."

How did the people receive this harsh reply?
With the greatest indignation, they immediately renounced their allegiance to him, and made Jeroboam (who had returned on Solomon's death) king over ten tribes. From this time the kingdoms of Juda and Israel continued separate. (8 Kings xii.)

Did Roboam make any attempt to recover the kingdom?
He did; assembling 180,000 chosen men, he made preparations for war, but was forbidden to proceed by Semeias, a holy man, sent by God to inform him that what occurred was by divine appointment, in punishment of Solomon's sin.

What tribes continued faithful in their allegiance to Roboam?
Juda, Benjamin, and Levi. The cities originally given to the priests were exclusively confined to Juda and Benjamin, with the exception of two or three in Simeon, which bordered immediately on Juda. (Jos. xxi.) On the separation of the kingdoms of Juda and Israel, the Levites left their possessions in the different tribes, and went to Jerusalem and Juda, because Jeroboam prevented them from exercising their functions. (2 Par. xi.)

How did Roboam govern Juda?
During the first three years of his reign he succeeded in all his undertakings, because during them he was faithful to God. He applied diligently to the fortification of most of the cities in his dominions, and to storing them with provisions.

How did God punish Roboam and the people of Juda when they were guilty of idolatry?
By means of Sesac, king of Egypt, who took several cities of Juda, and even entered Jerusalem, which

he plundered of its most valuable effects; but God, being appeased by the repentance of Roboam and the princes, who humbled themselves and acknowledged the justice of their punishment on the reproach made them by Semeias, the prophet, did not suffer Sesac utterly to destroy Jerusalem. (2 Par. xii.)

How long did Roboam reign?
Seventeen years; the greater part of which he spent in wars. He died at the age of fifty-eight.

Who succeeded Roboam?
His son Abia, who reigned only three years.

In the beginning of his reign what happened?
In the beginning of his reign, being about to fight Jeroboam, who brought against him an army twice the number of his, he invoked the assistance of God, who gave him a signal victory; nevertheless, after that he sinned, for which he was cut off by God, who yet for David's sake permitted his son Asa to succeed him. (2 Par. xiii., 3 Kings xv.)

What was the character of Asa?
He was an excellent and pious king. He destroyed all the remains of idolatry, and re-established the splendor of divine worship, for which God rewarded him by a long and prosperous reign of forty-one years, during which he gave him victory over all his enemies, the chief of whom was Zara, king of the Ethiopians, who brought an army of more than a million of men against him. (2 Par. xiv.)

Of what faults was Asa guilty towards the close of his reign?
Being invaded by Baasa, king of Israel, he, through want of confidence in God, called on the king of Syria for assistance, for which the prophet Hanani reproached him, reminding him of the victory God had given him over the more numerous army of the Ethiopians. In his last sickness also he placed more

reliance on the skill of physicians than in the power of God. (2 Par. xvi.)

CHAPTER XLVIII.

CONTEMPORARY KINGS OF ISRAEL.

What kings reigned in Israel from the time of its separation until the close of Asa's reign, a period of sixty-one years?
Jeroboam, Nadab, Baasa, Ela, Zamri, and Amri.

How did Jeroboam act when in possession of the kingdom of Israel?
He presently forsook God who had exalted him, banished the Levites, and set up idols, for which he made priests, sometimes officiated himself, and, by the force of his example, led the greater part of the nation into idolatry which ultimately caused their ruin, and is the reason that his name is always reprobated when mentioned in Holy Scripture. (1 Par. xi.)

What induced Jeroboam to act so impiously?
An ambitious, political motive. Fearing that the people would resume their allegiance to Roboam if suffered to go to sacrifice in Jerusalem, he set up two golden calves, one in Dan, the other in Bethel, to which he offered sacrifice with solemnities similar to those used in Jerusalem, and told the people—"Go no more to Jerusalem, behold thy gods, O Israel, who brought thee out of the land of Egypt." (3 Kings xii.)

What occurred the first time that Jeroboam sacrificed to the calf at Bethel?
A prophet of Juda, expressly sent by God, cried out to the altar: "Behold a child shall be born to the house of David, Josias by name, and he shall immolate upon thee the priests of the high places, who

now burn incense upon thee, and he shall burn men's bones upon thee, and this shall be the sign that the Lord hath spoken, the altar shall be rent and the ashes that are on it shall be poured out.

When was this prophecy fulfilled?
About three centuries afterwards by Josias, king of Juda.

What did Jeroboam on that occasion?
Stretching forth his hand against the prophet, he ordered him to be seized; but his hand immediately withering, he was unable to draw it back, and it was only at the prophet's prayer that he again received the use of it.

Was Jeroboam converted by the miracle?
No; he persevered in idolatry for which Ahias the prophet, who had foretold his exaltation to the throne, prophesied that his entire family should be exterminated, which was fulfilled about a year after his death, in the reign of his son Nadab. Jeroboam reigned twenty-two years. (3 Kings xiv. and xv.)

Who succeeded Jeroboam?
His son Nadab, who reigned little more than a year, when he was killed by Baasa, who usurped the throne and exterminated the family of Jeroboam, as predicted by the prophet Ahias. Baasa reigned twenty-four years.

Who succeeded Baasa?
His son Ela, who reigned about two years, when he and all the family of Baasa were killed by Zamri, captain of the horse, who committed suicide after a reign of only seven days, fearing to fall into the power of Amri, general of the army, whom the Israelites elected king.

How long did Amri reign?
Twelve years, four of which were contested by a competitor named Thebni. Amri built the city of Samaria.

CHAPTER XLIX.

KINGS OF JUDA, JOSOPHAT, JORAM, OCHOZIAS, AND JOAS.

Who succeeded Asa in the kingdom of Juda?
His son Josophat, who, like his father, was a pious good king. God rewarded him with a twenty-five years' reign of great glory and magnificence, and enabled him to overcome all his enemies. On one occasion when the Edomites, Moabites, and Ammonites combined against him, he and all the people prostrated themselves before God, who told them by the mouth of a prophet to go out confidently on the morrow and they should see that he would fight for them. Accordingly the next day, the enemies rising from their several ambuscades attacked and slew each other, on which Josophat and his people carried off the spoils and returned with joy and thanksgiving to Jerusalem.

Who succeeded the good king Josophat in the kingdom of Juda?
His eldest son Joram, at the age of thirty-two; he was a wicked, idolatrous king, and married Athalia, daughter to Achab, the impious king of Israel, who inherited her father's impiety.

What did Joram do?
He slew all his brethren and introduced idolatry, for which God commissioned Elias to foretell him the punishment decreed for him, a painful, lingering distemper, of which he died, after a troubled reign of eight years. He was buried in the city of David, but without honor, and not in the sepulchres of the kings. (2 Par. xxi.)

Who succeeded the impious Joram in the kingdom of Juda?
His youngest and only surviving son Ochozias, at

the age of twenty-two; all the rest being killed in an incursion of the Arabians. (4 Kings viii. 26: 2 Par. xxii.)

How long did Ochozias reign?
Only one year; on his way to visit his kinsman, Joram, son of Achab, king of Israel, he and all who attended him were slain by Jehu, who was at that ime extirpating the house of Achab. (2 Par. xxii.)

What was the character of Ochozias.
He was idolatrous and wicked like the house of Achab, being urged on by his mother Athalia.

How did Athalia act when Ochozias was slain?
Having killed all the royal family except Joas, the infant son of Ochozias, whom Josabeth, sister to Ochozias and wife to Joida, the High Priest, hid in the Temple, she made herself queen and reigned with uncontrolled sway nearly seven years, when Joida assembled the princes and people, presented Joas to them as their king, and had Athalia put to death. (2 Par. xxii. and xxiii.)

What was the character of Joas?
As long as Joida lived he was pious and zealous in the service of God, but on the death of the venerable High Priest, he chose evil counsellors and with them fell into idolatry. (2 Par. xxiv.)

How old was Joida the High Priest when he died?
One hundred and thirty years, and on account of the great services he had rendered the kingdom he was buried in the sepulchres of the kings.

What ungrateful and wicked act was Joas guilty of soon after the death of Joida?
He caused Zacharias, the son of Joida, to be stoned in the court of the Temple, because he had admonished him of his sin in forsaking the service of God for that of idols. (2 Par. xxiv.)

How did Joas end his life?
He was murdered by two of his servants after a

reign of forty years, the latter part of which was troubled; for God permitted him to be harassed by the Assyrians from the time he forsook his service. Joas, like his grand-father, Joram, was not buried in the sepulchres of the kings.

CHAPTER L.

CONTEMPORARY KINGS OF ISRAEL.

What kings reigned in Israel during the eighty years included from Josophat's ascending the throne to the end of the reign of Joas?
Achab, Ochozias, Joram, Jehu, and Joachas.

Whom did Achab succeed in the throne of Israel?
His father Amri; he married a wicked woman named Jezabel, and more impious than his predecessors, added the worship of Baal to his other crimes.

For what unjust and cruel act of Achab and Jezabel did God decree the extirpation of the family?
Achab, wishing to enlarge his garden, was anxious to procure a vineyard that immediately adjoined, but Naboth, to whom it belonged, would by no means part with his inheritance, which so annoyed Achab that he refused to taste food.

What did Jezabel do?
Jezabel, understanding the cause, determined to gratify him though at the expense of conscience and justice; and sending to the chief men and judges, commanded them to suborn false witnesses against Naboth and have him executed, which was accordingly done.

What sentence did Elias pronounce?
Achab having gone to take possession of the vineyard, God sent Elias to pronounce this sentence: "That in the place where the dogs had licked Naboth's blood, they should also lick his, that his race

should be utterly extirpated, and Jezabel devoured by dogs.

Was that sentence immediately executed?
No; for Achab humbled himself before God, who, in consequence, deferred the execution of the sentence until after his death, which happened in battle about two years after, when his chariot being brought to the pool of Samaria to be washed, his blood was licked by the dogs in the same place that they had licked Naboth's. Jezabel survived about thirteen years when, by the orders of Jehu, she was thrown from a window, and was devoured by dogs in the place where she fell; the remainder of the prophecy was accomplished by Jehu. (4 Kings x.)

How long did Achab reign?
Twenty-two years.

Who succeeded Achab?
His son Ochozias, who died from the effects of a fall after a reign of two years, and was succeeded by his brother Joram, who reigned twelve years, and was killed by Jehu, who exterminated the house of Achab and killed Jezabel.

Did Jehu ascend the throne when he exterminated the house of Achab?
He did, and reigned twenty-eight years. For the zeal he evinced in extirpating the worship of Baal, God promised that his children, to the fourth generation, should fill the throne of Israel; his son Joachaz succeeded him and reigned seventeen years (4 Kings xiii.)

CHAPTER LI.

THE PROPHETS.—ELIAS AND ELISEUS.

What great prophets flourished in Israel during the above-named eighty years?
Elias and his disciple Eliseus; the former was con-

temporary with Josophat and Achab, and was taken up into heaven in the reign of Joram; the latter lived until the beginning of the reign of Joas, son of Joachez, and grandson to Jehu.

How did Elias act when he saw that Israel was overrun with idolatry, promoted and sanctioned by Achab and Jezabel?

By his prayers he prevented rain from falling for three years, which caused a famine, during which he was at first miraculously fed by ravens that carried him food morning and evening, and afterwards by a poor widow who lived in Sarephta. (3 Kings xvii.)

How was the poor widow employed when Elias was sent to her by God?

Collecting a few sticks to cook what she believed would be the last meal for herself and son, for she had only a little meal and some oil in a cruse, which she nevertheless shared with the prophet; and from that day until the famine left the land neither the meal nor oil lessened.

What miracle did Elias perform whilst in the widow's house?

He restored her son to life by his prayers.

What miracle did Elias perform to prove that there is only one true God, whom he served, and that Baal and the others were false gods?

He requested Achab to assemble the people at Mount Carmel, and to send for the prophets of Baal, 456 in number; then desiring to have two bullocks brought, he proposed to the prophets of Baal to choose one, whilst he, the only prophet present of the true God, took the other; and addressing the people, he implored them no longer to hesitate between the worship of God and Baal, but to serve him who should prove himself God by sending fire from heaven to consume the victim.

Did the people assent to this?

Yes, they all readily assented to the proposal, and the prophets of Baal called in vain on their god from morning until noon, whilst Elias rallied them, desiring them to call louder, as their god was, perhaps, on a journey, or at an inn, or asleep.

When the time arrived, what did Elias do?
He called the people to assist in building up the altar to God, on which he laid the victim, and ordered a quantity of water to be poured over it, until the trench round the altar was filled; then calling on God to manifest his power and let the people see that he alone is God, fire fell from heaven, which immediately consumed, not only the holocaust, but the altar and water, at which the people fell on their faces and adored. Then, by command of Elias, they put all the false prophets to death, and God sent a plentiful supply of rain. (3 Kings xviii.)

Whither did Elias flee to avoid the vengeance of Jezabel, who, in revenge for the death of her prophets, had resolved on his death?
To Mount Horeb, by the direction of an angel, who gave him food, in the strength of which he walked forty days and forty nights across the desert, until he reached Horeb.

What do the holy Fathers say of this part of the life of Elias?
That the sudden vicissitude he experienced from courage to timidity, demonstrates the inconsistency and weakness of the human heart, when not supported by strength from above; and the food given him by the angel they consider emblematic of the Blessed Eucharist which nourishes our souls, imparting strength and vigor to them during our moral pilgrimage.

In what manner was Elias taken up into Heaven?
Having with his disciple Eliseus crossed the east side of the Jordan, through which he miraculously

made a passage by striking the water with his cloak, he was suddenly separated from Eliseus by a fiery chariot, and fiery horses, and carried up to heaven, when going up his cloak fell, which his disciple took, and with it made himself a passage across the Jordan as Elias had done. Eliseus inherited the double spirit of prophecy and miracles possessed by Elias.

CHAPTER LII.

What was the first use Eliseus made of his gift of miracles when he recrossed the Jordan?
At the request of the inhabitants he cured the waters of Jericho, which were very bad, and removed the barrenness of the land.

Relate some other miracles wrought by Eliseus?
He procured a supply of water to refresh the united armies of Juda, Israel, and Edom, in a war with the Moabites, who had revolted, and whose overthrow was effected according to his prediction.

What was his second miracle?
He relieved the widow of one of the prophets by miraculously increasing her little store of oil. This poor woman was in debt, which she had no means of paying. Her creditor was urgent, and threatened to seize her sons. In her distress, she had recourse to Eliseus, whose pity she excited; when, on inquiry, he discovered that her only possession was a little oil, he desired her to borrow a number of empty vessels and pour the oil into them. She obeyed, and filled so many vessels with it, that she was enabled to pay her creditor and support the family.

What was the third miracle?
He restored to life the son of a devout woman, who had often received him into her house.

What was the fourth miracle?
During a famine he multiplied food for a great number who resorted to him.

What was the next miracle?
He restored to perfect health Naaman, general of the Syrian army, who was afflicted with leprosy, and transferred the leprosy to his own servant Giezi, who, through covetousness, had obtained money and raiment from Naaman in the prophet's name.

What remarkable punishment did God inflict on some wicked boys who mocked the servant of God, calling him "Bald head?"
Two bears came out of the wood, and killed forty-two of them.

Was Eliseus gifted with the spirit of prophecy?
Yes, of which there are some instances related. First, when the Syrians, intending to invade Israel, made many attempts, and formed several ambuscades, of which Eliseus constantly informed the king of Israel, thus enabling him to counteract the enemy, who were at length obliged to withdraw.

Can you relate another instance?
Some time after, when the Syrians besieged Samaria, Joram blindly imagining that the holy prophet was instrumental to the great sufferings of the besieged, which were occasioned principally by famine, sent a man before, whom he followed immediately, with a determination to behead the prophet. Eliseus foresaw and prevented their evil design; and at the same time comforted the king, assuring him that by that hour next day there would be such an abundance of provisions, that a bushel of fine flour would be sold in the gate of Samaria for a stater, and two bushels of barley for the same price. (4 Kings vi. and vii.)

In what manner was that prophecy fulfilled?
Four lepers, who were at the gate of Samaria, being

pressed by famine, and thinking they might as well
run the risk of being killed, as to die of want, resolved to go to the camp of the Syrians. On their
arrival, they were surprised to see no one, and at
first thought only of satisfying their hunger, and
possessing themselves of the wealth which surrounded them; but after some time, reflecting that they
ought to make their fellow-citizens partakers of their
own good fortune, they returned to the city, and
announced that the Syrians had deserted their camp.

What did the king do?
The king received this news warily, and fearing that
it was an artifice of the enemy, sent messengers to
discover the truth. They confirmed the statement,
and found the roads covered with valuables which
the Syrians had cast away in their flight; for God
had struck them with a panic, and made them think
that they heard a great army approaching. In
their terror, they fled, leaving all they possessed
after them. The spoils were brought into Samaria
next day, and caused the abundance foretold by the
prophet.

*Was any one punished for incredulity on that oc-
casion?*
Yes, a nobleman, who was present with the king
when Eliseus predicted the great plenty, and said,
doubtingly, "Could that be, if God made flood-
gates in heaven?" Eliseus replied that he should
see, but not partake of the blessing; and the next
day, having been intrusted by the king with the
charge of the gate, he was crushed to death by the
multitude.

*What great person visited Eliseus when in his
last sickness?*
Joas, son of Joachaz, and grandson of Jehu, king
of Israel, who having testified great affliction for
losing him whom he revered as his father and guide

was comforted by Eliseus with the assurance that he would be victorious over the Syrians in three different engagements. (4 Kings xiii.)

Were the relics of Eliseus instrumental in performing any miracle?
Yes; a dead man who was being conveyed to the grave by his friends was thrown by them into the sepulchre of Eliseus in a panic caused by a sudden incursion of the Moabites; and he no sooner came into contact with the bones of the holy prophet than he was restored to life.

CHAPTER LIII.

KINGS OF JUDA, AMASIAS AND AZARIAS.

Who succeeded Joas in the kingdom of Juda?
His son Amasias, at the age of twenty-five. He was successful in all his undertakings whilst he continued to serve God, but growing proud of his success, he foolishly worshipped the idols of the very nations which God had enabled him to conquer. And when in the pride of his heart, he challenged and fought with Joas, king of Israel. He was utterly defeated and led back to Jerusalem by that king, who broke down a considerable part of the walls, and carried away the treasures of the Temple. Amasias survived this defeat about fifteen years. He was killed in a conspiracy after a reign of twenty-nine years. (2 Par. xxv.)

Who succeeded Amasias?
His son Azarias, sometimes called Ozias, then sixteen years of age; he reigned fifty-two years, during which he fortified Jerusalem, built several cities, and was successful in all his wars and undertakings whilst he was faithful to God.

How did he offend God and what was his punishment?

Being elated with prosperity, he assumed an office to which he was not called; he presumed to offer incense in the Temple, notwithstanding the remonstrances of the High Priest; God therefore struck him with a leprosy, from which he never recovered, and he was obliged to live alone for the remainder of his life. (2 Par. xxvi.)

CHAPTER LIV.

CONTEMPORARY KINGS OF ISRAEL.

What kings reigned in Israel whilst Amasias and Azarias reigned in Juda, (a space of eighty-one years)?
Joas, Jeroboam II., Zacharias, Sellum, Manahem, and Phaceia.

To whom did Joas succeed?
His father, Joachaz; he reigned sixteen years, and defeated the Syrians in three engagements, as predicted by Eliseus, leaving the kingdom in peace to his son Jeroboam.

How long did Jeroboam II. reign?
Forty-one years; he was valiant, but like those who preceded him, an idolator—(in his reign Jonas prophecied);—he was succeeded by his son Zacharias, after an interregnum of eleven years.

How long did Zacharias reign?
Only six months, when he was killed by Sellum, and thus ended the race of Jehu, to whom God had promised that his children to the fourth generation should reign in Israel.

How long did Sellum enjoy his newly-acquired dignity?
One month, when he was killed by Manahem, who reigned ten years, and was succeeded by his son Phaceia, who was killed, after a reign of two years, by Phacee. (4 Kings xv.)

CHAPTER LV.

THE PROPHET JONAS

Who was Jonas?
Jonas was son to Amathi, the prophet, a native of Geth Opher, in Galilee, and prophesied in the reign of Jeroboam II.

What is related of him?
Having been commissioned by God to preach to Ninive and to threaten it with destruction, on account of its crimes, he was unwilling to undertake the mission, and endeavored to fly from the face of God by sailing to Tharsis; but the ship had scarcely got to sea when God sent a tempest which endangered its safety.

What is said of the crew?
The crew, in great alarm, cast lots to discover which of them excited the anger of God, and the lot falling on Jonas, he acknowledged his fault, and desired them to throw him into the sea. They were unwilling to do so, and exerted themselves to reach the land by rowing, but found it impossible to succeed; and perceiving their danger every moment increasing, they threw him overboard, on which the sea immediately became calm.

What did God cause?
God, whose design was mercy, not destruction, caused Jonas to be swallowed up by a great fish, in which he remained for three days and three nights, during which he humbly and earnestly called on God, who graciously heard his prayer, and commanded the fish to cast him on shore.

What did the Lord renew and what followed?
The Lord then renewed his command, and Jonas no longer disobedient, went to Ninive. Having entered one day's journey into the city, and announced the

impending judgments of God, all the people, from
the king to the meanest, repented, and did penance
in fasting and in sackcloth, on which Almighty God,
who only desired their repentance, forgave them.

What is related of Jonas and the ivy?
Jonas fearing that he might pass for a false prophet,
was angry at the clemency of God, and left the city.
He sat at some distance, when God caused an ivy to
grow up and shade him, to the great joy of Jonas,
who was fatigued and oppressed by the heat of the
sun. God was willing to instruct his people, and
caused a worm to settle in the ivy, which on the following day destroyed it, leaving Jonas exposed to the
heat, at which, when he complained, God expostulated with him for grieving at the loss of that which
he had not reared, and which was the growth of only
a day; adding, "Shall not I then spare Ninive, that
great city in which are a hundred and twenty thousand, who know not how to distinguish between their
right hand and their left."

*Of what was Jonas's imprisonment in the whale
and his miraculous coming forth alive after three
days a figure?*
Of the burial and glorious resurrection of our Lord
Jesus Christ. (Matt. xii. 40.)

CHAPTER LVI.

KINGS OF JUDA—JOATHAN, ACHZ, EZECHIAS.

Who succeeded Azarias, (or Ozias,) king of Juda?
His son Joathan, at the age of twenty-five, a good
and pious king. He reigned sixteen years, during
which he ornamented the Temple, built several cities,
and made the Ammonites tributary. (2 Par. xxvii.)

Who succeeded Joathan?
His son Achaz, at the age of twenty, who also reigned

sixteen years. He was an impious, idolatrous king He removed the sacred vessels, shut up the Temple, and built altars to idols in several parts of Jerusalem. For his great impiety, God permitted him to be grievously harassed by the kings of Israel, Syria, and Assyria, though he sought to make the latter his ally by great presents. (2 Par. xxviii.)

Who succeeded Achaz in the throne of Juda?
His son Ezechias, at the age of twenty-five, who, on coming to the throne endeavored to plant true virtue and religion where impiety and superstition had flourished. He re-opened the Temple, caused it to be purified, and invited all Israel to celebrate the Pasch. Many Israelites accepted the invitation, though the greater number derided the piety of the king; but all Juda were faithful, and the Pasch was celebrated with greater solemnity and magnificence than it had been from the time of Solomon.

What did he assemble and re-establish?
Ezechias assembled the priests and Levites, who were dispersed, and re-established the primitive order and observances of divine worship. Having performed the duty he owed to God, the good king next turned his attention to the happiness and security of his subjects and the independence of his dominions. With the assistance of God strengthening him in all his undertakings, he recovered the cities that had been taken from Juda, and shook off the Assyrian yoke, which was imposed in the reign of Achaz.

CHAPTER LVII.

CONTEMPORARY KINGS OF ISRAEL TO THE ASSYRIAN CAPTIVITY.

What kings reigned in Israel from the first year of the reign of Joathan to the sixth of Ezechias?
Phacee and Osee. Phacee reigned twenty years.

During his reign, what happened?
During his reign, Theglathphalasar, king of Assyria, invaded Israel, and carried away a great number of captives.

What was the fate of Phacee?
Phacee was killed by Osee, who, after an interregnum of nine years, came to the throne and reigned nine years, the first three of which he was contemporary with Achaz, king of Juda, (4 Kings xvii.,) and the last six with Ezechias.

What is related of Osee?
In a fruitless attempt to free himself from a tribute he had undertaken to pay to the Assyrians, he lost the kingdom, for Salmanasar invaded it, and took Samaria after a siege of three years, abolished the kingdom of Israel, and led the people into captivity. (4 Kings xvii.)

Where did Salmanasar locate the captives?
He placed some in Ninive, others he scattered through Media.

How did Salmanasar re-people the land of Israel?
He sent thither people from Babylon, Cutha, and other places, who being on their arrival grievously harassed by wild beasts, he sent them, by the advice of his counsellors, a priest to instruct them in th worship of God, but they united the worship of the true God with that of their idols, their descendants continued the worship of both, and this was the reason why the Jews would not communicate with them.

How long did the kingdom of Israel last?
Two hundred and sixty years, from the time of its separation from Juda by the impious Jeroboam until the Assyrian captivity in the ninth year of Osee.

What was the characteristic sin of all the kings, and of the generality of the people of Israel?
Idolatry, to which they were always prone, but which from the time of Jeroboam they openly professed and

almost unanimously practised; therefore God delivered them into the power of their enemies, and cast them out of the land of their inheritance. He had repeatedly, but ineffectually warned them; and more than a century before the destruction of Israel, there could be counted only seven thousand faithful servants of God in all the kingdom. (3 Kings xix. 18.)

CHAPTER LVIII.

PROPHETS.

What prophets lived from the reign of Amasias, king of Juda and Jeroboam II., king of Israel, to the captivity of Israel, a space of one hundred years?
Jonas, Amos, Osee, Isaias, Micheas, Joel, and Abdias. Jonas, Amos, and Osee, began to prophesy in Israel, whilst Jeroboam II. reigned. (4 Kings xiv. 25, Amos i. 1, Osee i. 1.) Osee and Isaias continued to prophesy for nearly a century, the former in Israel, the latter in Juda.

When did Isaias begin to prophesy?
Isaias began to prophesy in the reign of Azarias, and continued until the reign of Manasses, when, according to the Hebrew tradition, he suffered martyrdom by being sawed asunder, in the persecution which was raised by that wicked king.

Where did Micheas begin?
Micheas began in Juda, in the reign of Joathan, and continued until the reign of Ezechias. (Micheas i. 1.)

What is supposed concerning Joel and Abdias?
Joel and Abdias, the former of Juda, the latter of Israel. are supposed to have been contemporary with the above-mentioned. Both most pathetically exhorted the people, and threatened them with the impending judgments of God.

Of what did Isaias prophesy?
Besides some matters of minor importance, he foretold the Assyrian and Babylonian captivity; and described the coming, life, and passion of our Lord Jesus Christ with such precision that his prophecy appears more like a history of past transactions, than the foretelling of events of future and distant ages.

Were any faithful servants of God to be found in Israel at the time of the captivity?
There were several, one in particular named Tobias, whose history has been preserved, was distinguished for his piety to God and charity to his neighbor.

CHAPTER LIX.

HISTORY OF TOBIAS.—HIS VIRTUES AND AFFLICTIONS.

Who was Tobias?
Tobias was a good and holy man of the tribe of Nephtali, who, notwithstanding the bad example of those who surrounded him, never adored the golden calves set up by Jeroboam, but was faithful to God from his youth, and went regularly to Jerusalem to sacrifice.

What is said of his wife and son?
His wife, named Anna was of the same tribe, and his son, an only child called also Tobias, was most carefully instructed by him in the law of God.

What was related of Tobias at Ninive?
When Salmanasar led Israel into captivity, Tobias was taken with the rest; but even in Ninive he continued equally faithful to God, and observant of his law as far as his state permitted, for which God gave him favor in the sight of the king, who not only allowed him to go from one city to another, but bestowed money on him, which enabled him to relieve the wants of his brethren. On one occasion having

gone to Rages, a city of Media, he saw one of his kindred named Gabelus, in distress, and lent him all he had with him, amounting to ten talents of silver, for which he took Gabelus' acknowledgment in writing.

On the death of Salmanasar, what is said of Tobias?

On the death of Salmanasar, Tobias' fortune changed, for Senecharib who succeeded his father in the empire, persecuted the Israelites, especially after his return from an unsuccessful attack on the kingdom of Juda; and Tobias, from the charity he evinced towards his brethren, became an object of his special hatred; he confiscated his property, and would have taken his life, had he not fled and remained concealed until the tyrant's death; but no sooner was the immediate danger over than Tobias resumed his charitable labors, though remonstrated with by his friends, who feared for his safety.

Can you relate an instance of his great zeal in burying the dead?

Yes; on one occasion in the midst of an entertainment he had made for several of his tribe, he heard, as he was sitting down to dinner, that an Israelite lay dead in the street, and immediately going out sought the body and concealed it in his house until night when he buried it.

What misfortune happened to him?

One day being more than usually tired from his pious labors, he lay down to rest near a wall in which was a swallow's nest, and fell asleep, during which droppings from the nest falling on his eyes blinded him. This trial was permitted by God that posterity might have an example of patience in him as well as in holy Job; like that patriarch he too was reviled by his friends, who asked to what end he had performed so many works of mercy, since God per-

mitted so great an affliction to befall him. But
Tobias was as faithful in adversity as he had been in
prosperity, and God having tried his servant for a
little time abundantly rewarded him.

*When he thought himself near his death, what did
he do?*
When Tobias thought himself near death he gave
his son advice as to his future conduct, informed him
of the money he had lent to Gabelus, and desired
him to procure a guide to conduct him to Rages in
order to receive it. The obedient son promised to
abide by his father's instructions and went to seek a
guide, whom God, mindful of the charity of old
Tobias, and his patience in affliction, gave him in the
angel Raphael, who, under the name and form of
Azarias, undertook to conduct him to Rages, and
bring him back safely to his father, whom he comforted by assuring him that his cure was at hand.

CHAPTER LX.

**THE YOUNG TOBIAS IS CONDUCTED BY AN ANGEL.—HIS
MARRIAGE AND RETURN TO HIS FATHER.**

*When Tobias reached the river Tigris, what hap-
pened to him?*
Accompanied by his heavenly guide, the young
Tobias set out on his journey; on the first night he
reached the river Tigris, where going to bathe he was
terrified by a monstrous fish that seemed ready to devour him, on which he cried out to his guide, who desired him to take hold of it and draw it ashore; he
obeyed, and by the angel's direction kept the heart,
liver and gall as useful medicines; then cooked part
of the fish and salted the rest as provision for their
journey.

When he arrived at Rages, what took place?

When they arrived at Rages (not the place of their destination, but a town of the same name) the angel said they would lodge at the house of Raguel, a kinsman of Tobias, a wealthy citizen, whose only daughter, named Sarah, he should demand in marriage. Tobias was startled at the proposal, as he knew that she had been given already to seven husbands, who were all killed on the day of their marriage, through the malice of the evil spirit, and he feared that if the same thing happened to himself his parents might die of grief; but the angel calmed his fears, and instructed him how to sanctify his marriage.

On entering the house, what did Raguel remark?
On entering the house Raguel remarked the likeness that the young man bore to his kinsman Tobias, and being informed by the angel that he was his son, he received him with joy and prepared a feast for him, of which however, Tobias refused to partake until Raguel had promised him his daughter Sarah in marriage.

What did Raguel at first do?
Raguel at first hesitated on account of the sudden death of her former husbands; but the angel having removed his fears, he consented and gave half his property with her, settling the remainder on Tobias at his death. When the marriage was agreed to, the old people so earnestly begged Tobias to remain with them for a fortnight that he could not refuse, but unwilling to cause anxiety to his parents by the least unnecessary delay, he requested his guide to, go to Gabelus and receive the money; the angel did so, and brought Gabelus with him to the feast, who rejoiced at the prosperity of his friend's son, and gratefully returned what had been lent him.

When the fortnight had elapsed, what did Tobias do?
When the fortnight had elapsed, Tobias prepared to

return to his parents with his wife and property; on reaching Charan, which was about half way, the angel reminded him of the state in which he had left his father, and recommended him to hasten with himself on before, and let his wife and family journey by easy stages; the advice pleased Tobias, and they were still at a distance when they were descried by Anna, who, in anxiety for her son, used to go every day to the top of the hill to watch his coming.

What did she do?

She immediately announced his approach to his aged father, who, through joy, ran stumbling to meet him, and his son by the angel's direction anointed his eyes with the gall of the fish, by which his sight was restored to his own inexpressible joy and that of all his neighbors, who united with him in returning thanks to God.

CHAPTER LXI.

DEATH OF TOBIAS.

What did Tobias do on his return?

Seven days after the return of Tobias, his wife and family arrived. In the meantime, he recounted to his father the many favors the guide had done him, and both agreed that half their property would be an inadequate recompense, which, however, they begged him to accept.

What did the angel reply?

The angel replied, "Bless ye the Lord of heaven, give glory to him in the sight of all that live, because he hath shown his mercy to you; for it is good to hide the secret of a king; but honorable to reveal and confess the works of God. Prayer is good with fasting and alms more than to lay up treasures of gold........I discover then the truth to you, and I will not hide the secret from you. When thou didst pray with tears, and didst bury the dead, and didst leave thy dinner, and hide the dead by day in thy house, and bury them by night, I offered thy prayer to the Lord. And because thou wast acceptable to God, it was necessary that temptation should prove thee and now the Lord hath sent me to heal thee, and to deliver Sarah, thy son's wife, from the devil; for I am the angel Raphael, one of the seven, who stand before the Lord."

On hearing this, what did Tobias and his son do?
On hearing this, Tobias and his son fell prostrate on the ground; but the angel encouraged them, and desired them not to fear, but to bless God, and publish all his wonderful works, saying which, he vanished; after which, they continued prostrate in prayer for three hours, then rising they published the wonderful works of God.

How long did Tobias live after his sight was restored?
Tobias lived forty-two years after his sight was restored, and terminated a long and holy life by a happy death, having foretold the approaching destruction of Ninive, and enjoined his son to leave it with his children and grandchildren, as soon as he should have buried his mother in the same grave with him

What is said of young Tobias?
The younger Tobias punctually obeyed his father's commands; and when he had paid the last duty to his mother he removed with all his family to the house of his father and mother-in-law, to whom he performed the part of an affectionate and dutiful son. He lived to the age of ninety-nine, esteemed and respected by all who knew him.

CHAPTER LXII.

KINGS OF JUDA, AFTER THE ASSYRIAN CAPTIVITY—CONTINUATION OF THE REIGN OF EZECHIAS—MANASSES.

What miraculous intervention prevented Senecharib (son of Salmanasar) from attacking Jerusalem, when he invaded the kingdom of Juda in the fourteenth year of the reign of Ezechias?
Almighty God, moved by the prayer of Ezechias, sent an angel into the Assyrian camp, who killed in one night 185,000 of the most valiant, including the chief officers. This dreadful visitation obliged Senecharib to return to Ninive with the remnant, where he was killed by his sons in the temple of his idol. (4 Kings xix. 35; Tobias i. 24.)

What great prophet was counsellor to Ezechias?
The prophet Isaias, who began to prophesy in the reign of Azarias, and continued during the reign of Joathan, Achaz, and Ezechias.

What occurred to Ezechias soon after Senecharib's invasion?
He fell dangerously ill, and was desired by Isaias, on the part of God, to prepare for death, but he earnestly and with many tears besought God to prolong his life, who graciously heard his prayer, and commanded Isaias to tell him that he had prolonged his life for fifteen years; and as a sign of the fulfilment of this promise he, at the prophet's prayer, made the shadow go back ten degrees on the sun dial of Achaz.

What imprudent act did Ezechias commit through pride?
He exhibited all his treasures to the ambassadors of Berodach Baladin, King of Babylon, who came to congratulate him on his recovery; for which God sent Isaias to foretell him that they would be seized and carried to Babylon; but, at the entreaty of Eze-

chias, the evil did not occur in his days. Ezechias reigned twenty-nine years; six before the captivity of Israel and twenty-three after.

CHAPTER LXIII.

MANASSES.

Who succeeded Ezechias in the throne of Juda?
His son Manasses, who began to reign when he was twelve years old: he reigned fifty-five years and was an impious and cruel king, he re-erected the places of idolatrous worship which his father had pulled down, and carried his wickedness so far as to erect altars to idols in and about the Temple, besides which he put to death a great number of just persons, amongst whom, according to the Hebrew tradition, was the great prophet Isaias, who is said to have been sawed in two for reproving him.

What did God send him?
God sent him repeated warnings in vain, and at length caused him to be carried captive to Babylon, where, in his distress he humbly and contritely called upon God, who heard him, and restored him to his kingdom. On his return Manasses cast out all the idols, and restored the worship of God. (4 Kings xxi.; 2 Par. xxxiii.)

What venerable person was instrumental in saving the city of Bethulia and the kingdom of Juda about this time?
Judith, widow of a wealthy citizen of Bethulia, illustrious for her piety, mortification, charity, and fortitude.

CHAPTER LXIV.

HISTORY OF JUDITH.—SIEGE OF BETHULIA.

What is said of Nebuchodonozer?
Nebuchodonozer, king of the Assyrians, having defeated the Medes in the twelfth year of his reign, formed the ambitious design of subjecting all nations

of the earth to his dominion, and of making them
adore him as their god, for which he gave directions
to Holofernes, his general, not only to subdue the
people, but to destroy their temples, idols and groves

What did the Jews determine?
Many kingdoms submitted, being unable to oppose
the immense army he sent against them; but the
Jews, encouraged by the exhortations of the High
Priest, determined to defend the Temple. To prevent access to Jerusalem, they took possession of the
mountain passes, and fortified all their towns, at the
same time humbling themselves in fasting and prayer
before God.

In the meantime, what did Holofernes do?
In the meantime, Holofernes, with his almost count-
less host, approached Judea, expecting the same
submission he had received from the neighboring
kingdoms; but his surprise and indignation were
excessive, when he found them prepared to resist, and
Bethulia, a town in the mountains, in a state of defence.

What did he inquire?
Assembling the officers of the Moabites and Ammonites, who, amongst others, had come to surrender, he
haughtily inquired who these people were, and in
what they trusted to oppose his hitherto invincible
army.

What did Achior relate and conclude?
Achior, general of the Ammonites, related what he
knew of the Jewish nation, the miracles God had
wrought at different times for their defence or preservation, and concluded by advising Holofernes to
inquire before attacking them whether they were
guilty of any impiety, for in that case only could he
succeed against them: but if they were not, their
God would surely defend them, and make him and
his army a reproach to the whole earth.

What did Holofernes do?
At these words, Holofernes and his captains were highly incensed and causing Achior to be bound, sent him to Bethulia to await his doom with the inhabitants of the place, not doubting that they would soon be masters of it.

What is said of the Bethulians?
The Bethulians, understanding the cause of his being sent to them, comforted him with the hope of seeing Bethulia triumph over the pride of Holofernes, and having refreshed him, passed the whole night in prayer, imploring God to take compassion on their low condition, and to humble the pride of their adversaries, who trusted in their numbers and strength.

What followed?
Next morning, Holofernes gave orders to attack the town, but seeing the determination of the inhabitants, he resolved to starve them into submission, and accordingly cut off their aqueduct, and placed guards at the springs, which reduced them to such distress that at the end of twenty days, they tumultuously called on Ozias, the governor, to surrender, declaring that they would rather die by the sword than await the lingering death which appeared prepared for them. Ozias endeavored to console and encourage them, but at length promised to comply, if they were not relieved within five days.

What is related of Judith?
Judith, the widow of a wealthy citizen, who, since her husband's death, had passed her days in retirement, prayer, and mortification, hearing what Ozias and the ancients had agreed to, expostulated with them for their want of confidence, and represented to them that they did ill in appointing a time for the mercy of God, that the present chastisement was less than their sins deserved, and given rather for their amendment than destruction.

How did she exhort the people?
She exhorted them to encourage the people by a remembrance of the miracles God had heretofore wrought for their deliverance when in as great danger, and begged of them to unite in fervent prayer for the success of an undertaking she meditated.

What did she then do?
Judith then retired to her oratory. Clothed in haircloth, with ashes on her head, and prostrated before God, she implored the divine assistance, rising with renewed confidence in divine help, she put off her penitential garb, and arrayed herself in her richest ornaments, God adding to her beauty, and making her appear incomparably lovely, as her dressing was not from vanity but virtue.

CHAPTER LXV.

THE SIEGE RAISED BY THE FORTITUDE OF JUDITH.—DEATH OF HOLOFERNES.

What is related of Judith?
Attended by her maid, who carried some provisions, Judith passed the gate of Bethulia, where Ozias and the ancients were, who fervently blessed her undertaking. Praying all the way, she descended the hill on which the town was built, and towards break of day reached the advanced guard of the enemy

Where did they conduct her?
They conducted her to the general, whom she complimented on the renown he had acquired, and by flattering him, procured a delay of hostilities, with permission for herself and maid to go in and out of the camp when they pleased, for the space of three days.

How did she use the permission?
The use Judith made of this permission was, to go

every evening to the neighboring valley, where, after bathing, she spent some time in retirement and recollection, humbly begging of God to direct and enable her to accomplish the deliverance of his people. Holofernes, charmed with her beauty, grace, and wisdom, treated her with great respect, and ordered her to be lodged where his treasures were stored.

On the fourth day, what did he do?
On the fourth day after her arrival he made a splendid entertainment to which he invited her; Judith accepted the invitation, but such was her respect for the least observances prescribed by the law, and her holy fear of offending God, that she partook only of the food which her maid had brought and prepared for her: circumstanced as she was, alone, in the midst of pagan enemies, she professed her faith openly, and adhered to a religious practice, that many in such circumstances would consider themselves more than justified in dispensing with.

Towards the close of the entertainment what happened?
Towards the close of the entertainment, Holofernes, who had drank to excess, fell asleep; all retired by degrees, leaving Judith alone, who, immediately taking advantage of the opportunity afforded her, placed her maid at the door to watch, and praying to God to strengthen her, cut off the head of Holofernes with his own sword, and wrapping it in his rich canopy, gave it to her maid to carry, on which both went out of the camp as on the preceding evenings.

What is related when she drew near the city?
When they drew near the gate of Bethulia, Judith called to the watchmen to open, saying: "God is with us, who has shown his power in Israel." On hearing her voice they called the ancients, and the whole town was in motion to receive her; by the

light of torches they conducted her to a high place, whence, silence being procured, she exhorted them to return thanks to God for his manifest protection in strengthening her to cut off their most powerful enemy, and producing the head of Holofernes, directed them to hang it on their walls, and at sunrise to make a vigorous attack on the enemy, who would be in confusion at the loss of their general, and so be easily dispersed.

What is said of the event?
The event verified her prediction; the Assyrians were completely routed, and the Bethulians enriched with their spoils, while Achior, convinced that the God of Israel was the true and only God, professed himself a Jew. The High Priest, with all the ancients, came from Jerusalem to see and congratulate Judith, whom they styled, "The glory of Jerusalem, the joy of Israel, and the honor of the people." Far from being elated with the praises bestowed on her, she gave the glory of the victory to God, to whom she consecrated the remainder of her life in prayer, mortification, and holy retirement. The invasion by Holofernes is supposed to have occurred in the reign of Manasses.

CHAPTER LXVI.

KINGS OF JUDA, FROM MANASSES TO THE ELEVENTH YEAR OF SEDECIAS, WHEN THE REMNANT OF THE PEOPLE WERE CARRRIED CAPTIVE TO BABYLON.

Who succeeded Manasses?
His son Amon, at the age of twenty-two, who imitated his father in his sins, but not in his repentance. He was murdered by his servants, after a reign of two years. (2 Par. xxxiii. 21.)

Who succeeded Amon?
His son Josias, who was only eight years old when

he began his reign. Holy Scripture testifies of him that no king before or after him so exactly fulfilled all the laws of Moses, and he most zealously exerted himself to extirpate idolatry and restore the worship of God.

What did he do?
He purified the temple and commanded the Levites to replace the ark in the sanctuary, whence it was probably removed in one of the late impious reigns. This is he whom the prophet foretold to Jeroboam, king of Israel, when sacrificing at Bethel, 350 years before, who should destroy the altar of Bethel and burn the bones of the idolatrous priests on it, which Josias fulfilled.

How did Josias end his life?
He was, to the great grief of the entire nation, killed in a battle in which he unadvisedly engaged with Pharaoh Necho, king of Egypt, having reigned thirty-one years. (4 Kings xxii; 2 Par. xxxv.)

Who succeeded the good king Josias?
His son Joachaz, at the age of twenty-three, who reigned only three months; he was a wicked king, and was carried captive to Egypt by Pharaoh Necho, who appointed his brother Eliakim, king instead, having changed his name to Joakim. (2 Par. xxxvi.)

How long did Joakim reign?
Eleven years. He also was a wicked king, for which he was punished during the course of his reign by the repeated incursions of his enemies. In the third year of his reign, he was, with many princes and children of the principal families, amongst whom was the prophet Daniel, then a child, carried captive to Babylon by Nebuchodonozer II.; but after some time Joakim was released. The seventy years' captivity begins its date from the time of Joakim's being carried to Babylon.

Who succeeded Joakim?
His son Joachin, at the age of eighteen, who imitated his father's impiety, and was carried captive to Babylon, after a reign of only three months, together with the principal inhabitants, and the best artificers; in all about ten thousand persons. At the same time, the sacred vessels of the Temple were likewise carried to Babylon, together with the king's treasures, as had been foretold to Ezechias.

Whom did Nebuchodonozer appoint instead of Joachin?
His uncle Sedecias, son of Josias; but, unlike his good father, he was impious and wicked. Regardless of the oath of allegiance he had taken to Nebuchodonozer, he revolted, and he and his people cruelly ill-treated the prophet Jeremiah and the other prophets whom God sent to exhort them to repentance before his just and often threatened judgments would overtake them. (2 Par. xxxvi.)

How long did Sedecias reign?
Eleven years. In the ninth year of his reign Nebuchodonozer began the siege of Jerusalem, and took it in the eleventh. Having killed the children of Sedecias in his presence, he had his eyes pulled out and sent him bound to Babylon; then plundered and burned the Temple, and all Jerusalem with it, put the high priest to death, and led into captivity all that remained of the kingdom of Juda, except some husbandmen and vine dressers, over whom he placed Godolias governor; but he gave directions to Nabuzardan, his general, to spare the prophet Jeremiah, and permit him to go wherever he pleased. (4 Kings xxv., and Jer. xxxix.)

How many years after the dispersion of Israel was Juda led into captivity?
One hundred and thirty-three years.

CHAPTER LXVII.

THE PROPHET JEREMIAH.

What circumstance led to the dispersion of the few Jews whom Nebuchodonozer left?
A wicked man, named Ismahel, having killed Godolias, the people, fearing the vengeance of Nebuchodonozer, fled into Egypt, though Jeremiah endeavored to dissuade them, assuring them that no evil would befall them if they remained; at the same time he foretold the miseries that would overtake them in Egypt, as Nebuchodonozer would invade that country; and represented also the danger they would there be exposed to of falling into idolatry; but they would not be dissuaded.

Did Jeremiah accompany them in their flight to Egypt?
Yes, they obliged him and his secretary, the prophet Baruch, to go with them, promising to be guided in all things by Jeremiah, but soon, to his inexpressible grief, they declared themselves idolators, and, according to the Hebrew tradition, stoned him and Baruch to death.

Was Jeremiah advanced in years at his death?
He was; his age is not recorded, but he must have been very old, as he prophesied for nearly a century, having begun in the thirteenth year of the reign of Josias, and he survived the release of Joachin from prison in the thirty-seventh year of his captivity.

What prophets preached between the Assyrian and Babylonian captivity?
Besides those already mentioned, Jeremiah, Nahum, Sophonias, and Habacuc, preached in Judea, and Daniel and Ezechiel in Babylon.

What became of the Tabernacle, ark of the Covenant and Altar of Incense?

Jeremiah, by the command of God, had them carried to Mount Nebo, and there concealed in a cave, the entrance to which he locked up, and would not suffer the place to be marked, saying, "The place shall be unknown till God gather together the congregation of the people, and receive them to mercy." (2 Mac. ii.)

What did Jeremiah order to be done with the sacred fire?
He directed the priests to take it from the altar, and hide it in a deep dry pit, where it remained undiscovered until the return from the captivity. (2 Mac. i. 19.)

Of what did Jeremiah prophesy?
Of the coming of our Lord, and the perpetuity of the priesthood. He foretold the Babylonian captivity, a punishment inflicted for the idolatry and obstinate impenitence of the Jews, their return to Jerusalem after seventy years, and the destruction and perpetual desolation of Babylon on account of the iniquity of its people. (Jer. xv., xxix., xxxii., xxxiii.)

CHAPTER LXVIII.

THE PROPHET EZECHIEL.

Of what did Ezechiel prophesy?
He foretold in Babylon what Jeremiah did in Jerusalem, the approaching desolation of that city, and the captivity of its king and people: with their restoration and the rebuilding of the Temple. Ezechiel also foretold the coming of our Lord, who would himself be the shepherd of his people. (Ez. xii., xvii., xxxiv., xxxix.)

What exemplification did God give Ezechiel of the deliverance of his people from captivity, and their restoration to their former greatness?

He placed him in spirit in the midst of a plain which was covered with dry bones, and having made him consider them attentively, asked "Dost thou think these bones shall live:" to which Ezechiel replied "O Lord, thou knowest:" then God desired him to command the bones to come together, and resume their former position. Having done so, the bones with noise and commotion came, each one to its joint as he spoke, the sinews and flesh came on them, and the skin was stretched over them.

Then by divine command what did Ezechiel do?
Then by the divine command Ezechiel called on the spirit to reanimate them, and they stood up, an exceedingly great army. "These bones," said Almighty God, "represent the house of Israel, they say, our bones are dried up, and our hope is lost, and we are cut off; therefore prophecy, and say to them, thus saith the Lord God: Behold I will open your graves, and will bring you out of your sepulchres, O my people, and will bring you into the land of Israel."

Relate the vision Ezechiel had in the fifth year of the captivity of King Joachin?
Being on the bank of the great river Chobar or Euphrates, he perceived a whirlwind rising from the north, which enlightened the atmosphere around. In the midst of the fiery cloud appeared four living creatures, who in shape and body had the likeness of a human figure; but their heads and feet were of a very singular appearance.

What is said of their faces?
Each one had four faces in an opposite direction, looking towards the four points of the heavens. The face of a man was on the fore part of all the four; the face of a lion on the right. On the left was the face of an ox, and behind was the face of an eagle rising somewhat higher. They had four wings,

one on every side, and under each wing a hand, resembling that of a man; their legs were straight, and the sole of their foot was like that of a calf. Two of their wings covered each one's body, and the other two were extended and lifted up as it were, ready for flight. Whenever they moved, and they moved as the impulse of the Spirit directed them, their motion was straightforward, and they ran and returned like flashes of lightning. Neither did they turn about when they went, each one having his face always pointing forward. Their whole figure glowed with the appearance of burning coals and bright flaming lamps.

What is said of Ezechiel, at the sight of this vision?
At the sight of this awful vision, Ezechiel fell upon his face. The Lord bade him rise, and announce his judgments to the children of Israel. (Ez. xxxvii.)

CHAPTER LXIX.

THE PROPHET DANIEL IN THE COURT OF NEBUCHODONOSOR.

Of what did Daniel prophesy?
He foretold not only the coming of our Lord, but the time in which he would come; the rebuilding of Jerusalem, its final destruction, the cessation of the Jewish sacrifices, and the rise and fall of several great empires. (Dan. ix. 24, and xi. 31.)

In what manner did Daniel live in the court of Nebuchodonosor, when selected with other Hebrew children to wait on the king, and be instructed in the learning of the Chaldees?
He lived most frugally and abstemiously, though surrounded with every delicacy, despising all that he might serve God faithfully. The Lord therefore blessed him and his companions that followed his example,

made them look better than those who were nourished with exquisite meats, and gave them understanding and wisdom beyond all who were educated with them. To Daniel also, he added the gift of prophesy. (Dan. i.)

How was Daniel specially introduced to the notice of the king?
Nebuchodonosor had a dream which greatly terrified him, but having forgot it when he awoke, he sent for his wise men and soothsayers, and commanded them, under pain of death and confiscation of property, to inform him both of the dream and its interpretation. They remonstrated, saying, that he required an impossibility; but said they would interpret the dream if he related it. This he considered an attempt to gain time, and deceive him, and accordingly gave orders for their immediate execution: several were put to death before Daniel heard of it, and as the sentence extended to all the wise men, Daniel and his companions were included; he immediately went to the king and begged some respite, then returning to his house, he and his three companions Ananias, Azarias and Misael united in fervent prayer to God who graciously heard them, and revealed the dream to Daniel that night. Having returned thanks to God he went to the king and interpreted his dream; for which he raised him to great dignity, and at his request placed Ananias, Azarias and Misael over the works of Babylon. Daniel was known to the Chaldees by the name of Baltassar, and his companions as Sidrach, Misach and Abdenago. (Dan. ii.)

What was the dream of Nebuchodonosor?
He dreamed that he saw a terrible colossal statue, the head of which was made of gold, the breast and arms of silver, the body of brass, the legs of iron, the feet partly of iron, partly of clay. Having observed it some time, a stone not cut with hands rolled from

a mountain, and struck the statue on the feet, broke
it in pieces, and crumbled the whole into dust, which
was blown away by the wind; and the stone became
a mountain which filled the whole earth.

What was the interpretation of the dream?
Such, O king, said Daniel, was your dream; and
this is the interpretation: the head of gold denotes
you and your kingdom; another less powerful than
you shall succeed you as denoted by silver, which
shall be followed by a third of brass; and the fourth
shall be of greater strength, as denoted by iron; but
it shall be divided, being partly strong and partly
weak, as denoted by iron mixed with clay. Then
shall God raise a fifth, which shall last for ever, and
shall utterly destroy and consume those that preceded
it. (Dan. ii.)

CHAPTER LXX.

PRESERVATION OF THE HEBREWS WHEN CAST INTO THE FIERY FURNACE.

Relate what you remember of the miraculous preservation of Sidrach, Misach, and Abdenago, when cast into the fiery furnace?
Nebuchodonosor having made a great golden statue,
erected it in a plain near Babylon, and ordered the
nobles, magistrates, rulers, and all in authority to
attend at its dedication; and at a signal given by
musical instruments, to fall down and adore it, commanding that any one who refused should be cast
into a fiery furnace. When the signal was given,
all prostrated except the Hebrews, who being immediately brought before the king, he, in great anger,
repeated his command and threat, asking, "Who is
the God that shall deliver you out of my hand?"
To which they replied, "Our God whom we worship
is able to save us from the furnace of burning fire

and to deliver us out of thy hands, O king; but if he will not, be it known to thee, O king, that we will not worship thy gods, nor adore the golden statue which thou hast set up."

What did Nebuchodonosor then do?
Then Nebuchodonosor, in great rage, ordered the furnace to be heated seven times more than it was, and the strongest men in his army to bind Sidrach, Misach, and Abdenago, and cast them in.

What is related of the three Hebrews?
The king's servants threw in pitch, tow, and other combustibles, until the flame arose forty-nine cubits above the furnace, and killed all who were near it, with the men who cast in the three Hebrews; but they walked in the midst of the fire unhurt, praising, and blessing God, who had sent an angel with them into the furnace to drive out the flame, and render it cool and pleasant.

What did Nebuchodonosor do?
Nebuchodonosor seeing the miracle that was wrought, called on them to come forth, gave them full liberty to exercise their religion, and published an edict throughout his dominions in praise and acknowledgment of the wonderful works of God. (Dan. iii.)

CHAPTER LXXI.

BEL AND THE DRAGON.

What means did Daniel take to prove to the king and people the absurdity of idolatry?
The favorite idol of the Babylonians was called Bel, to which they erected a magnificent temple, and sent into it daily, for the use of the idol, a large quantity of fine flour, forty sheep, and sixty vessels of wine. The king went daily to the temple to adore it, and one day asked Daniel why he did not. Daniel replied that he did not adore idols, the work of men's

hands; but that he adored the living God who made
heaven and earth. The king expressed surprise at
his doubt of Bel being a living God, seeing that he
consumed so much provisions. Daniel assured him
that he was deceived, that Bel never ate, and that he
could prove it. The king ordered him to do so, and
decreed that in case he did, the priests of Bel should
die, but that if he failed, he should die himself for
blaspheming Bel. The provisions being placed in
the temple, the king sealed the door with his own
seal, and went away, Daniel having first taken the
precaution of sifting fine ashes over the floor. The
next morning, the king, accompanied by Daniel, went
to the temple, and having opened the door, seeing
that the place was empty, began to extol Bel, but
Daniel directed his attention to the prints of feet in
the ashes. The king, seeing the footsteps of men,
women, and children, sent for the priests, and obliged
them to show the secret door, by which they entered
and carried away the provisions. Then, being greatly
incensed, he condemned them to death, and permitted Daniel to destroy Bel and the temple.

Did the Babylonians pay divine honor to any other object besides Bel?
They did, to a great dragon which, next to Bel, was
held in the greatest veneration by them. This, the
king told Daniel he ought to have no objection to
worship, as he could not deny that it had life; to
which Daniel replied, that if he permitted him, he
would kill the dragon without sword or club. The
king having assented, he gave it a composition, on
eating which it burst; and Daniel took that opportunity to point out the absurdity of worshipping such
things. (Dan. xiv.)

How did the Babylonians act when they heard what Daniel had done?
They assembled seditiously, and threatened to de-

stroy the king and his house unless he delivered Daniel to them. He reluctantly yielded, not being able otherwise to appease them, and they immediately threw Daniel into the lion's den, where he remained six days. On the seventh, the king went to lament him, but seeing him sitting in the midst of the lions, had him instantly taken out and glorified the God whom he adored. He then caused Daniel's enemies to be thrown in, and the lions immediately devoured them.

How was Daniel supplied with food while in the lion's den?

By a prophet of Judea, named Habacuc, who having prepared a dinner for some reapers, was carrying it to them, when an angel desired him to take it to Daniel, who was in the lion's den in Babylon, and on his replying that he never saw Babylon, nor knew the den, the angel took him up by the hair and carried him thither. After Daniel had partaken of the food thus miraculously conveyed, the angel presently set Habacuc again in his own place. (Dan. xiv.)

What impending judgment did Daniel foretell to Nebuchodonosor II?

That he would be cast out from the society of men for seven years, and have for his companions the beasts of the field until he acknowledged the power of God, and his entire dependence on him.

How did Daniel advise him to avert it?

Daniel advised him to redeem his sins with alms, and his iniquities with works of mercy to the poor that God might forgive him.

At the end of a year, what happened to Nebuchodonosor?

At the end of a year, Nebuchodonosor walking in his palace, and beholding with delight the glory that

Note.—This is the Nebuchodonosor who led the Jews into captivity. He was son to Nabopolaser, and father to Evil Merodach.

surrounded him, in the pride of his heart, attributed all to his own excellence and power; then a voice from heaven pronounced the sentence which Daniel had predicted, and Nebuchodonosor became a companion for beasts, and was driven from the society of men for seven years. When they had expired his reason was restored, and he blessed the hand that chastised him, acknowledging the power, the justice, and wisdom of God, who then restored to him his kingdom with additional majesty. (Dan. iv.)

CHAPTER LXXII.

BALTASSAR'S FEAST.

What is related of Baltassar?
Baltassar, who is believed to be the son of Evil Merodach, in the seventeenth and last year of his reign, made a splendid entertainment for a thousand of his nobles, during which, he ordered the sacred vessels that were brought from the Temple of Jerusalem, to be produced for the use of himself and guests.

What happened when they had drunk out of the sacred vessels?
Scarcely had he and they profanely drunk out of them, when the fingers of a man's hand appeared writing characters on the wall, which none of the wise men could decipher, and the king in great trouble anxiously sought for one who could read and interpret the mysterious writing, promising to clothe in purple, and exalt to the third dignity in the kingdom any who could do so. The queen hearing of the king's disquiet came into the banquet-room and endeavored to calm his agitation; at her suggestion Daniel was sent for, to whom the king renewed his promises of reward.

What did Daniel reply?
Daniel replied, "Thy rewards be to thyself, and the

gifts of thy house, give to another, but the writing I will read to thee, O king, and show thee the interpretation thereof. Then reminding Baltassar of the punishment that befell Nebuchodonosor for his pride, and representing to him that notwithstanding his being aware of it, he had lifted himself up against the Lord of heaven, and profaned the consecrated vessels of his Temple.

What was the interpretation of the writing?
The words on the wall were "*Mane, Thecel, Phares,*" and Daniel thus interpreted it: "*Mane,* God hath numbered thy kingdom, and hath finished it. *Thecel,* thou art weighed in the balance and found wanting. *Phares,* thy kingdom is divided, and given to the Medes and Persians." (Dan. v.)

How soon was the prediction fulfilled?
That very night the Medes gained an unexpected entrance into Babylon, Baltassar was slain, and Darius ascended the throne.

How was that great city Babylon taken in one night?
Cyrus, general of the combined forces of the Medes and Persians at the time besieging Babylon, seeing that on account of the great strength and extent of the city there was little probability of being able to take it unless by stratagem, devised an extraordinary way to gain an entrance. The great river Euphrates ran through the centre of the city, and Cyrus meditated no less than turning its course and marching

Note.—Daniel was at this time about eighty-seven years old, being eighteen when carried to Babylon with Joakim, the year before Nabopolaser's death, whose son Nebuchodonosor II. reigned forty-three years; his son, Evil Merodach, two years, and Baltassar seventeen. Between Baltassar and Evil Merodach two kings of a different line reigned, one for four years, the other nine months. Daniel survived to the reign of Cyrus, who succeeded Darius the Mede. The latter is supposed to have reigned but one year in Babylon.

his army through the dry bed of the river: accordingly, with great labor he had a deep ditch cut half round the city connected with the Euphrates below Babylon, and separated above only by a dam. The night of Baltassar's feast he put his project in execution; breaking the dam, and turning the river into the channel he had cut for it, he led his army without opposition into the centre of the city, by what the Babylonians considered their best defence, whilst they were engaged in banqueting, not thinking an enemy could approach them.

CHAPTER LXXIII.

PROPHECIES OF THE CAPTURE OF BABYLON.

Was the taking of Babylon foretold long before by the prophets?
Yes, nearly 200 years before by Isaias; also by Jeremiah, with the manner in which it should be taken, the people who should overthrow it, and the name of the general who should command them, together with the occurrence that should bring the vengeance of God on the city.

Repeat the prophecies that describe the manner of its capture?
"I have caused thee to fall into a snare, and thou art taken, O Babylon, and thou wast not aware of it, (Jer. l. 24,) thou that dwellest upon many waters, (Jer. li. 13,) a drought is upon them, (Jer. l. 38,) the fords are taken, and the marshes burned with fire, and the men of war are affrighted. (Jer. li. 32.) The king of Babylon hath heard the report of them, and his hands are grown feeble. (Jer. l. 43.) I will make her princes drunk, and her wise men, and her captains, and her rulers, and her valiant men, and they shall sleep an everlasting sleep." (Jer. li. 57.)

Repeat the prophecy that mentions the names of the combined forces that should attack Babylon?

"Go up, O Elam, besiege, O Mede.... Babylon is fallen, she is fallen, and all the graven gods thereof are broken unto the ground?" (Isaias xxi. 2, 9; and Jer. li. 28.)

Repeat the prophecy which names the general who took Babylon?

"Thus saith the Lord to my anointed Cyrus, whose right hand I have taken hold of to subdue nations before his face, and to turn the backs of kings, and to open the doors before him, and the gates shall not be shut, I will go before thee, and humble the great ones of the earth, I will break in pieces the gates of brass, and burst the bars of iron, and I will give thee hidden treasures, and the concealed riches of secret places, that thou mayest know that I am the Lord who call thee by thy name, the God of Israel, for the sake of my servant Jacob, and Israel my elect, I have even called thee by thy name, I have made a likeness of thee, and thou hast not known me." (Isaias xlv.)

Repeat the prophecies of the occurrences which brought the judgment of God on Babylon?

"Get thee into darkness, O daughter of the Chaldeans, who sayest, 'I am, and there is none else besides me.' "I was angry with my people, and gave them into thy hands, and thou hast shown no mercy to them. Behold I come against thee, thou proud one, saith the Lord of hosts." (Isaias xlvii. Jer. l. 81.) "The Lord hath raised up the spirit of the kings of the Medes, and his mind is against Babylon to destroy it, because it is the vengeance of the Lord, the vengeance of his Temple." (Jer. l 11.) "It shall be no more inhabited for ever, and it shall not be founded unto generation and generation." (Isaias xiii. 20.)

CHAPTER LXXIV.

DANIEL IN THE LION'S DEN.

How was Daniel treated by Darius?
With every mark of esteem, which excited the envy of the courtiers, who consulted together in order to discover something to accuse him of, and not succeeding, devised a plan by which they hoped to gratify their unjust hatred.

What plan did they devise?
Waiting on Darius, they prevailed with him to issue a decree forbidding all under pain of death to present any petition to God or man for the space of thirty days. Daniel, though aware of the decree, performed his daily devotions as usual. This his enemies expected, and reported to the king, requiring the immediate execution of the edict. Darius, in great trouble, sought to deliver him, but the nobles would not suffer it, as (according to the laws of the Medes and Persians) a decree published by the king could not be annulled. Darius with much grief then gave orders for Daniel's being cast into the lions' den; and through grief could neither eat nor sleep that night.

In the morning, what did the king do?
Early in the morning, going to the den, he cried in a mournful voice, "Daniel, servant of the living God, hath thy God, whom thou servest always, been able to deliver thee from the lions?"

What did Daniel reply?
Daniel replied, "O king, my God hath sent his angel, and hath shut up the mouths of the lions, and they have not hurt me, forasmuch as before him justice hath been found in me; yea, and before thee. O king, I have done no offence."

What did the king then do?
Then the king with great joy had him taken out of the den, and his accusers with their wives and children immediately cast in, who were killed by the lions before they so much as reached the bottom of the den. (Dan vi.)

How long did the Babylonian captivity last?
Seventy years, as foretold by the prophet Jeremiah, "And all this land shall be a desolation . . . . . and shall serve the king of Babylon seventy years." (Jer. xxv. 2.)

How did Daniel act when the seventy years had nearly expired?
He humbled himself in prayer and fasting, earnestly imploring of God to restore his people and rebuild the city whereon his name was invocated. Whilst Daniel persevered in prayer, he was favored by the angel Gabriel appearing to him, and assuring him not only of the deliverance of the people from bondage, but also from the slavery of sin, by the coming and death of Christ, which he foretold him would take place in the seventieth week (of years) from the going forth of the decree to rebuild Jerusalem. (Dan. ix. 11.)

SIXTH AGE OF THE WORLD.

From the return from the Babylonian captivity under Cyrus to the birth of Christ, a space of 546 years.

CHAPTER LXXV.

THE TEMPLE OF JERUSALEM REBUILT.

By whom was the decree to rebuild the Temple published?
By Cyrus, in the first year of his reign. The seven-

ty years' captivity being ended, he (as was foretold by Isaias) gave permission to all to contribute to the rebuilding of the Temple, and he restored the sacred vessels that had been carried out of it. The principal families of Juda and Benjamin, together with the priests and Levites to the number of 42,360, availed themselves of his permission to return to Jerusalem, and with 7360 servants marched under the conduct of Zorobabel, grandson to king Joachin, and accompanied by Josue, the High Priest, and the Prophets Aggeus and Zacharias. (Esdras i.)

Did any people impede the rebuilding of the Temple?
The Samaritans did. At first, they offered to assist the Jews in rebuilding it; but their services being declined, they exerted all their influence to counteract it, and by their representations to the court of Persia, succeeded during the reign of three successive kings (a space of about sixteen years); but in the reign of Darius Hystaspes, the prophets Aggeus and Zacharias encouraged Zorobabel and the people to proceed with it, and Darius himself contributed large sums of money.

How did the ancients act who remembered the former Temple, when they saw the foundations of the new?
They wept so bitterly, and cried so loud, that their lamentations nearly drowned the acclamations of the young people who rejoiced at seeing the building, (Esdras iii. 12); but God sent the prophet Aggeus to comfort and assure them that though that house was not to be compared to the former in magnificence, it should nevertheless surpass it in glory; that in a little time God would move heaven and earth and *the desired of all nations come,* and that house be filled with glory. (Aggeus ii.)

Whilst the Jews who returned from captivity were

in danger from the enmity of the Samaritans, with what danger were their brethren who remained after them threatened?

With utter extermination, from the fury of a wicked man named Aman, but God counteracted his devices, and raised a protector for his people in the person of Esther, one of their own nation, whom the king raised to the dignity of queen for her superior merit.

CHAPTER LXXVI.

HISTORY OF ESTHER.

What is related of Assuerus?
Assuerus, king of the Medes and Persians, made a great feast in the third year of his reign for all the nobles and princes of his empire; and in order to exhibit his riches prolonged it for one hundred and eighty days; at the end of which he made another feast of seven days, to which he invited all the citizens of Susan, the capital of his empire; he sent also to Vasthi, the queen, whom he requested to come arrayed in her royal robes, that the nobles and people might admire her, for she was exceedingly beautiful; but it being unusual for Persian women of rank to appear at banquets, the queen refused.

What did the king do?
The king thinking himself slighted in the presence of his nobles, resented the queen's refusal, and consulted some of his wise men as to how he should act; they inflamed his resentment, advising him to divorce her and select from amongst the most beautiful women of the empire one who would be worthy to reign instead. In accordance with this advice, officers were sent through all the provinces, and of all who were presented to the king none pleased him so much as Esther, whom he crowned, and

their nuptials were celebrated with royal magnificence.

What is said of Esther?
Esther had been left an orphan when very young, and was brought up in sentiments of great piety by her uncle Mordochai, to whom she was as obedient when queen as during her childhood; soon after her coronation a plot was laid against the king's life, which Mordochai discovered and disclosed to Esther, who in his name informed the king of it, and the matter being inquired into, the conspirators were executed; but Esther did not say that Mordochai was related to her, because he had forbidden her to make known her country or people.

What is said of Mordochai?
After Esther was made queen, Mordochai usually sat at the palace gate, yet even in that humble position acquired the enmity of a powerful courtier named Aman, who being used to the servile homage paid him by the king's servants, was mortified at not receiving the same from Mordochai, and discovering that he was a Jew, determined to be revenged not only on him but on all his countrymen.

What did Aman do?
Accordingly, he took occasion to represent to Assuerus that the Jews scattered over his dominions despised his ordinances; and used laws and ceremonies peculiar to themselves, which rendered it expedient to exterminate them all, and begged the king to issue a decree to that effect: to which Assuerus assented, as he believed the statement made on such authority. Aman immediately proceeded to put his wicked design in execution, but first, superstitiously cast lots for the day on which the general massacre should take place, and having drawn the thirteenth of the twelfth month, ordered the king's scribes to write to all parts of the king-

dom, and to command the judges and lieutenants to cause all the Jews young and old to be killed on that day.

At the announcement, what is said of Mordochai?
At the announcement of this sorrowful news, Mordochai put on sackcloth, and weeping bitterly went to the gate of the palace, of which Esther being informed she sent in great anxiety to know the cause of his grief, and he sent her a copy of the edict, with an injunction to petition the king in behalf of her people. Esther humbly represented that none could go into the king's inner court unsent for, under pain of instant death, unless the king held out the golden sceptre in token of clemency; she had not yet made known that she was a Jewess on account of Mordochai's prohibition, but he now removed it telling her that God had probably raised her to the throne that she might be ready to assist her people in their distress; and that at such a time she ought to think of saving other lives besides her own.

What did Esther do after hearing the reasoning of Mordochai?
Esther yielding to his reasons, consented to risk her life for the sake of her people, but first desired that he, and all the Jews in Susan should unite with her in prayer and fasting for three days. At the end of that time laying aside her penitential garb, and begging of God to put a suitable speech in her mouth when in the king's presence, she arrayed herself in her royal robes, and taking two maids with her, entered the inner court in which the king was seated on his throne, surrounded by the ensigns of royalty.

What happened, when she came into the king's presence?
Surprised at the unexpected appearance of the queen,

Assuerus looked at her angrily, at which, she turning pale, sank down; at that moment God changed the king's spirit into mildness, hastily descending from the throne, he raised her, and laying the golden sceptre on her neck told her the law was not made for her, and encouraged her to ask what she desired, assuring her that if it were half the kingdom she should have it: when sufficiently recovered to answer him, Esther requested him to partake of the banquet she had prepared for him, and to bring Aman to it: with which the king immediately complied.

What reply did Esther make to enquiries of the king at the feast?
Being greatly pleased at the entertainment, Assuerus again asked Esther what she wished, and renewed the promise to grant it whatever it might be: she replied that she would open her mind to him on the following day, if he and Aman would again favor her by coming to her feast; to this the king consented.

What is said of Aman?
Aman went out highly pleased at the honor done him; but when he saw Mordochai his former discontent revived to such a degree, that as he told his wife and friends, his wealth, children, and honors appeared nothing to him as long as he saw Mordochai sitting at the king's gate.

What was he advised to do?
They advised him to erect a gibbet fifty cubits high, and in the morning to speak to the king to have him hanged on it; Aman immediately began to act on this advice, his pride and resentment not enduring the delay of his revenge until the day appointed for the general massacre of the Jews.

How were his designs defeated?
God who watches over his servants defeated the designs of the proud Aman; that night, the king not

being able to sleep commanded the annals of his reign to be read for him; on hearing the part in which it was mentioned that Mordochai discovered the plot against his life, he asked what reward he had received; and being told that he had got none, desired to know who waited in the court. Aman had just come to procure the order for Mordochai's execution, and was instantly called to the king, who asked him how the man should be honored whom the king wished to honor.

What reply did Aman make?
Aman supposing none could be intended but himself, replied, that he should be clothed in royal robes, with the crown on his head, and seated on the king's horse, the first of the nobles holding the bridle, and proclaiming as they advance: "Thus shall he be honored, whom the king hath a mind to honor."

How did the king answer?
"Make haste," said the king, "take the robe and the horse, do as you have said to Mordochai, the Jew, and fail not in any particular."

What followed this answer?
This mortification was but a prelude to Aman's destruction; that day, whilst in company with the king and queen, Assuerus again asked Esther to mention her petition. "If I have found favor in thy sight, O king," she replied, "and if it please thee, give me my life for which I ask, and my people for which I request, for we are given up to be slain; if we were to be sold as slaves we should only have mourned in silence, but now the cruelty of our enemy redoundeth on the king."

What is said of Assuerus?
Assuerus, in surprise asked whom she meant, and who had power to do what she said? The queen replied, "It is Aman who is our adversary and most wicked enemy." Aman's perturbation confirming

the statement, Assuerus in great anger arose, and went into the garden.

What did Aman do?
Perceiving that his life was in danger, and overwhelmed with fear, Aman fell at Esther's feet to beg for pity.

What did Assuerus order?
Assuerus returned whilst he still remained in that position, and being already incensed became still more so at what he considered rudeness to the queen, and one of the attendants mentioning the gibbet that Aman had prepared for Mordochai, the king ordered him to be hanged on it forthwith; which was accordingly done.

What followed the death of Aman?
Assuerus gave Aman's house to Esther, and invested Mordochai with the dignity Aman had enjoyed, by another decree counteracted the former, and restored peace to the Jewish people; on seeing which wonderful deliverance many professed themselves Jews, and worshipped the one only true God.

CHAPTER LXXVII.

EDICT OF ARTAXERXES TO REBUILD THE WALLS OF JERUSALEM.—NEHEMIAS APPOINTED GOVERNOR.

When did Esdras the priest leave Babylon for Jerusalem?
In the seventh year of the reign of Artaxerxes, grandson to Darius Hystaspes, about eighty years after Zorobabel's return, and a number of the Jews, who had until then remained in Babylon accompanied him. Esdras was invested with authority from Artaxerxes to carry the presents offered by the king and others for the service of the Temple, to appoint judges and magistrates, and to establish good order in Judea. of which he held the government thirteen

years, until Nehemias was sent with a new commission from the Persian court.

When was the order given to rebuild the walls of Jerusalem?
In the twentieth year of the reign of Artaxerxes, at the prayer of Nehemias his cup-bearer, whom he appointed governor, and who proved himself worthy of the trust reposed in him, being unremitting in the discharge of his public duties, and most charitable and kind to the poor, whom he protected from the exactions of the rich. Both by exhortation and example he strove to induce the wealthy to remit the debts due to them; and not only gave up the pension allowed him as governor but contributed largely out of his private fortune to the wants of the poor.

What prophet lived after the rebuilding of the Temple?
Malachias, the last of the prophets; there was no prophet from his time until St. John Baptist, whom he foretold. (Mal. iii.)

Of what did Malachias prophecy?
Of the coming of Christ, the rejection of the Jews and their sacrifices, and the call of the gentiles, who should in every place offer to God an acceptable sacrifice.

How many prophets left writings bearing their names?
Sixteen: they are divided into two classes, the great and the minor prophets.

Name the great prophets.
Isaias, Jeremiah, Ezekiel, and Daniel, who are designated the great, on account of the length of their prophecies.

Note.—From this date the seventy weeks (of years) foretold by Daniel are begun to be counted; there being sixty-nine weeks of years, or four hundred and eighty-three years from this to the baptism of our Lord.

Name the twelve minor prophets.
Jonas, Osee, Amos, Abdias, Micheas, Nahum, Joel, Sophonias, Habacuc, Aggeus, Zacharias, and Malachias.

Why is not Baruch named among them?
Because the prophecy which bears his name was for a long time thought to be the work of Jeremiah; and is even still supposed to be dictated for the most part by Jeremiah, though penned by Baruch.

What space of time was included between the first and last of the above-named prophets?
About four hundred years.

How did Nehemias procure hallowed fire after the rebuilding of the Temple?
He sent some descendants of the priests, who by command of Jeremiah, had hidden the sacred fire, to seek it; but they found only thick water, which Nehemias desired them draw up and bring to him; and having caused the altar and victims to be sprinkled with it, it ignited and consumed the sacrifice. (2 Mac. i.

CHAPTER LXXVIII.

CIVIL DISTURBANCE.—FOREIGN INVASION.

How was the kingdom of Juda governed from the time of Nehemias?
By High Priests, of whom a regular succession was maintained from the beginning. The kingdom was nevertheless subject to Persia, but had full enjoyment of religious liberty, and a long and prosperous peace, during which Jerusalem was in a great degree restored to its ancient splendor, and the Temple adorned by the gifts of several kings; but after the conquest of Persia by Alexander the Great, and the subsequent division of his empire, the peace of Ju

was disturbed partly by civil dissensions, and partly by the tyranny of the kings of Asia.

What occasioned the building of the temple on Mount Gerezim in Samaria, and the schism that followed?

Manasses, brother to Jaddua, the High Priest, married the daughter of a powerful man of Samaria, named Sanballat, contrary to the law which prohibited priests marrying out of their own nation. This disqualified him from performing the sacred duties of the ministry, and whilst he was undecided whether to renounce his sacerdotal dignity or send away his wife, Sanballat, anxious to gratify him for his daughter's sake, promised to build him a temple at Gerezim, like that at Jerusalem, and to make him priest of it. He engaged also to procure the approbation of Darius; but that king being conquered by Alexander, Sanballat transferred his allegiance, and obtained Alexander's sanction for the intended temple. The edifice was quickly raised, and thenceforward, for about two hundred years, it was resorted to by those Jews who were unwilling to be restrained by the strictness of the law, and by priests, who, like Manasses, had married pagan wives. (Josephus, Book II., c. 8 and 9.)

What gave rise to the attempt of Seleucus, king of Asia, on the treasury of the Temple at Jerusalem?

The overseer of the Temple, a wicked man of the

Note.—Those denominated kings of Asia were some of Alexander's successors who shared in the division of his conquered dominions. The disputes between them and the kings of Egypt made them occasionally seek alliance with the Jews; at other times they claimed Palestine as a province.

Note.—Fifty years after the erection of the Samaritan temple, Ptolemy Philadelphus, sent to Jerusalem to Eleazer, the high priest, (grandson to Jaddua,) for a copy of the Jewish law which he gave, and with it six interpreters from each tribe, who translated it into Greek. This is what is called the Septuagint translation.

tribe of Benjamin named Simon, being opposed in
an unjust design by Onias the High Priest, gave
information, out of a spirit of revenge, that immense
sums of money were deposited in the treasury of the
Temple, which could be converted to the king's use.
Seleucus immediately sent Heliodorus, his commis-
sary, with orders to seize it, and notwithstanding the
remonstrances of the High Priest, who represented
that the money was the property of widows and or-
phans who placed it there for safety, he proceeded to
take possession of it.

*How was Heliodorus prevented from possessing
himself of the money?*
When the reason of his arrival in Jerusalem was
made known, Onias and all the people earnestly besought Almighty God to prevent the profanation of
the sanctuary; he mercifully heard their prayer, and
when Heliodorus, surrounded by his guards, attempted to enter, he and they were struck with sudden terror and faintness at the appearance of a horse
with a terrible rider, richly adorned and clad in
golden armor, which ran fiercely at Heliodorus and
struck him with his fore feet, while two young men,
in rich attire, standing at either side, severely
scourged him. Heliodorus fell speechless on the
ground, and was carried out nearly dead, but at the
prayer of Onias God restored him, and on his return
to the king he gave testimony of the power of God.
(2 Mac. iii.)

What became of the good Onias?
He was deposed from the office of High Priest by
the intrigues of his brother Jason, who procured it
for himself by giving a large sum of money to Antiochus Epiphanes, successor to Seleucus; but he
enjoyed his ill-gotten dignity only three years, during which he introduced many heathen customs

He was displaced by the still more impious Menelaus, brother to the above-mentioned Simon, of the tribe of Benjamin.

What is related of Menelaus?
Menelaus being reproved by Onias for his sacrilegious robberies and other crimes, procured his murder; and then, having no one to check his impiety, brought great misery on the people; but he was, not long after, put out of office, for not paying what he stipulated for the dignity, and was succeeded by his equally wicked brother Lysimachus. (2 Mac iv.)

What civil disturbances arose about this time in Judea?
On a false rumor of the death of Antiochus, the impious Jason made an attempt to recover the dignity of High Priest, for which purpose he assembled about a thousand followers, and took Jerusalem by assault; but after having killed a great number of the inhabitants he was at length compelled to fly.

What did Antiochus do on hearing of these events?
Antiochus hearing what was done, and fearing that the Jews would forsake his alliance, returned out of Egypt, where he had been at war, and stormed Jerusalem, which he took, and spared neither young nor old, so that in the space of three days he killed 80,000, made prisoners of 40,000; and sold 40,000 more for slaves. (2 Mac. v.)

How did Menelaus act on that occasion?
He led the impious Antiochus into the Temple, who sacrilegiously took the sacred vessels in his hands, and robbed the treasury of the Temple of 1,800 talents. (2 Mac. v.)

What directions did Antiochus give the governors he appointed in Judea?
To oppress and afflict the people; and, on his return to Antioch, he sent Appolonius, whose hatred of the Jews was well known, with an army of 22,000, and

directions to kill all the men and sell all the women and children.

What means did Appolonius take to execute his cruel orders?
Pretending peace, he went to Jerusalem, and there, waited until the Sabbath, when he armed his soldiers, and killed a great multitude without opposition; for the Jews, through respect for the Sabbath, suffered themselves to be killed without making any resistance.

CHAPTER LXXIX.

MARTYRDOM OF ELEAZER AND OF THE SEVEN MACHABEES.

What further marks of hatred did Antiochus give?
He commenced a furious persecution on account of religion, placed an idol in the Temple, defiled the altar, put a great number to death, who refused to conform to the superstitions of the heathens, and struck such universal terror, that many had not fortitude to profess their religion, and apostatized, while others fled and hid themselves in caves. (1 Mac. i, and 2 Mac. vi.)

Relate some particulars of that persecution?
Among the most remarkable persons who suffered martyrdom during it, was Eleazer, one of the chief scribes, who was ninety years of age, beloved and venerated by all for his great piety. In the heat of the persecution, some of his friends, through mistaken pity, endeavored to induce him to elude the edict of Antiochus, by eating lawful meat under pretence that it was swine's flesh, which was forbidden by the law of Moses; but he generously refused, saying that it would ill become him at his age to dissemble, and for the preservation of a corruptible life, to scandalize the young, and bring on himself the inevitable judgment of God, whilst, by suffering

death courageously, he would prove his fidelity to God, and leave to his brethren an example of fortitude.

What followed?
He was immediately led to execution, and, when about to expire, prayed in these words, "O Lord, who hast the holy knowledge, thou knowest manifestly that whereas I might be delivered from death, I suffer grievous pains in body, but in soul am well content to suffer these things because I fear thee.".

What other distinguished persons suffered martyrdom about the same time?
Seven brothers, usually called the Machabees, and their mother; Antiochus presided at their trial, and used every effort to shake their constancy. Beginning with the eldest, he had him cruelly tortured and finally put to death in presence of his mother and brethren: he acted towards the rest in like manner, until only the youngest remained, the mother animating and courageously exhorting them, all the time, to persevere.

What is said of the tyrant?
The tyrant exasperated at their constancy, resolved to overcome the youngest, and for that purpose, omitted neither caresses nor threats; he promised to make him his friend, to enrich and load him with honors, and confirmed his promises with an oath; but seeing him still unshaken, he desired his mother to prevail on him to save his life by complying.

What did she do?
She, endued with fortitude from God, bent towards her last surviving child, and, in the most tender and pathetic manner, exhorted him to enliven his faith and confidence in God, to despise the threats or promises of a mortal man, and to imitate the glorious example of his brethren, that so she might have

the consolation of receiving them all in a glorious immortality.

What did he cry out to the executioners?
Whilst she continued to exhort him, he cried out to the executioners, "For whom do you wait, I will not obey the king, but I will obey the law of God, and offer my life for it like my brethren, who now, after undergoing a short pain, are in possession of eternal life." Antiochus, greatly incensed, added new torments to those inflicted on his brethren, which the young man endured with equal constancy, and like them, attained the crown of martyrdom. Then the admirable mother, after witnessing the martyrdom of her seven sons, was found worthy of a like crown, and was united to them in eternal life. (2 Mac. vii.)

In what other way did Antiochus manifest his hatred of the Jewish religion?
He destroyed the sacred writings, and put those to death with whom they were discovered. (1 Mac. i. 59.)

What remarkable declaration did the youngest of the Machabees make when about to die?
That the wickedness of the nation was the cause of God sending that scourge on them for their chastisement, but not for their utter destruction. (2 Mac vii. 33.)

CHAPTER LXXX.

HISTORY OF THE ASAMONEAN FAMILY.—MATHATHIAS.

Whom did God raise to assist his people?
A holy priest named Mathathias, who with his family and kindred determined to die rather than renounce their fidelity to God. Leaving Jerusalem, he retired to his native city, Modin, but the perse-

cutors arriving there soon after, he being a ruler in the city, was called on to give an example of compliance to his fellow-citizens. This he steadfastly refused, and being transported with zeal, slew an Israelite who had just come to sacrifice to an idol, threw down the altar, killed the officer who had caused the man's apostacy; and calling on all who were zealous for the law of God to follow him, fled to the mountains, where being joined by a great number, he soon found that he had sufficient force to attack the enemy, of whom he slew a great many, put more to flight, and preserved those who were zealous for the law in comparative peace to the end of his life. (1 Mac. ii.)

What instructions did he give his children when he was near death?
He exhorted them to be faithful observers of the law of God, and willingly to sacrifice their lives, if necessary in its defence, he reminded them of the covenant God made with their forefathers, and the repeated miracles he had performed on behalf of those who were faithful to him; he cautioned them not to fear the words of sinful man, who to-day is and to-morrow will have returned to the earth whence he came. Mathathias then appointed Simon adviser of his brethren, for he was endued with the spirit of counsel, and named Judas Machabeus, who was valiant from his youth, general of the army. (1 Mac. ii. 49.)

How many sons had Mathathias?
Five; Judas, who succeeded him in the government, (1 Mac. iii.,) Eleazar, who was crushed in battle by an elephant, which he slew, thinking that Antiochus Eupator was on it, and hoping by his death to terminate the evils of his country, (1 Mac. vi. 43,) John who was treacherously killed by the children of Zamri, (1 Mac. ix. 36,) Jonathan and Simon

(1 Mac. xiii. 8,) who successively governed Juda
with wisdom and piety, restored the strict observance of religion as prescribed by Moses, made their
country respected among nations, and formed leagues
of friendship with the Romans, Greeks, Egyptians
and Asiatics.

*How did Antiochus Epiphanes act when he heard
of the victories gained by Judas Machabeus over his
generals?*

He immediately set out for Judea, vowing to make
Jerusalem a grave for the Jews, and resolving to revenge on them the disgrace of a defeat he received
in Persia. But God checked his pride. Falling
from his chariot, which in his excessive anger he had
driven with the greatest violence, he was so much
hurt that he had to be carried in a litter; and God
at the same time struck him with a painful incurable
distemper, worms swarmed from his body which
emitted such a stench that it became intolerable to
himself and to the whole army.

What did he then do?

Then entering into himself, he acknowledged the
power of God and his just judgment, and begged for
his life, promising to treat the Jews with clemency,
and even to confer dignities on them, to adorn the
Temple which before he had robbed, to become a Jew
himself, and to go through the world proclaiming the
power of God. But his sorrow being extorted only
by pain came not from the heart, and was not accepted, which should teach us that repentance deferred to the last hour though accompanied with all
the verbal protestations of Antiochus, is not to be
relied on.

CHAPTER LXXXI.

MATHATHIAS IS SUCCEEDED IN THE GOVERNMENT BY HIS SON JUDAS MACHABEUS.

What was the first care of Judas Machabeus after he had driven the enemy from his country?
He repaired and refurnished the Temple, erected a new altar of holocausts, carefully collected the sacred writings which were scattered during the war, and caused the sacrifices and other observances to be resumed. He also fortified Mount Sion. (2 Mac. x.)

In what manner did Judas Machabeus usually prepare for battle?
By prayer, fasting, and mortification, which procured him the blessings and manifest protection of God, enabling him on several occasions with a few soldiers to defeat the great armies that came against him. (2 Mac. ii. 14.)

On what occasion did Judas Machabeus procure sacrifice to be offered for the dead?
After a signal victory he had gained over Antiochus Eupator's general, having come to bury some of his soldiers who were killed in battle, he discovered under their clothes the donaries of idols, and seeing that their death was in punishment of that sin, (for the Jews were strictly prohibited by God to keep any thing belonging to idolatrous worship,) he, and the survivors united in earnest supplication to God for their forgiveness, and making a collection, Judas Machabeus sent 12,000 drachms of silver to Jerusalem to have sacrifice offered for them. (2 Mac. xii.)

Note.—Antiochus Eupator was the son of Antiochus Epiphanes, and left, by him when he went into Persia, under the guardianship of Lysias the Regent, who had him proclaimed king on his father's death. Both were put to death some time after by order of Demetrius, who claimed the throne on a claim prior to Eupator's, and being joined by a number of followers, succeeded.

What remark does Holy Scripture make on that act of Judas Machabeus?
That he "thought well and religiously concerning the resurrection," and "that it is a holy and wholesome thought to pray for the dead that they may be loosed from their sins."

After Judas Machabeus had governed Juda, and prevailed over the enemies of his country for three years, what wicked person caused fresh miseries in the kingdom?
Alcimus, a priest, who, being ambitious of the High Priesthood, went to King Demetrius at the head of a number of persons devoted to his interest, accused Judas and his brethren, and so incensed Demetrius against them, that he sent him with a great army commanded by Bacchides, one of his generals, to execute vengeance on the Jews, and establish him High Priest.

How did Alcimus then act?
Alcimus, supported by an army, did what he could to maintain his ill-gotten dignity; but finding that Judas prevailed, notwithstanding all his exertions, he went back to the king and procured a greater army with Nicanor, a powerful man, and a great enemy of the Jews to command it. (2 Mac. xiv.)

How did Nicanor act on entering Judea?
At first, awed by the valor and boldness of the Jews, he thought it prudent to make terms of peace, which were accepted; and for some time Judas and he were on friendly terms, at which Alcimus was displeased, and accused him to Demetrius as attached to foreign interests, which so incensed Demetrius that he commanded Nicanor to break the league immediately, and send Judas prisoner to Antioch.

What is then related of Judas?
At their next interview, Judas perceiving that evil was intended, withdrew, and concealed himself; but

Nicanor resolved to execute his commission, left nothing undone to discover him, and suspecting that the priests had some part in concealing him, imperiously commanded them to deliver him up. On their declaring that they knew not where he was, Nicanor stretched out his hand to the Temple, and swore that if they would not deliver up Judas to him, he would break the altar, and dedicate the Temple to Bacchus, on returning from the battle which he then proclaimed against the Jews. (2 Mac. xiv.).

What was the result of that battle?
Judas was victorious, Nicanor's immense army being put to flight, and himself slain in the first onset. His head was carried to Jerusalem by command of Judas; and the hand which he had impiously stretched out against the Temple was hanged up opposite to it. The kingdom of Juda, after this, enjoyed peace, until Alcimus, by fresh intrigues, obtained from Demetrius another army under the command of Bacchides. (1 Mac. ix. and 2 Mac. xv.)

What was the result of the battle fought between Judas and Bacchides?
Bacchides was victorious. The men of Juda, forgetful of the victories God had given them over armies as numerous, yielded to discouragement, and sought their individual safety by flight, until only 800 remained, who vainly endeavored to dissuade Judas from engaging, but though greatly dispirited, he was resolved to hazard the battle, saying, "If our time be come let us die manfully for our brethren." And encouraging his little troop, the battle commenced, which was fought hard from morning until evening. Many fell on both sides, and among the rest, to the inexpressible grief of the whole nation, Judas was slain. (1 Mac. ix.)

How did Alcimus end his wicked life?
He died in great torment of palsy with which God

struck him whilst he was engaged in destroying the works of the prophets, after having thrown down part of the walls of the Temple. (1 Mac. ix.)

CHAPTER LXXXII.

JUDAS MACHABEUS SUCCEEDED BY HIS BROTHERS JONATHAN AND SIMON.

Whom did the Jews elect to govern them in place of Judas Machabeus?
His brother Jonathan, who was equally devoted to the interests of religion. He overcame Bacchides twice, and then made a treaty with him; after which, the kingdom of Juda enjoyed peace for nearly fourteen years. Kings sought the friendship of Jonathan. Demetrius and Alexander, (son of Antiochus,) rivals for the kingdom, vied with each other in honoring him; and the latter conferred on him the High Priesthood. (1 Mac. x. 21.)

What first disturbed this peace?
Demetrius, being killed in a battle with Alexander, was succeeded by his son Demetrius, who appointed Apollonius, the known enemy of the Jews, his general. At the head of a large army, he entered Judea, determined to make it tributary, but was defeated by Jonathan, and the remnant of his army obliged to fly. After Alexander's death, Demetrius became Jonathan's ally, though not a sincere one.

On occasion of a revolt in Antioch, what did he do?
On occasion of a revolt in Antioch, he sent to him to request he would assist in quelling it, promising in return to remove those of his subjects who held the castle of Jerusalem and other strong places whence they annoyed the peaceable inhabitants; but when Jonathan had succeeded in restoring Deme-

trius to the peaceable possession of his throne, instead of a reward he received great annoyance from him. (1 Mac. x. and xi.)

With whom did Jonathan renew treaties of peace and friendship?
With the Romans and Lacedemonians.

By what means was the peace of the kingdom again disturbed?
By the intrigues of an ambitious man named Tryphon, who was originally of king Alexander's party, after whose death he joined Demetrius; but perceiving that he was unpopular, left him, and procured the young Antiochus, son of Alexander, to be proclaimed king; he next desired the sovereignty for himself, but, through fear of Jonathan, durst not attempt anything against the young Antiochus, who, as well as his father, was an ally of the Jews. Tryphon therefore determined to remove Jonathan, and entered Judea with a considerable army, but finding Jonathan prepared to meet him, he had recourse to treachery, and under pretence of friendship got him into his power, and made him prisoner. (1 Mac. xii.)

How did Jonathan's brother Simon act when he heard of Tryphon's treachery?
He went to Jerusalem, assembled the people, and offered himself as their leader in place of his brother, which offer they joyfully accepted, and promised him obedience.

What was Simon's first care on being appointed High Priest and judge?
He fortified Jerusalem, finished its walls, and placed a garrison in Joppa.

How did Tryphon act when he understood that Simon prepared for war with him?
He sent messengers to him to say that he detained Jonathan because he owed money to the king; and

that he would liberate him on condition that Simon would pay one hundred talents of silver, and send Jonathan's two sons to him as hostages, to secure that their father would not revolt when set at liberty.

Did Simon believe him?
No; but nevertheless he was constrained to yield to Tryphon's demand, lest the people should murmur, supposing Jonathan lost, because the money and children were not delivered for him. (1 Mac. xiii.)

How did Tryphon act when he got the children and money into his possession?
He would not liberate the father, and entered into the country intending to lay it waste, but being every where prevented by Simon, he slew Jonathan with his two sons; and returning home soon after, made himself king in place of the young Antiochus, whom he treacherously murdered.

How long did Simon govern the kingdom of Juda?
About nine years, during which he completed what his father and brothers had begun for the good of the kingdom, repaired and rebuilt what had been destroyed by the wars in Jerusalem, restored the city and Temple nearly to their ancient splendor, renewed the treaties of friendship and alliance that were made with the Romans and Greeks, successfully opposed all invaders of his country, administered justice impartially, and established the kingdom in peace.

How did Simon end his life?
He was murdered with two of his sons by the contrivance of Ptolemy, his son-in-law, who committed this act through the ambitious desire of governing (1 Mac. xvi.)

CHAPTER LXXXIII.

SIMON SUCCEEDED BY HIS SON JOHN HYRCANUS—CONCLUSION OF THE HISTORY.

Which of Simon's sons succeeded him?
John, surnamed Hyrcanus, whom his father had appointed general of the army during his lifetime; he dwelt at Gazara, and got notice of the murder of his father and brothers in time to guard against the treachery of Ptolemy, who sought his life also. He was as valiant and pious as the other members of his family, and distinguished himself while his father still lived by a victory over a great army sent by Antiochus (son of Demetrius) to invade Judea.

How long did John Hyrcanus govern the kingdom?
About thirty-one years. Soon after coming to the government he capitulated with Antiochus to raise the siege of Jerusalem; after which he subdued the neighboring nations which had harassed the Jews. He destroyed the schismatical temple, already alluded to, which, two hundred years before, was built by Sanballat on Mount Gerizim. (Josephus, Book I, chap. 2.)

Who succeeded John Hyrcanus?
His son Aristobulus, who, wishing to change the form of government, placed a crown on his head, being the first who did so from the time of the Babylonian captivity. He reigned only one year, and was odious for cruelty to his family, having murdered his mother and one of his brothers. He was succeeded by his brother Alexander Jannæus, who died after an unquiet reign of twenty-seven years, and left two sons, Hyrcanus and Aristobulus. (Josephus, Book I., c. 3 and 4.)

To whom did Alexander leave the sovereign power?
To Alexandra his queen. She reigned nine years,

and caused her elder son Hyrcanus to be made High Priest. After her death, the younger son Aristobulus, who was of a bold active disposition, disputed the sovereignty with Hyrcanus, who was a quiet, unambitious person, and after a contest, in which Aristobulus was victorious, they made an agreement, confirmed by oath, that Aristobulus should reign, and Hyrcanus retire to his estate.

What disturbed the harmony which then existed between the brothers?
An Idumean named Antipater possessed of considerable wealth and influence in his own country, and a friend to Hyrcanus, never ceased to represent to him that his life was in danger from Aristobulus, and that he was unjustly deprived of his birthright until he induced him to apply for foreign aid, and so involved the nation in war.

What is said of the Romans?
The Romans at length restored Hyrcanus to his dignity, made Aristobulus prisoner, and appointed Herod, Antipater's son, Tetrarch of Galilee, and afterwards king. By the transgression of the law which prohibited the Jews having a king of any but Jewish race, two remarkable prophecies were fulfilled, one which foretold that Esau (Edom) would shake off his brother's yoke; and the other, that the sceptre departing from Juda was to be the immediate prelude to the coming of the Messiah.

NEW TESTAMENT.

CHAPTER I.

THE INCARNATION OF OUR DIVINE LORD—VISIT OF THE BLESSED VIRGIN TO ST. ELIZABETH.—A. M. 4000.

How long after the fall of our first parents did Jesus Christ become man?
About four thousand years.
Of what lineage was he?
Of the tribe of Juda, and family of David; his mother was Mary, the ever blessed Virgin, foretold by Isaias; his reputed father was Joseph, the holy spouse of the Virgin Mary, by trade a carpenter; their residence, previous to our Lord's birth, was Nazareth.
What circumstances attended the incarnation of our Divine Lord?
"The angel Gabriel was sent by God into a city of Galilee, called Nazareth, to a virgin espoused to a man whose name was Joseph, of the house of David, and the virgin's name was Mary. And the angel being come in, said unto her, Hail, full of grace, the Lord is with thee, blessed art thou among women, Who having heard, was troubled at his saying, and thought with herself what manner of salutation this should be."
What did the angel say to her?
"And the angel said to her, Fear not, Mary, for thou hast found grace with God; behold thou shalt conceive in thy womb and shalt bring forth a son, and thou shalt call his name *Jesus*. He shall be great and shall be called the Son of the Most High, and

the Lord God shall give him the throne of David his father, and he shall reign in the house of Jacob for ever, and of his kingdom there shall be no end."

What did Mary reply?
"And Mary said to the angel, How shall this be done, because I know not man? And the angel answering said to her, the Holy Ghost shall come upon thee, and the power of the Most High shall overshadow thee, and therefore also the Holy which shall be born of thee shall be called the Son of God." (Luke i.)

How did the Blessed Virgin express her consent?
"Behold the handmaid of the Lord, be it done unto me according to thy word."

Of what did the angel inform the Blessed Virgin on that occasion?
That her cousin, St. Elizabeth, already far advanced in years, would also give birth to a son, and that this was the sixth month with her; on hearing which the Blessed Virgin Mary went to visit her, and remained with her about three months.

How did St. Elizabeth receive the visit of her holy relative?
With great joy, acknowledging her great unworthiness to entertain so great a guest, on hearing whose salutation she was endowed with the spirit of prophecy, and her unborn son endued with reason.

What did St. Elizabeth say to the Blessed Virgin on that occasion?
"Blessed art thou among women, and blessed is the fruit of thy womb; and whence is this to me that the mother of my Lord should come to me?"

How did the Blessed Virgin reply?
"My soul doth magnify the Lord and my spirit hath rejoiced in God my Saviour, because he hath regarded the humility of his handmaid, for behold from henceforth all generations shall call me blessed.

Because he that is mighty hath done great things to me, and holy is his name, and his mercy is from generation to generation to them that fear him. He hath showed might in his arm, he hath dispersed the proud in the imagination of their hearts. He hath deposed the mighty from their seat and hath exalted the humble; he hath filled the hungry with good things, and the rich he hath sent away empty. He hath received Israel his child, being mindful of his mercy; as he spoke to our fathers, to Abraham and his seed for ever."

CHAPTER II.

THE BIRTH OF ST. JOHN THE BAPTIST.

Who was St. Elizabeth?
She was wife to a holy priest, named Zachary, and was also herself descended from Aaron.

What remarkable circumstances preceded and attended the birth of their son?
Whilst Zachary, in the exercise of his ministry, offered incense in the Temple, the angel Gabriel appeared, standing at the right side of the altar of incense, and announced to him that his wife should give birth to a son, whom he should call John; that he would be filled with the Holy Ghost from his birth, would convert many of the children of Israel to the Lord, and go before him in the spirit and power of Elias.

What did the angel say to Zachary on his expressing incredulity?
On Zachary's expressing incredulity, the angel told him that he should lose the use of speech and remain dumb until the fulfilment of the prophecy; he immediately lost the power of utterance, and continued dumb until his son, at circumcision, received the name foretold by the angel.

Repeat the canticle of Zachary on recovering the use of his speech?
"Blessed be the Lord God of Israel, because he hath visited and wrought the redemption of his people, and hath raised up a horn of salvation to us in the house of David his servant, as he spoke by the mouth of his holy prophets, who are from the beginning. Salvation from our enemies and from the hand of all that hate us. To show mercy to our fathers and to remember his holy covenant, the oath which he swore to Abraham our father that he would grant to us; that being delivered from the hand of our enemies, we may serve him without fear, in holiness and justice before him all our days. And thou, child, shall be called the prophet of the highest, for thou shalt go before the face of the Lord, to prepare his ways; to give knowledge of salvation to his people unto the remission of their sins, through the bowels of the mercy of our God, in which the Orient from on high hath visited us; to enlighten them that sit in darkness and in the shadow of death, to direct our feet in the way of peace."

Where did St. John pass his youth?
In the desert, until the time for commencing his mission had arrived, when he got the surname of Baptist from his office. He was the precursor of our Lord, foretold by Isaias.

What kind of life did he lead?
One of retirement, prayer, and mortification. His food was locusts and wild honey; his garment was of camel's hair, fastened by a leathern girdle.

CHAPTER III.

THE BIRTH OF OUR DIVINE LORD.

Did the Blessed Virgin inform St. Joseph of the wonderful dignity to which God had raised her?

No, she never spoke of what might tend to her own commendation.

How was the mystery of the incarnation made known to him?
By an angel sent by God for that purpose, who removed his anxiety respecting the appearance of his holy spouse, and told him he should give the name of Jesus to the Holy One who would be born of her.

Where was our Blessed Lord born?
In Bethlehem, as foretold by Micheas.

What circumstance caused the Blessed Virgin St. Joseph to go to Bethlehem?
The Roman emperor Augustus published an edict commanding all to repair to the cities of their respective families in order to be enrolled, on which Mary and Joseph being descendants of David repaired to his city Bethlehem. Unable to procure a lodging on their arrival, the inn being full, they retired to a stable, where Mary brought forth the Redeemer of the world, and laid him in a manger.

At what season of the year was our Blessed Lord born?
In the depth of winter, the 25th of December, and at night.

Who were the first adorers of the infant Saviour?
Poor shepherds, who were at the time keeping the night watches over their flocks.

How was his birth made known to them?
"An angel of the Lord stood by them, and the brightness of God shone round about them, and they feared with a great fear. And the angel said to them, Fear not, for behold I bring you good tidings of great joy, that shall be to all the people; for this day is born to you a *Saviour*, who is *Christ* the *Lord*, in the city of David; and this shall be a sign to you, you shall find the infant wrapped in swaddling clothes, and laid in a manger. And suddenly there

was with the angel a multitude of the heavenly army, praising God and saying, glory to God in the highest, and on earth peace to men of good will."

What did the shepherds as soon as the angels disappeared?
They went with haste to Bethlehem, where they found all things as the angel had told them, for which they glorified and praised God.

Repeat Isaias's prophecy of our Lord's nativity?
"Behold a virgin shall conceive and bear a son, and his name shall be called *Emmanuel.* * * * A child is born to us, and a son is given to us, and the government is upon his shoulder; and his name shall be called *Wonderful, Counsellor, God* the *Mighty, the Father of the world to come,* the *Prince of Peace.*" (Is. vii. 14, ix. 6.)

When was the saving name of Jesus given our Divine Lord?
Eight days after his birth, when he was circumcised. This ceremony is commemorated by the Church on the first of January.

What do the Apostles Saints Peter and Paul say of the holy name of Jesus?
St. Peter says, "There is no other name under heaven given to man, whereby we must be saved." (Acts iv. 12.) And St. Paul, "He humbled himself, becoming obedient unto death, even to the death of the cross; for which reason God also hath exalted him, and hath given him a name which is above all names; that in the name of *Jesus* every knee should bow, of those that are in heaven, on earth, and under the earth, and that every tongue should confess that the Lord *Jesus Christ* is in the glory of God the Father." (Phil. ii. 8.)

CHAPTER IV.

OUR SAVIOUR'S BIRTH MADE KNOWN TO THE GENTILES BY A STAR.

How was our Saviour's birth made known to the gentiles?
By a star, whose guidance certain wise men, or as they are sometimes designated kings, followed from the East, until they reached Jerusalem, where it disappeared. Entering the royal city, they thought their journey at an end, and directing their steps to the palace, inquired, "Where is he that is born King of the Jews, for we have seen his star in the East and are come to adore him."

How did king Herod act when he heard this inquiry, which troubled not only him but all Jerusalem?
He assembled the chief priests and scribes, and inquired of them where *Christ* should be born, who answered, "In Bethlehem of Judea, for so it is written by the prophet." Then Herod sending the wise men to Bethlehem, desired them to seek diligently for the child, and when they had found him, to bring him word that he also might go and adore him.

How did the wise men discover the house in which our Blessed Lord was?
As soon as they resumed their journey the star reappeared to their great joy, and went before them until it conducted them to where the child was, and entering into the house they found the child with Mary his mother, and falling down they adored him, and opening their treasures, offered him gifts, gold, frankincense, and myrrh.

What was Herod's motive in desiring the wise men to bring him intelligence concerning the child?
To destroy him, lest he should deprive him of his kingdom. But his malicious designs were frustrated,

for the wise men were admonished in sleep not to return to him, and they went back by another road to their own country.

What mystical signification is attached to the offerings presented by the wise men?
The offering of myrrh is considered by interpreters as an acknowledgment of the humanity of Christ, on account of myrrh being used in embalming the bodies of the dead and therefore implying mortality; it is also a figure of mortification, as incense is of prayer, and gold of charity.

By what name is the feast known which commemorates the adoration of the wise men, and when is it celebrated?
It is known by the name of the Epiphany, and is celebrated on the sixth of January.

CHAPTER V.

THE PURIFICATION OF THE BLESSED VIRGIN, AND THE PRESENTATION OF OUR DIVINE LORD.

With what rite of the Mosaic law did the Blessed Virgin Mary comply on the fortieth day after the birth of our Lord?
Her own purification, and her divine son's presentation to his eternal father in the temple.

What sacrifice did she offer on that occasion?
That prescribed for the poor, a pair of turtle doves, or two young pigeons.

What holy persons acknowledged our Lord on his presentation?
A holy old man, named Simeon, and Anna a prophetess. The former had received a promise from God, that he should not die until he had seen Christ, and the latter served day and night in the temple, in prayer and fasting.

Repeat the canticle of Simeon on seeing the infant Jesus, and taking him into his arms?
"Now thou dost dismiss thy servant, O Lord, according to thy word in peace; because my eyes have seen thy salvation, which thou hast prepared before the face of all people; a light to the revelation of the gentiles, and the glory of thy people Israel."

What words did Simeon address to the holy mother of Jesus?
"Behold this child is set for the fall, and for the resurrection of many in Israel, and for a sign which shall be contradicted. And thy own soul a sword shall pierce, that out of many hearts thoughts may be revealed."

How do you understand the first part of this prophecy?
Simeon here prophesies what would come to pass, that many, through their own wilful blindness and obstinacy, would not believe in Christ, nor receive his doctrine, that therefore he would become by their abuse of his grace a cause of ruin to them; but to others a resurrection by their believing in him and obeying his commandments.

On what day does the Church commemorate the purification of the Blessed Virgin Mary, and the presentation of our Lord?
On the second of February, on which day tapers are blessed and distributed to the faithful, who hold them lighted in their hands during the gospel and until the communion, in honor of Christ who is the true light, and who is called by holy Simeon, "a light," &c.

CHAPTER VI.

THE MASSACRE OF THE HOLY INNOCENTS, THE FLIGHT OF OUR DIVINE LORD INTO EGYPT, AND HIS RETURN.

How did Herod act when he perceived that the wise men had deluded him?
He most cruelly caused all the male children in Bethlehem and its vicinity, who were two years old and under, to be put to death.

How did our Blessed Lord escape?
An angel appeared in sleep to St. Joseph, after the departure of the wise men, and said, "Arise, take the child and his mother and fly into Egypt, and be there until I shall tell thee; for it will come to pass that Herod will seek the child to destroy him." St. Joseph immediately arose and took the child and his mother that night and retired to Egypt, where he remained until Herod's death.

How many years did the Holy Family reside in Egypt?
About eight years, as is generally supposed.

How did they know when to return?
An angel appeared in sleep to St. Joseph in Egypt, informed him of Herod's death, and desired him to take the child and his mother back to the land of Israel. He did so immediately, but hearing that Archelaus, Herod's son, reigned in Judea, he was afraid to go thither, and being admonished in sleep went to Galilee.

In what city did he fix his residence?
In Nazareth, that the prediction of the prophets might be fulfilled in our Lord, viz., that he should be called a Nazarite.

How did our Blessed Lord spend his time at Nazareth?
It is supposed that he worked at St. Joseph's trade.

The Evangelists make no special mention of what he did until his baptism, except that, when he was twelve years of age, his parents took him to Jerusalem according to their custom to celebrate the pasch, and on their return he remained behind, which they did not discover until they had gone a day's journey: and after seeking him for three days, they found him in the Temple in the midst of the doctors, hearing them and asking them questions, his wisdom being the astonishment of all.

What did his mother say to him on that occasion?
"Son, why hast thou done so to us, behold thy father and I have sought thee sorrowing." To which he replied, "How is it that you sought me, did you not know that I must be about my Father's business." Then returning with them to Nazareth he was subject to them, and as the Evangelist adds, he advanced in wisdom, and age, and grace, with God and men.

What would our Blessed Lord have us learn from his example in these particulars?
To be humble and obedient, and continually to advance in the way of virtue.

Did the wisdom of our Divine Lord admit of increase?
No; but he made it more manifest as he advanced in age. The Evangelist, in saying that he advanced, only accommodated himself to our mode of speech.

CHAPTER VII.

THE BAPTISM OF OUR DIVINE LORD, THE PREACHING AND MARTYRDOM OF ST. JOHN THE BAPTIST.

Where did St. John Baptist open his mission?
In the desert of Judea, and he prepared himself for

the important object by prayer, fasting, and retirement.

What was the subject of his preaching?
"Do penance, for the kingdom of heaven is at hand."

Did many resort to his instructions?
Yes, great multitudes, whom he baptised in the Jordan.

What opinion had the people of St. John?
That he was a great prophet; some even doubted whether he were not the Messiah.

What did St. John say when asked by the Pharisees to give an account of himself?
"I am the voice of one crying in the wilderness, make straight the way of the Lord."

What answer did he give when they further asked, "Why then dost thou baptise, if thou be not Christ, nor Elias, nor the prophet."
"I baptise with water; but there hath stood one in the midst of you, whom you know not. The same is he that shall come after me, who is preferred before me; the latchet of whose shoe I am not worthy to loose."

What did St. John Baptist when he saw our Divine Redeemer coming to be baptised by him?
He stayed him, saying: "I ought to be baptised by thee, and comest thou to me." But on our Lord replying, "Suffer it to be so now; for so it becometh us to fulfil all justice," St. John baptised him.

What testimony did our Lord receive from heaven on his being baptised?
The heavens were opened, and the Holy Ghost descended on him in the form of a dove; while a voice from Heaven proclaimed, "This is my beloved Son in whom I am well pleased."

What did St. John Baptist say when he saw our

Lord coming towards him on the day after his baptism?

"Behold the Lamb of God; behold him who taketh away the sins of the world. This is he of whom I said, after me there cometh a man who is preferred before me, because he was before me and I knew him not; but that he may be made manifest in Israel, therefore am I come baptising with water...... I saw the Spirit coming down as a dove from heaven, and he remained upon him; and I knew him not, but he who sent me to baptise with water said to me, he upon whom thou shalt see the Spirit descending and remaining upon him, he it is that baptiseth with the Holy Ghost; and I saw and I gave testimony that this is the Son of God. (John i. 29—34.)

What did St. John reply to some of his disciples, when on a dispute arising between them and the Jews concerning purification, they came to him saying, "Rabbi, he that was with thee beyond the Jordan, to whom thou gavest testimony, behold he baptiseth, and all men come to him," (though Jesus himself did not baptise but his disciples?)

"A man cannot receive anything unless it be given him, from heaven. You yourselves do bear me witness that I said I am not Christ, but that I am sent before him. He that hath the bride, is the bridegroom; but the friend of the bridegroom, who standeth and heareth him, rejoiceth with joy because of the bridegroom's voice. This my joy therefore is fulfilled. He must increase, but I must decrease. * * * * The Father loveth the Son, and he hath given all things into his hand. He that believeth in the Son hath life everlasting; but he that believeth not the Son shall not see life, but the wrath of God abideth in him."

What happened St. John the Baptist soon after this?

He was cast into prison by Herod the Tetrarch, because he reproved him for marrying Herodias, his brother's wife, and he was detained there until Herod's birthday, when by the contrivance of the wicked Herodias, he was beheaded.

What message did St. John whilst in prison send to our Lord, when he was told of the miracles he performed and the fame he had acquired?
He sent two of his disciples to ask, "Art thou he that art to come, or look we for another."

What answer did our Divine Lord give?
"Go and relate to John what you have heard and seen; the blind see, the lame walk, the lepers are cleansed, the deaf hear, the dead rise again, the pooi have the gospel preached to them. And blessed is he that shall not be scandalized in me." (Matt. xi 2, Luke vii. 19.)

What did our Lord say of St. John Baptist when his disciples had returned?
That amongst those born of women there was not a greater prophet than John the Baptist; that he was a prophet and more than a prophet, and of him was written, "Behold I send my angel before thy face who shall prepare thy way before thee."

Relate the particulars of the martyrdom of St. John the Baptist?
"Herod made a supper for his birthday for the princes and tribunes and chief men of Galilee; and when the daughter of Herodias had come in, and had danced, and had pleased Herod and those that were at table with him, the king said to the damsel, Ask of me what thou wilt and I will give it thee. And he swore to her, whatsoever thou shalt ask I will give thee, though it be the half of my kingdom."

What did she say when she went out?
"When she was gone out she said to her mother What shall I ask? But she said, The head of John

the Baptist. And when she was come in immediately with haste to the king, she asked saying, I will that forthwith thou give me in a dish the head of John the Baptist."

What is said of the king?
"And the king was struck sad, yet because of his oath, and because of them that were with him at table, he would not displease her; but sending an executioner, he commanded that his head should be brought in a dish. And he beheaded him in prison, and brought his head in a dish, and gave it to the damsel, and the damsel gave it to her mother." (Mark vi. 21.)

CHAPTER VIII.

OUR DIVINE LORD'S FAST AND TEMPTATION IN THE DESERT.—THE OPENING OF HIS MISSION.

What was our Lord's age at baptism?
Thirty years.
What did he immediately after baptism?
He retired to the desert, where he remained forty days and forty nights, during which he ate nothing.
Repeat St. Matthew's account of the temptation endured by our Divine Lord at the close of his retreat?
The tempter coming said to him: "If thou be the Son of God, command that these stones be made bread. Who answered and said: It is written, *Not in bread alone doth man live, but in every word that proceedeth from the mouth of God.*"
Then what did the devil do?
"Then the devil took him up into the holy city and set him upon the pinnacle of the Temple, and said to him, If thou be the Son of God, cast thyself down, for it is written, *That he hath given his angels charge over thee, and in their hands shall they bear thee up, lest perhaps thou dash thy foot against a stone.* Jesus

said to him it is written again, *Thou shalt not tempt the Lord thy God.*"

What did the devil again do?
"Again the devil took him up into a very high mountain, and showed him all the kingdoms of the world, and the glory of them, and said to him, All these will I give thee, if falling down thou wilt adore me. Then Jesus saith to him, Begone Satan; for it is written, *The Lord thy God shalt thou adore and him only shalt thou serve.* Then the devil left him, and behold angels came and ministered to him."

Whither did our Lord go when the temptation had ended?
To Galilee, where he taught in the Synagogues, and his fame spread throughout the country.

What was the subject of the first instruction he gave in the Synagogue at Nazareth?
That the prophecy of Isaias was that day fulfilled, which says, "*The spirit of the Lord is upon me. Wherefore he hath anointed me to preach the gospel to the poor; he hath sent me to heal the contrite of heart, to preach deliverance to the captives and sight to the blind, to set at liberty them that are bruised, to preach the acceptable year of the Lord and the day of reward.*"

Why did our Lord leave Nazareth?
Because the people thought to throw him from the brow of the hill on which their city was built.

How did he escape from them?
The Evangelist only says, that, "passing through the midst of them, he went his way."

CHAPTER IX.
THE CALL OF THE APOSTLES, AND CHRIST'S FIRST MIRACLE.

Who were the first disciples of Christ?
St. Andrew and another, whose name is not men-

tioned; these, hearing S. John Baptist, whose disciples they were, say of our Lord, "Behold the Lamb of God!" immediately followed him.

Whom did St. Andrew bring to our Lord?
His brother Simon, telling him that they had found the Messiah, which is, being interpreted, the Christ.

What did our Lord say on seeing Simon?
"Thou art Simon, the son of Jona, thou shalt be called Cephas, which is interpreted Peter." (John i. 42.)

Who were the two next disciples of our Lord?
James and John, the sons of Zebedee; who on our Lord's gracious invitation immediately left all and followed him.

How were they employed when called by our Lord?
Mending their nets in the ship with their father; for they as well as Peter and Andrew were fishermen (Mark i. 20.)

Whom did our Lord call on the following day?
Philip, who had scarcely attained the knowledge of our Lord, when desirous of bringing others to him, he told Nathaniel, "We have found him of whom Moses in the law and the prophets did write, Jesus, the son of Joseph of Nazareth." On Nathaniel replying, "Can any good come out of Nazareth?" Philip said, "Come and see."

Who was Nathaniel?
A good and holy man, "an Israelite without guile."

What testimony did Nathaniel bear to our Lord?
That he was the Son of God, the King of Israel.

How did our Lord employ himself whilst he remained in Galilee?
Preaching in the synagogues, and confirming the doctrine he preached by miracles; he also, during his stay there, selected his apostles.

Note.—Some commentators think that Nathaniel is another name for Bartholomew the Apostle.

Name the apostles?
Peter, and Andrew, his brother; James and John; Philip and Bartholomew; Matthew and Thomas; James, the son of Alpheus; and Simon, who is called Zelotes; and Jude, the brother of James; and Judas Iscariot, who was the traitor." (Luke vi. 14.)

Where did our Lord perform his first miracle?
In Cana, of Galilee, at the request of his holy Mother.

Relate the history of it?
Whilst in Cana, of Galilee, our Lord was invited, with his disciples, to a marriage feast; Mary, his mother, was also there. During the entertainment the wine failed; the failure was observed by the Blessed Virgin, who mentioned it to Jesus, being fully aware that to make known a want to him was enough to dispose him to supply it.

What is said of his reply to her request, and what did she say?
He replied to the request conveyed in her representation that his hour was not yet come. Knowing that those who trust in him are never confounded, and confidently hoping that though his hour was not come he would anticipate it, rather than disappoint her, she said to the waiters, "Whatsoever he shall say to you, do."

What did our Lord do?
Her hope was not frustrated; our Divine Lord could not overlook the confiding love of his holy Mother, the most exalted of his creatures; turning to the waiters, he desired them to fill with water six large stone pitchers which stood near. They filled to the brim. "Draw out now and carry to the chief steward," said our Lord.

What did the chief steward say?
They did so, and the chief steward, having tasted and not knowing whence the wine came, remon-

strated with the bridegroom for having kept the best wine to the last, instead of producing it at the beginning of the entertainment. But the waiters who had drawn the water knew whence the wine came, and the faith of our Lord's disciples was strengthened by the evidence of the miracle.

Whither did our Lord go after this?
To Caphernaum, a city on the sea coast, in the borders of Zabulon and Nephtali, by which was fulfilled what was said by the prophet Isaias: "Land of Zabulon and Nephtali, the way of the sea beyond the Jordan, Galilee of the gentiles; the people that sat in darkness hath seen great light, and to them that sat in the region of death light is sprung up."

CHAPTER X.

THE CENTURION'S SERVANT—THE WIDOW'S SON OF NAIM.

Relate the miracle performed in Caphernaum by our Lord on the centurion's servant?
"The servant of a certain centurion, who was dear to him, being sick, was ready to die; and when he had heard of Jesus, he sent unto him the ancients of the Jews, desiring him to come and heal his servant. And when they came to Jesus they besought him earnestly, saying to him: he is worthy that thou shouldst do this for him, for he loveth our nation and he built us a synagogue.

As Jesus approached the house, what did the centurion say?
And Jesus went with them; and when he was now not far from the house, the centurion sent his friends to him, saying, Lord, trouble not thyself, for I am not worthy that thou shouldst enter under my roof, for which cause neither did I think myself worthy to come to thee; but say the word and my servant shall be healed: for I also am a man subject to

authority, having under me soldiers, and I say to one: go and he goeth; and to another: come and he cometh; and to my servant, do this, and he doeth it.

On hearing this, what did Jesus say?
Which Jesus hearing, marvelled, and turning about to the multitude that followed him, he said: Amen I say to you I have not found so great faith, not even in Israel. And they who were sent being returned to the house, found the servant whole who had been sick." (Luke vii. 2.)

Relate the miracle performed by our Lord soon after going into Naim.
"When he came nigh to the gate of the city, behold a dead man was carried out, the only son of his mother and she was a widow, and a great multitude of the city was with her; whom, when the Lord had seen her, being moved with mercy towards her, he he said to her: Weep not; and he came near and touched the bier, and they that carried it stood still. And he said, Young man, I say to thee, arise; and he that was dead sat up and began to speak, and he gave him to his mother. And there came a fear upon them all, and they glorified God, saying, A great prophet has arisen amongst us, and God hath visited his people." (Luke vii. 11.)

CHAPTER XI.

SERMON ON THE MOUNT.

Repeat a portion of the discourse known as our Lord's Sermon on the Mount, which he preached from an eminence in the neighborhood of Capharnaum?
"Blessed are the poor in spirit, for theirs is the kingdom of heaven. Blessed are the meek, for they shall possess the land. Blessed are they that mourn,

for they shall be comforted. Blessed are they that hunger and thirst after justice, for they shall have their fill. Blessed are the merciful, for they shall obtain mercy. Blessed are the clean of heart, for they shall see God. Blessed are the peace-makers, for they shall be called the children of God. Blessed are they that suffer persecution for justice' sake, for theirs is the kingdom of heaven."

What did our Lord say in that sermon of the perfection required of Christians?
"Unless your justice abound more than that of the Scribes and Pharisees, you shall not enter into the kingdom of heaven."

What was the nature of the justice, or righteousness, which the Scribes and Pharisees made profession of?
They were most exact observers of the letter of the law, and of the entire ceremonial; they were so particular in paying tithes, that they even tithed the herbs of their gardens; they fasted rigorously, made long prayers, and bestowed abundant alms. But they performed these things ostentatiously, in order to gain the reputation of holiness, and they preferred themselves before others.

What lessons of fraternal charity did our Divine Lord give in that sermon?
That if any of them should remember, when offering his gift at the altar, that his brother had any thing against him, he should leave there his gift, and go first to be reconciled before offering it. That they should not swear, nor seek revenge; but love their enemies, do good to them that hate, bless them that curse, and pray for them that persecute and calumniate them.

CHAPTER XII.

ON PRAYER.

In what manner did our Lord teach his disciples to pray?
Without ostentation, and in these words—"Our Father, who art in heaven, hallowed by thy name; thy kingdom come; thy will be done on earth as it is in heaven. Give us this day our daily bread; and forgive us our trespasses as we forgive them who trespass against us; and lead us not into temptation but deliver us from evil." Amen.

In what manner should we pray?
With great attention and devotion, and in a respectful posture, on bended knees.

When should we pray?
Every morning and every night, in all dangers, temptations, and afflictions; besides which, in order to comply with our Divine Lord's precept, that "we ought always pray," we should offer to God all our thoughts, words, and actions, and keep ourselves in the state of grace.

What did our Lord say of prayer as a remedy for temptation?
During his agony in the garden he said to the apostles whom he had chosen as witnesses of it, "Pray, lest ye enter into temptation." On another occasion he said to St. Peter, "Behold, Satan hath desired to have thee, that he may sift thee as wheat; but I have prayed for thee, that thy faith fail not." (Luke xxii. 31.)

What conditions are necessary to render our prayers acceptable?
We must offer them with a contrite and humble heart, with fervor and perseverance, with confidence in God's goodness, with resignation to his will, and in the name of Jesus Christ.

What dispositions did our Lord exhort his disciples specially to in prayer?
Faith, and the forgiveness of injuries; telling them that all things they asked with a firm undoubting faith should be granted, were it the removal of a mountain; and that, if they forgave the offences of others, their heavenly Father would forgive theirs; but if they would not forgive, neither would their Father forgive them.

What parable did our Lord speak to correct those who prided themselves on their uprightness, and to show that humility is a necessary disposition for prayer?
"Two men went up into the Temple to pray; the one a pharisee, and the other a publican. The pharisee, standing, prayed thus with himself: O God, I give thee thanks that I am not as the rest of men, extortioners, unjust, adulterers, as also is this publican; I fast twice a week, I give tithes of all that I possess. And the publican, standing afar off, would not so much as lift up his eyes towards heaven, but struck his breast saying, O God, be merciful to me a sinner. I say to you this man went down into his house justified rather than the other; because every one that exalteth himself shall be humbled, and he that humbleth himself shall be exalted." (Luke xviii.)

What did our Lord say to exemplify that prayer ought to be filial and confiding?
"Behold the birds of the air, for they neither sow, nor do they reap, nor gather into barns, and your Heavenly Father feedeth them: are not you of much more value than they?........Be not solicitous, therefore, saying, what shall we eat, or what shall we drink, or wherewith shall we be clothed, for after all these things do the heathens seek; for your father knoweth that you have need of all these

things. Seek ye, therefore, first the kingdom of God and his justice, and all these things shall be added unto you....... What man is there among you, of whom, if his son shall ask bread, will he reach him a stone; or if he shall ask him a fish, will he reach him a serpent? If you then, being evil, know how to give good gifts to your children, how much more will your father who is in heaven give good things to them that ask him." (Matt. vi. and vii.)

CHAPTER XIII.

ON PERSEVERANCE IN PRAYER.

What did our Lord say to show his disciples the benefit of perseverance in prayer?
"Which of you shall have a friend, and shall go to him at midnight, and shall say to him, friend, lend me three loaves, because a friend of mine is come off his journey to me, and I have not what to set before him. And he from within should answer and say, trouble me not; the door is now shut and my children are with me in bed, I cannot rise and give thee. Yet if he shall continue knocking, I say to you, although he will not rise and give him because he is his friend, yet because of his importunity he will rise and give him as many as he needeth. And I say to you, ask, and it shall be given you; seek and you shall find; knock and it shall be opened to you." (Luke xi. 5.)

What miracle did our Lord perform in reward of humility and perseverance?
Our Lord being in the neighborhood of Tyre and Sidon, was met by a woman of Canaan, who cried out to him, "Have mercy on me, O Lord, thou Son of David, my daughter is grievously troubled by a devil. Who answered her not a word; and his dis-

ciples came and besought him, saying: Send her away, for she crieth after us.

What did he answer?
And he answering, said: I was not sent but to the sheep that are lost of the house of Israel. But she came and adored him, saying, Lord, help me. Who answering, said, it is not good to take the bread of the children and cast it to the dogs. But she said, yea, Lord, for the whelps also eat of the crumbs that fall from the table of their masters. Then Jesus answering, said to her, O woman, great is thy faith, be it done to thee as thou wilt. And her daughter was cured from that hour." (Matt. xv. 22.)

What comment does St. John Chrysostom make on this miraculous cure?
Our Blessed Saviour, said he, refused at first to listen to the petition of this Canaanean woman, that, by her example, he might instruct us with what faith, humility, and perseverance we ought to pray. To make his servants the more sensible of his mercy, and the more eager to obtain it, he often seems to pay no attention to their prayers until he has exercised them in the virtues of humility and patience.

What instruction did our Lord give in his Sermon on the Mount respecting alms-deeds and fasting?
"Take heed that you do not your justice before men, to be seen by them; otherwise you shall not have a reward of your father who is in heaven........But when thou dost alms, let not thy left hand know what thy right hand doth, that thy alms may be in secret; and thy father, who seeth in secret, will repay thee......And when you fast, be not as the hypocrites, sad......But anoint thy head and wash thy face, that thou appear not to men to fast, but to thy father who is in secret; and thy father, who seeth in secret, will repay thee." (Matt. vi.)

Would our Lord, by these instructions, inculcate that his disciples should do no good works in public, and make no profession of piety?

No; but he would have them purify their motive, performing all the good in their power, with the sole intention of pleasing God, for in another place he says, "By this shall all men know that you are my disciples, if you have love one for another." (John xiii. 35.) "Every one, therefore, that shall confess me before men, I will also confess him before my father who is in heaven. But he that will deny me before men, I will also deny him before my father who is in heaven." (Matt. x. 32.) And, "So let your light shine before men, that they may see your good works and glorify your father who is in heaven." (Matt. v. 16.)

What illustration did our Lord give some time after that it was not the value of the gift he regarded so much, as the good-will with which it was offered?

Once, when looking at the people casting their offerings into the treasury of the Temple, many of the rich gave much, and a poor widow cast in two brass mites, (about the value of a farthing.) Turning to his disciples, our Lord said, "Verily I say to you, that this poor widow hath cast in more than they all; for all these of their abundance have cast into the offerings of God, but she of her want hath cast in all the living that she had." (Luke xxi.)

What did our Lord say of those who hear his words and profit of them?

"Every one, therefore, that heareth these my words and doth them, shall be likened to a wise man that built his house upon a rock; and the rain fell, and the floods came, and the winds blew, and they beat upon that house, and it fell not, for it was founded on a rock." (Matt. vii. 25.)

To what did our Lord compare those who heard his words and did them not?
To a foolish person who built his house upon sand, and which consequently fell as soon as the rain and wind beat upon it.

CHAPTER XIV.

OUR LORD INSTRUCTS HIS APOSTLES.—HE CASTS THE BUYERS AND SELLERS OUT OF THE TEMPLE.

What directions did our Lord give his Apostles?
To preach the gospel, and confirm the doctrine inculcated by miracles; the power of working which, he imparted to them.

What did he foretell them?
That they would suffer persecution; but he comforted them, by telling them not to be solicitous as to what they should say when brought before governors and kings for his sake; for that a proper speech would be put into their mouths, and the spirit of their father would speak in them. He reminded them of what he suffered, adding that they could not expect to be treated better than their master, and that they ought not to fear those who could kill only the body, but rather fear him who could cast both soul and body into hell.

Had our Lord any other disciples beside the twelve Apostles?
Yes; he appointed also seventy-two, whom he sent before him, two and two into every city and place whither he himself was to come. On them also he conferred the gift of miracles.

What did he say to them on their returning to him and recounting with joy that the evil spirits were subject to them in his name?
"I saw Satan like lightning falling from heaven

Behold I have given you power to tread upon serpents and scorpions, and upon all the power of the enemy; and nothing shall hurt you. But yet rejoice not in this, that spirits are subject to you; but rejoice in this, that your names are written in heaven." (Luke x. 18.)

Were any persons of distinction disciples of our Lord?

Yes; many, but in secret, for fear of the Pharisees, lest they might be cast out of the synagogue; two are specially mentioned, Joseph of Arimathea and Nicodemus; the latter came to our Lord at first by night for instruction; and received it from our benign Redeemer. (John iii.)

On what did our Lord instruct Nicodemus?

On the necessity of regeneration by baptism; on the love of God for the world in giving his only begotten Son to redeem it; on his (our Divine Lord's) approaching passion and death, prefigured by the serpent erected by Moses, and of the necessity of all believing in him.

What manifestation of zeal did our Divine Lord exhibit on finding buyers and sellers in the Temple when he went on one occasion to celebrate the Pasch?

He made a scourge of little cords and drove out the sheep and the oxen, poured out the money of the money-changers, overthrew their tables; and said to the sellers of doves, "Take these things hence, and make not the house of my father, a house of traffic." (John ii. 14.)

What did the Jews say on seeing him act thus?

"What sign dost thou show us seeing thou dost these things?" To which our Lord replied, "Destroy this temple, and in three days I will raise it up." He spoke of the temple of his body, but they imagining he spoke of the temple of worship, said, "six and forty years was this temple in building, and wilt thou raise it up in three days." But his disciples remembered this word when he was risen from the dead.

What did our Lord prophesy concerning the Temple?
That it would be utterly demolished, so that one stone would not remain on another. This prophecy was partly fulfilled at the taking of Jerusalem by Titus after a siege of ten years; and entirely accomplished by Julian the Apostate, who, thinking to make void the words of our Divine Redeemer, dug out the very foundation intending to rebuild the Temple. But God frustrated his impious design and made him instrumental to the fulfilment of the prophecy; for when every stone was removed, fire issued from the foundations which hindered the workmen from approaching and finally obliged them to desist.

What effect had the destruction of the Temple on the religion of the Jews?
With the temple their sacrifices ceased, for they were prohibited from offering sacrifice in any place but in front of it.

CHAPTER XV.

CHRIST INSTRUCTS THE SAMARITAN WOMAN—HE HEALS THE RULER'S SON.

What occurred when our Lord was on his way back to Galilee from Jerusalem?
When he had reached Sichar, a city of Samaria, he sat on Jacob's well to rest, for he was fatigued from the journey, while his disciples went into the city to buy provisions. In the meantime a Samaritan woman came to the well to draw water, of whom our Lord asked to drink, which request surprised her, as the Jews did not communicate with the Samaritans.

What did our Divine Redeemer then do?
Our Divine Redeemer, ever solicitous for the salva-

tion of souls, improved her first emotion into a desire of knowing his doctrine, and attaining life everlasting; and having mentioned to her some acts of her past life, elicited from her that she believed him to be a prophet; after which she immediately consulted him on the matter in dispute between the Jews and Samaritans, whether God should be adored in Jerusalem or on Mount Gerezzim.

What did our Lord reply?
To which our Lord replied that salvation was of the Jews, yet that in a little time the divine worship would not be confined to any particular place, because God being a spirit sought true adorers, who would adore him in spirit and in truth.

What is then related of the woman?
The woman having answered that she knew the Messiah when come would instruct them in all things, our Lord said to her: "I am he who am speaking with thee. On hearing which she left her pitcher, and going immediately to the city, brought several of the inhabitants to Jesus, telling them what he had said to her, and adding, "Is not he the Christ." (John iv.)

How did the Samaritans act when they came to our Lord?
They entreated him to remain some time with them, to which he consented; and during his stay he converted many, who then told the woman, "We now believe, not for thy saying, for we ourselves have heard him, and know that this is indeed the Saviour of the world."

What miracle did our Lord perform on his return to Cana?
He restored to health, at the distance of a day's journey, a ruler's son, who was at the point of death from fever; by which the father and entire family were converted.

How did our Divine Lord spend the time from his retreat in the desert until his death?
Going about the cities and towns doing good to all; instructing the ignorant, healing the sick, preaching in the temple, in the synagogues, or in the open air, and confirming his doctrine by miracles.

In what form did our Blessed Lord usually convey his instructions to the people?
In parables, by which the prophecy was fulfilled, "*I will open my mouth in parables.*" (Matt. xiii. 35.)

How did the Scribes and Pharisees act when they saw that multitudes in admiration of the doctrine and miracles of our Divine Lord, followed him?
They sent their disciples to ensnare him, if possible, in his speech by proposing questions to him. The Sadducees did the same, for though widely differing in doctrine and practice, they combined to oppose our Divine Lord.

Repeat some of their questions?
They asked, "Is it lawful to give tribute to Cæsar or not?" Our Lord knowing their wiliness replied, Show me the coin of the tribute. They offered him a penny; Jesus said to them, Whose image and inscription is this? They answered, Cæsar's. Then, he replied, Render therefore to Cæsar the things that are Cæsar's, and to God the things that are God's." A little after this, they again endeavored to ensnare him; the Sadducees, by proposing difficulties on the doctrine of the resurrection; the Pharisees, by questioning him on the law; but he silenced both.

What answer did our Blessed Lord give them when on a Sabbath day they showed him a man with a withered hand, and asked, Is it lawful to heal on the Sabbath day?
"What man shall there be among you that hath one sheep, and if the same fall into a pit on the Sabbath

day, will he not take hold on it and lift it up. How much better is a man than a sheep? Therefore it is lawful to do a good deed on the Sabbath day. Then he said to the man, Stretch forth thy hand, and he stretched it forth, and it was restored to health even as the other." (Matt. xii. 10.)

CHAPTER XVI.
MIRACLE AT THE POND OF PROBATICA AND CURE OF THE MAN BLIND FROM HIS BIRTH.

Do you remember any other miraculous cures effected by our compassionate Redeemer on the Sabbath day?
Yes, he cured a man who had been infirm thirty-eight years; gave sight to another who had been blind from his birth, and restored a woman to health after eighteen years' illness.
Mention the particulars of the first?
There was at Jerusalem a pond called Probatica, in Hebrew Bethsaida, having five porches, in which lay a multitude of persons afflicted with divers diseases waiting for the moving of the water; for an angel descended at certain times into the pond, and the water was moved, and whoever went down first into the pond after the moving of the water was cured. Our Lord visiting this place on the Sabbath day, and seeing a man there who had been thirty-eight years sick, asked him did he wish to be cured; the man replied that he had no person to put him into the water when it was troubled, for while he was going another went down before him. Our benign Lord, moved with compassion, desired him to rise, take up his bed and walk, which he immediately did, being restored to perfect health. (John v.)
What did the Jews say to this miracle?
They accused the man of breaking the Sabbath by

taking up his bed, and persecuted our Lord for performing miracles on that day.

Mention the particulars of the blind man's cure?
Our Lord, walking with his disciples, saw a blind man begging, and being asked by them whether it was in punishment of his own, or his parents' sins that the man was born blind, answered, Neither; but that the works of God might be manifested; then spitting on the ground he made clay of the spittle, and applying it to the blind man's eyes, desired him to go to the pool of Siloe and wash, which he did, and immediately recovered his sight.

What did the Pharisees say of our Divine Lord when they beheld this miraculous cure?
Some said, that he could not be of God, as he committed what they considered a breach of the Sabbath: others said, How can a man that is a sinner do such miracles? and appealing to the blind man for his opinion he replied, "He is a prophet."

Were they then satisfied?
No, but sending for the parents of him who was cured, they inquired was he their son who was born blind, and by what means he had acquired his sight. The parents admitted that he was the same, but referred them to himself for information as to the manner in which he obtained his sight; for they feared being cast out of the synagogue, which the Jews had agreed to do to any who confessed our Lord to be Christ.

Were they then convinced of the certainty of the miracle?
No, being willing to contest it, and still persisting in their obduracy, they endeavored to make the blind man retract the confession he had made in favor of our Lord. But failing in this, and only eliciting a more decided act of faith, and a confutation of their calumnies, they with great anger cast him out.

What did our Lord say to him on meeting him after this occurrence?

"Dost thou believe in the Son of God? The man having answered, Who is he, Lord, that I may believe in him. Jesus said, Thou hast both seen him and it is he that talketh with thee. On which he replied, I believe, Lord;" and, falling down, he adored him.

CHAPTER XVII.

MIRACLE PERFORMED ON THE WOMAN WHO HAD BEEN SICK EIGHTEEN YEARS.—CURE OF THE MAN AFFLICTED WITH DROPSY.

Can you tell the particulars of the miracle performed on the woman who had been eighteen years sick?

She was in the synagogue on a Sabbath day during our Lord's instructions: He, moved with compassion at her condition (for she was bowed together, and could not look up) called her and laying his hands on her, delivered her from her infirmity, and immediately she was made straight and glorified God (Luke xiii. 13.)

What did the ruler of the synagogue say on witnessing this miracle?

"Six days there are wherein you ought to work; in them therefore come and be healed, and not on the Sabbath day."

What did our Lord reply?

"Ye hypocrites, doth not every one of you on the Sabbath day loose his ox or his ass from the manger and lead them to water; and ought not this daughter of Abraham, whom Satan hath bound, lo these eighteen years, be loosed from this bond on the Sabbath day?"

What effect had this defence of our blessed Lord?

His adversaries were ashamed, and the people rejoiced at all things that were gloriously done by him.

Do you remember any other cure performed by our Lord on the Sabbath day?
Yes; that of a man afflicted with dropsy.

What are the particulars of it?
Our Lord being entertained at the house of one of the principal Pharisees, saw there a man who had a dropsy; turning to the lawyers and Pharisees, he asked, "Is it lawful to heal on the Sabbath day?" but they making no reply, he healed him, saying to them, "Which of you shall have an ass or an ox fall into a pit, and will not immediately draw him out on the Sabbath day." (Luke xiv. 1.)

How should we sanctify the Sabbath?
By prayer, assisting devoutly at the holy sacrifice, reading pious books, or hearing sermons: and performing any spiritual or corporal works of mercy in our power, particularly the instruction of the ignorant. We are bound also to avoid all unnecessary servile work, and whatever might hinder the due observance of the Lord's day, or tend to profane it.

What did our Lord answer when the Scribes and Pharisees demanded a sign of his heavenly mission?
That he would give them only that of Jonas the prophet; for as Jonas was in the body of the whale three days and three nights, so should the Son of Man be in the heart of the earth three days and three nights.

Who did our Lord say would rise in judgment with that generation and condemn it?
The people of Ninive, who did penance at the preaching of Jonas; and the queen of the south who travelled from the ends of the earth to hear the wisdom of Solomon; but the people of that generation had greater than either Jonas or Solomon to instruct them, yet profited very little of it.

CHAPTER XVIII.

PARABLES OF THE SOWER AND OF THE COCKLE.

Repeat some of the parables in which our Divine Lord instructed the people?
"The sower went forth to sow his seed, and whilst he sowed some fell by the way side, and it was trodden down, and the birds of the air devoured it. And other some fell upon a rock, and as soon as it was sprung up it withered away because it had no moisture. And other some fell among thorns, and the thorns growing up with it choked it; and other some fell upon good ground, and being sprung up yielded fruit an hundred-fold."

Where was our Divine Lord while speaking this parable?
In a boat near the shore, which he went into for the purpose of instructing the people who crowded on the shore.

What explanation did our Lord give his disciples of this parable?
"The seed is the word of God, and they by the way side are they that hear, then the devil cometh and taketh the word out of their heart, lest believing they should be saved. Now they upon the rock are they, who when they hear receive the word with joy; and these have no roots; for they believe for a while, and in time of temptation they fall away. And that which fell among thorns, are they who have heard, and going their way are choked with the cares and riches, and pleasures of this life, and yield no fruit. But that on the good ground, are they who in a good and very good heart hearing the word keep it, and bring forth fruit in patience." (Luke viii.)

Repeat the parable of the oversowing of the cockle?
"The kingdom of heaven is likened to a man that

owed good seed in his field; but while men were asleep, his enemy came and overspread cockle among the wheat and went his way. And when the blade was sprung up and had brought forth fruit, then appeared also the cockle; and the servants of the good men of the house coming said to him, Sir, didst thou not sow good seed in thy field, whence then hath it cockle? And he said to them, an enemy hath done this. And the servants said to him, Wilt thou that we go and gather it up?"

How did he answer the servants?

"And he said No, lest perhaps gathering up the cockle you root up the wheat also together with it. Suffer both to grow until the harvest, and in the time of the harvest I will say to the reapers, Gather up first the cockle and bind it into bundles to burn, but the wheat gather up into my barn."

How did our Lord expound this parable to his disciples?

"He that soweth the good seed is the Son of Man, and the field is the world. And the good seed are the children of the kingdom; and the cockle are the children of the wicked one; and the enemy that sowed them is the devil. But the harvest is the end of the world, and the reapers are the angels. Even as cockle therefore is gathered up and burnt with fire, so shall it be at the end of the world, the Son of Man shall send his angels and they shall gather out of his kingdom all scandals, and them that work iniquity, and shall cast them into the furnace of fire, there shall be weeping and gnashing of teeth. Then shall the just shine as the sun in the kingdom of their Father." (Matt. xiii.)

CHAPTER XIX.

THE STORM AT SEA.

Where was our Lord while giving these instructions?
In a ship with his disciples on the sea of Galilee, the people being assembled on the shore. (Matt. xiii. 1.)

What did our Lord direct his disciples to do when he had finished his instructions to the people?
To sail to the opposite coast, which they immediately did; but when they had gone some way a great storm arose, and the sea beat into the ship so that it filled and was in danger of sinking.

In the mean time where was our Lord?
In the mean time our Lord was asleep in the hinder part of the ship, when his disciples awoke him saying: "Master, doth it not concern thee, that we perish; and rising up he rebuked the wind and said to the Sea, Peace, be still."

What followed?
And the wind ceased, and a great calm ensued: and he said to them, Why are you fearful, have you not faith yet. And they feared exceedingly, and said one to another, Who is this thinkest thou, that both wind and sea obey him? (Mark iv. 35.)

What occurred when they arrived at the opposite coast, the country of the Gerasins?
Our Lord was met by a man possessed by an evil spirit, who falling down adored, crying out: "What have I to do with thee, Jesus, the Son of the Most High God, I beseech thee do not torment me," for our Lord had said, "Go out of the man thou unclean spirit."

What did our Lord ask?
Our Lord asked, "What is thy name?" he replied "Legion, for we are many," and they besought him that he would not command them to go into the abyss,

but to suffer them to enter into a herd of swine that was feeding near. He did so, and going out of the man they entered the swine, and the whole herd, to the number of about two thousand, ran into the lake and were stifled.

What is said of the Man?
The man was immediately restored to reason, became quite peaceable, and resumed his clothes, which he had not worn for a long time; having lived from the time he became possessed, in sepulchres, and having been so fierce, that he could not be approached, nor in any way restrained. In the commencement, some attempts were made to bind him even with chains, but he had broke through all. (Mark v.)

CHAPTER XX.

THE DAUGHTER OF JAIRUS RAISED TO LIFE.

What did our Lord after performing these miracles?
He recrossed the Lake to Galilee, for the Gerasins entreated him to leave their country, being terrified at what they had witnessed.

What miracles did he perform immediately after landing?
He raised to life the daughter of Jairus, a ruler of the synagogue, and cured a woman who had been twelve years infirm.

Relate the particulars?
As soon as our Lord landed, Jairus fell at his feet, earnestly entreating him to come to his house, and lay his hand on his only daughter who was at the point of death. Our Lord complied, and while going, a woman who had been twelve years ill, and had in vain spent all she had in endeavoring to procure relief, came behind and touched his garment,

saying within herself, "If I shall touch but the hem of his garment I shall be cured."

What followed?
Immediately on doing so, she was perfectly restored, and our Lord, turning to the crowd that surrounded him, asked: "Who hath touched my garments?" All denying, St. Peter said, "Master, the multitudes throng and press thee, and dost thou say who touched me?"

What did the Woman do?
But the woman seeing that she was discovered, fell at his feet and declared the truth, to whom our Lord said: "Daughter, thy faith hath made thee whole, go in peace."

While he was speaking, what happened?
Whilst he was speaking, a messenger came to Jairus to inform him of his daughter's death, but our Lord said to him: "Fear not, believe only, and she shall be safe;" and taking with him Peter, James, and John, he suffered no others but the father and mother of the girl to go with him into the house; and going to the place where she lay, he took her by the hand saying: "Maid arise;" and her spirit returned, and she rose immediately. (Luke viii. 41.)

CHAPTER XXI.

MULTIPLICATION OF THE LOAVES AND FISHES.—ST PETER UPON THE WATERS.

Whither did our Lord go soon after this miracle?
To a desert place together with his apostles, but being followed by multitudes, on whose infirmities and ignorance he had compassion, he healed the sick among them, and instructed all until evening, when his apostles begged of him to dismiss them as no food could be had in that desert place

What did he reply?
He replied: "They have no need to go, give you them to eat;" they answered: "We have only five loaves and two fishes;" "Bring them to me," said our Lord.

What did he then direct?
Then he directed the multitudes to be seated, in number about five thousand, and looking up to heaven he blessed the five loaves and two fishes, and desired his disciples to distribute them: they did so, and when all were satisfied, our Lord commanded the fragments to be collected that nothing should be wasted; and with these they filled twelve baskets.

What did the people say on witnessing this great miracle?
"This is of a truth the prophet that is to come into the world:" and they would have made him king, on which our Lord withdrew from among them.

Whither did our Lord send his disciples that evening?
Across the lake in the ship, he himself remaining alone to pray.

What occurred to them about the middle of the night, when they had gone a considerable distance?
The wind arose, and the ship was tossed, but our Lord seeing them laboring came to them walking on the water, whom when his disciples saw, they cried out, thinking it was an apparition; but he calmed their fears, saying, "It is I, fear not."

What did St. Peter say?
"Lord if it be thou, bid me come to thee upon the waters;" to whom our Lord said, "Come;" and St. Peter going down out of the ship walked upon the water to him, but the wind being high he was frightened, and when he began to sink, he cried out, "Lord save me;" on which our gracious Lord took

hold of him saying, "O thou of little faith, why didst thou doubt."

What testimony did those in the ship give, when they saw what was done, and that the storm subsided?
They adored our Lord, saying, "Indeed thou art the Son of God."

Relate the particulars of our Lord's feeding over four thousand people, who collected to hear his instructions and to be cured?
Being with his disciples on a mountain near the sea of Galilee, great multitudes resorted to him, and continued with him three days, at the end of which time he desired his disciples to give the people food saying, "I will not send them away fasting lest they faint in the way."

What did the disciples reply?
The disciples replied that they had only seven loaves and a few small fishes, which they brought to their Divine Master, who, having blessed, directed them to be distributed among the people, who all ate a sufficiency, yet left as much fragments as filled seven baskets.

CHAPTER XXII.

ST. PETER'S CONFESSION OF CHRIST.—TRANSFIGURATION OF OUR LORD.

What did the people think on seeing the stupendous miracles wrought by our Divine Lord?
Some thought he was John the Baptist risen from the dead: others that he was Elias; others, that he was Jeremiah, or one of the ancient prophets.

What did St. Peter answer when our Lord asked his disciples, "Whom do you say that I am?"
"Thou art Christ the Son of the living God."

What did our Lord say on this confession of St. Peter?

"Blessed art thou Simon Bar-Jona, because flesh and blood hath not revealed it to thee, but my father who is in heaven, and I say to thee that thou art Peter, and upon this rock I will build my Church, and the gates of hell shall not prevail against it. And I will give to thee the keys of the kingdom of heaven; and whatsoever thou shalt bind upon earth, shall be bound also in heaven; and whatsoever thou shalt loose upon earth, shall be loosed also in heaven" (Matt. xvi.)

What did our Lord foretell his disciples soon after this?

That he should go to Jerusalem, and suffer many things from the ancients and chief priests, and be put to death, and the third day rise again.

What did St. Peter on hearing this announcement of our Lord?

He expostulated with him, saying, "Lord be it far from thee, this shall not be unto thee;" but our Lord rebuked him for being still so worldly-minded, and not relishing the ignominy of the cross.

What miraculous occurrence took place about a week after this?

Our Lord taking Peter, James, and John, retired to a mountain, which is generally supposed to be Thabor, to pray: and whilst in prayer he was transfigured, assuming the appearance of a glorified body; his face shone as the sun, and his garments became white and glittering. And Moses and Elias appeared conversing with him on his approaching Passion and Death in Jerusalem.

What did St. Peter say on seeing him?

St. Peter seeing them, said, "Lord it is good for us to be here; let us make three tabernacles, one for thee, one for Moses, and one for Elias;" whilst he was speaking, a bright cloud overshadowed them, and a voice out of the cloud said, "This is my beloved Son, in whom I am well pleased, hear ye him." The disciples hearing this, fell with fear to the ground, but our Lord calmed them, and desired them to rise; on doing so they saw him only, who charged them not to speak of the vision until he should be risen from the dead.

CHAPTER XXIII.

INSTRUCTIONS ON ZEAL, HUMILITY, AND ON THE NECESSITY OF GIVING GOOD EXAMPLE.

What did our Lord soon after his transfiguration?
He set out with his disciples on his return to Jerusalem, having again foretold to them what he was to suffer there.

What happened in a Samaritan city which lay in our Lord's way, and through which he was to pass?
The inhabitants refused him entrance; on which James and John asked permission to call fire down from heaven to consume them; but the Lord rebuked them, saying, "You know not of what spirit you are, the Son of Man came not to destroy souls but to save." And they went into another town.

On what subjects did our Lord instruct his disciples on the way?
On the necessity of humility; on the danger of giving scandal, and the necessity of cutting off all occasions of sin; on the forgiveness of injuries; on charity, and on the evil of setting the heart on riches.

What exemplification did our Lord give of Christian humility?
He placed a little child in the midst, saying, "Unless you be converted and become as little children,

you shall not enter into the kingdom of heaven; whosoever therefore shall humble himself as this little child, he is the greater in the kingdom of heaven."

In what words did our Lord propose himself as their model in this virtue?

"Take up my yoke upon you and learn of me, because I am meek and humble of heart and you shall find rest to your souls, for my yoke is sweet and my burden light." (Matt. xi. 29.)

What did our Lord say of those who should give scandal to children?

"He that shall scandalize one of these little ones that believe in me, it were better for him that a millstone should be hanged about his neck, and that he should be drowned in the depth of the sea..........See that you dispise not one of these little ones, for I say to you that their angels in heaven, always see the face of my father who is in heaven."

What did our Lord say of removing the cause of scandal be it ever so near or dear?

"If thy hand or thy foot scandalize thee cut it off and cast it from thee. It is better for thee to go into life maimed or lame, than having two hands or two feet, to be cast into everlasting fire. And if thy eye scandalize thee, pluck it out and cast it from thee: it is better for thee having one eye to enter into life, than having two eyes to be cast into hell fire." (Matt. v. 29.)

Are these words to be understood literally?

No, as self-mutilation is unlawful; their meaning then is that we are to withdraw ourselves from those things and persons that are an occasion of sin to us; that we are to cast from us those objects, though dear to us as our eyes or hands, which we cannot cherish without offending God; that we are to renounce all sinful attachments and affections, no matter what pain the renunciation may cost us.

21

What is observed of the plucking out of the eye, &c.?

The plucking out of our eyes and cutting off of our hands are never necessary means to secure our salvation, as God on the one hand, gives us grace to avoid using them perversely, and on the other forbids us to destroy them. If therefore holy persons have, in some instances, acted up to the letter of this passage, by maiming themselves to escape guilt more surely; we must say either that they were excused by ignorance of the prohibition, whilst they are to be praised for their earnest zeal against sin, or, as appears to have been the case in some instances, that they were justified by a special inspiration of God, who, being supreme Lord of life and limb, could unquestionably authorize such actions, which we may therefore admire but not imitate.

CHAPTER XXIV.

ON FRATERNAL CORRECTION AND FORGIVENESS OF INJURIES.

What did our Lord say respecting fraternal correction?

"If thy brother shall offend against thee, go and rebuke him between thee and him alone. If he shall hear thee, thou shalt gain thy brother, and if he will not hear thee, take with thee one or two more, that in the mouth of two or three witnesses every word may stand, and if he will not hear them, tell the Church."

What does our Lord say of him who will not hear the Church?

"Let him be to thee as the heathen and the publican."

What did our Lord reply when asked by St. Pe-

how often he should forgive one who injured him, should he do so seven times?

"I say not to thee till seven times, but till seventy times seven times." (Matt. xviii.)

What parable did our Lord relate to exemplify the necessity of forgiving injuries?

"The kingdom of heaven is likened to a king who would take an account of his servants, and when he had begun to take the account one was brought to him that owed him ten thousand talents. And as he had not wherewith to pay it, his lord commanded that he should be sold, and his wife and children and all that he had, and payment to be made.

What did the servant do?

But that servant falling down, besought him, saying: Have patience with me and I will pay thee all; and the lord of that servant being moved with pity, let him go, and forgave him the debt. But when that servant was gone out, he found one of his fellow servants that owed him a hundred pence, and laying hold of him, he throttled him, saying: Pay what thou owest.

How did his fellow-servant answer?

And his fellow-servant falling down besought him, saying: Have patience with me and I will pay thee all. And he would not, but went and cast him into prison until he paid the debt. Now his fellow-servants, seeing what was done, were very much grieved, and they came and told their lord all that was done.

What did his lord then do?

Then his lord called him and said to him: Thou wicked servant I forgave thee all the debt because thou besoughtest me; shouldst not thou then have had compassion also on thy fellow-servant even as I had compassion on thee. And his lord being angry delivered him to the torturers until he paid all the debt. So also shall my Heavenly Father do to you if you forgive not every one his brother from your hearts." (Matt. xviii.)

CHAPTER XXV.

ON CHARITY, AND ON THE EVIL OF SETTING THE HEART ON RICHES.

What answer did our Lord give a certain lawyer who to tempt him asked, What must I do to possess eternal life?
Our Lord said, What is written in the law? On the lawyer's replying that it was written: Thou shalt love the Lord thy God with thy whole heart, and with thy whole soul and with all thy strength and with all thy mind, and thy neighbor as thyself." Thou hast answered rightly, said our Lord, this do and thou shalt live.

What parable did our Lord relate on the lawyer's asking, Who is my neighbor?
"A certain man went down from Jerusalem to Jericho and fell among robbers, who also stripped him, and having wounded him, went away leaving him half dead; and it chanced that a certain priest went down the same way, and, seeing him, passed by. In like manner, also, a Levite, when he was near the place and saw him, passed by.

What did the Samaritan do?
But a certain Samaritan being on his journey came near him, and seeing him was moved with compassion; and going up to him bound up his wounds, pouring in oil and wine, and, setting him upon his own beast, brought him to an inn and took care of him. And the next day, he took out two pence and gave to the host, and said: Take care of him, and whatsoever thou shalt spend over and above, I, at my return, will repay thee.

What did our Lord ask, and what did the lawyer reply?
Which of these three, in thy opinion, was neighbor to him that fell among the robbers? The lawyer replied: He that showed mercy to him. And Jesus said to him: Go, and do thou in like manner. (Luke x. 25.)

What answer did our Lord give another, who asked: What good shall I do, that I may have life everlasting?
"If thou wilt enter into life, keep the commandments:" The young man replying that he had kept them from his youth, but wished to know what was yet wanting to him, our Lord said: "If thou wilt be perfect, go sell what thou hast, and give to the poor, and thou shalt have treasure in heaven, and come follow me."

What did the young man do on hearing these words of our Lord?
He went away sad, for he had great possessions.

What did our Lord say to his disciples on seeing the rich young man go away sad?
"How hard is it for them that trust in riches to enter into the kingdom of God.... It is easier for a camel to pass through the eye of a needle than for a rich man to enter into the kingdom of heaven." (Matt. xix. and Mark x.)

What did our Lord reply to St. Peter when he said, "Behold we have left all things and have followed thee, what therefore shall we have?
"Amen I say to you, that you who have followed me, in the regeneration when the Son of Man shall sit on the seat of his Majesty, you also shall sit on twelve seats judging the twelve tribes of Israel. And every one of you that hath left house or brethren, or sisters, or father, or mother, or wife, or children, or lands, for my name's sake, shall receive an

hundred fold, and shall possess life everlasting.' (Matt. xix.)

CHAPTER XXVI.

PARABLE OF THE RICH MAN AND LAZARUS.

What parable did our Lord make use of to warn the rich against using their wealth only for their own indulgence?

"There was a certain rich man who was clothed in purple and fine linen, and feasted sumptuously every day. And there was a certain beggar named Lazarus who lay at his gate full of sores desiring to be filled with the crumbs that fell from the rich man's table, and no one did give him, moreover the dogs came and licked his sores."

What came to pass?

"And it came to pass that the beggar died and was carried by the angels into Abraham's bosom; and the rich man also died and was buried in hell. And lifting up his eyes when he was in torments, he saw Abraham afar off, and Lazarus in his bosom; and he cried and said: Father Abraham have mercy on me, and send Lazarus that he may dip the tip of his finger in water to cool my tongue for I am tormented in this flame?'"

What did Abraham say?

"And Abraham said to him: Son, remember that thou didst receive good things in thy lifetime, and likewise Lazarus evil things, but now he is comforted and thou art tormented. And besides all this, between us and you there is fixed a great chaos, so that they who would pass from hence to you cannot, nor from thence come hither." (Luke xvi. 19.)

What other parable did our Lord speak to show the folly of trusting in riches?

"The land of a certain man brought forth plenty of

fruits and he thought within himself, saying: What shall I do because I have no room where to bestow my fruits; and he said: This will I do; I will pull down my barns, and will build greater, and into them will I gather all things that are given to me, and my goods. And I will say to my soul: Soul thou hast much goods laid up for many years, take thy rest; eat, drink, make good cheer."

What did God say to him?
"But God said to him, Thou fool, this night do they require thy soul of thee, and whose shall these things be which thou hast provided." So is he that layeth up treasure for himself. and is not rich towards God. (Luke xii. 16.)

CHAPTER XXVII.

PARABLE OF THE BARREN FIG TREE, AND OF THE LABORERS IN THE VINEYARD.

What parable did our Lord speak to show the necessity of doing penance and performing good works?
"A certain man had a fig tree planted in his vineyard, and he came seeking fruit on it, and he found none; and he said to the dresser of the vineyard: Behold for these three years I come seeking fruit on this fig tree, and I find none; cut it down therefore, why cumbereth it the ground?"

What did he answer?
"But he answering, said to him: Lord, let it alone this year also, until I dig about it and dung it; and if happily it bear fruit, but if not, then after that thou shalt cut it down." (Luke xiii. 6.)

Repeat the parable of the laborers in the vineyard?
"The kingdom of heaven is like to a householder who went out early in the morning to hire laborers into his vineyard; and having agreed with the laborers for a penny a day, he sent them into his vineyard.

And going out about the third hour, he saw others standing in the market-place idle; and he said to them: Go you also into my vineyard and I will give you what shall be just; and they went their way. And again he went out about the sixth and the ninth hour and did in like manner; but about the eleventh hour he went out and found others standing, and he saith to them: Why stand you here all the day idle? They say to him: Because no man hath hired us. He saith to them: Go you also into my vineyard."

When evening was come what did the lord do?
"And when evening was come the lord of the vineyard saith to his steward: Call the laborers and pay them their hire, beginning from the last, even to the first. When, therefore, they were come that came about the eleventh hour, they received every man a penny: but when the first also came, they thought that they should receive more; and they also received every man a penny."

What did those who came first say?
"They murmured against the master of the house, saying: These last have worked but one hour, and thou hast made them equal to us that have borne the burden of the day and the heats."

How did the master answer?
"But he answering, said to one of them: Friend I do thee no wrong; didst thou not agree with me for a penny, take what is thine and go thy way; I will also give to this last even as to thee; or is it not lawful for me to do what I will; is thy eye evil because I am good. So shall the last be first, and the first last; for many are called but few chosen." (Matt. xx.)

What instruction may you derive from the above parable?
To labor diligently in performing the duties allotted without murmuring at the comparative ease enjoyed

by some; and knowing that labor is appointed by God, to acquit ourselves of the portion that devolves to us with such fidelity as will hereafter merit for us to hear: "Well done good and faithful servant, as thou hast been faithful over few things I will place thee over many, enter into the joy of thy Lord."

CHAPTER XXVIII.

PARABLE OF THE VINEYARD LET OUT TO HUSBANDMEN.

What parable did our Lord speak to forewarn the Jews that if they did not repent the kingdom of God should be transferred from them to the gentiles?
"There was a man, a householder, who planted a vineyard, and made a hedge round about it, and dug in it a press, and built a tower, and let it out to husbandmen, and went into a strange country. And when the time of the fruits drew nigh, he sent his servants to the husbandmen that they might receive the fruits thereof."

What did the husbandmen do?
"And the husbandmen laying hands on his servants, beat one, and killed another, and stoned another. Again he sent other servants more than the former, and they did to them in like manner; and last of all he sent to them his son, saying: They will reverence my son. But the husbandmen, seeing the son, said among themselves: This is the heir, come let us kill him and we shall have his inheritance, and taking him they cast him forth out of the vineyard and killed him." (Matt. xxi. 33.)

What answer did the Jews give when our Lord said: When therefore the lord of the vineyard shall come what shall he do to these husbandmen?
They replied: "He will bring these evil men to an evil end, and will let out his vineyard to other husbandmen that shall render him the fruit in due season."

What did our Lord say further?
"Have you never read in the Scriptures, *The stone which the builders rejected, the same is become the head of the corner. By the Lord this has been done, and it is wonderful in our eyes.* Therefore I say to you that the kingdom of God shall be taken from you, and shall be given to a nation yielding the fruits thereof."

Was the above parable calculated to remind the Jews of ancient prophecies and so lead them to reflect and repent?
It was; both Isaias and Jeremiah had compared them to a vineyard on which no trouble had been spared yet which produced only briers and thorns.

Repeat the prophecies?
"My beloved had a vineyard on a hill in a fruitful place; and he fenced it in, and picked the stones out of it, and planted it with the choicest vines, and built a tower in the midst thereof, and set up a wine press therein; and he looked that it should bring forth grapes, and it brought forth wild grapes. And now, O ye inhabitants of Jerusalem, and ye men of Juda, judge between me and my vineyard, what is there that I ought to do more for my vineyard, that I have not done to it.

What was the answer to this question?
"And now I will show you what I will do to my vineyard, I will take away the hedge thereof, and it shall be wasted; I will break down the wall thereof, and it shall be trodden down; and I will make it desolate, and it shall not be pruned and it shall not be digged, but briers and thorns shall come up; and I will command the clouds to rain no rain upon it.

What was the vineyard?
"The vineyard of the Lord of Hosts is the house of Israel, and the man of Juda his pleasant plant; and I looked that he should do judgment and behold

iniquity; and do justice and behold a cry." (Isaias v.) "Yet I planted them a chosen vineyard all true seed; how art thou turned unto me, into that which is good for nothing, O strange vineyard." (Jer. ii. 21.)

Ought not we likewise derive instruction and warning by the above parable and prophecies?
Yes; for though addressed to the Jews, they are applicable to Christians whom God has planted in his Church, fenced in with holy laws, and provided with the holy sacraments as so many conduits of his grace. In it he expects the faithful to prune all superfluities by mortification; to dig deeply into their souls by a profound knowledge of self; to root out by contrary acts the briers of vicious habits; and water with tears of compunction the dry affections of their hearts, that so they may render fruit in due season, and deserve praise instead of reproach from their heavenly master.

CHAPTER XXIX.

PARABLE OF THE MARRIAGE FEAST, AND OF THE TEN VIRGINS.

Repeat the parable of the marriage feast?
"The kingdom of heaven is likened to a king who made a marriage for his son; and he sent his servants to call them that were invited to the marriage, and they would not come. Again he sent other servants, saying: Tell them that were invited, Behold I have prepared my dinner, my beeves and fatlings are killed, and all things are ready, come ye to the marriage.

What did they do?
"But they neglected and went their ways, one to his farm and another to his merchandize, and the rest laid hands upon his servants, and having treated them contumeliously put them to death.

What did the king do, when he heard this?
"But when the king had heard of it, he was angry, and sending his armies he destroyed those murderers and burned their city. Then he saith to his servants: The marriage indeed is ready, but they that were invited were not worthy, go ye therefore into the highways, and as many as you shall find call to the marriage. And his servants going forth into the ways, gathered together all that they found both bad and good; and the marriage was filled with guests.

What is related of the king when he went in to see the guests?
"And the king went in to see the guests, and he saw there a man who had not on a wedding garment, and he saith to him: Friend how camest thou in hither, not having on a wedding garment, but he was silent. Then the king said to the waiters: Bind his hands and his feet, and cast him into the exterior darkness; there shall be weeping and gnashing of teeth; for many are called but few are chosen." (Matt. xxii. 1.)

What application may you make of this parable in order to derive fruit from it?
To approach the Holy Table at the appointed times with due preparation, humility and gratitude; and never to presume to do so unless clothed with the nuptial robe of charity, and the grace of God.

What parable did our Lord relate to warn his disciples to be always prepared for death?
"Then shall the kingdom of heaven be like to ten virgins, who, taking their lamps, went out to meet the bridegroom and the bride: and five of them were foolish and five wise. But the five foolish having taken their lamps, did not take oil with them, but the wise took oil in their vessels with the lamps. And the bridegroom tarrying, they all slumbered and slept; and at midnight there was a cry made:

Behold the bridegroom cometh, go ye forth to meet him; then all these virgins arose and trimmed their lamps: and the foolish said to the wise, Give us of your oil, for our lamps are gone out. The wise answered, saying: Lest perhaps there be not enough for us and for you, go ye rather to them that sell and buy for yourselves.

What happened while they went to buy?
"Now whilst they went to buy the bridegroom came, and they that were ready went in with him to the marriage, and the door was shut. But at last came also the other virgins, saying, Lord, Lord open to us; but he answering, said, Amen I say to you, I know you not. Watch ye, therefore, because ye know not the day nor the hour." (Matt. xxv. 1.)

CHAPTER XXX.

PARABLE OF THE LOST SHEEP AND OF THE PRODIGAL SON.

What parables did our Lord relate to encourage sinners to repent and return to their duties?
Those of the lost sheep and the prodigal son.

Relate the parable of the lost sheep?
"What man of you that hath an hundred sheep, and if he shall lose one of them doth he not leave the ninety-nine in the desert, and go after that which was lost until he find it. And when he hath found it, lay it upon his shoulders rejoicing; and coming home call together his friends and neighbors, saying to them: Rejoice with me because I have found my sheep that was lost. I say to you, that even so there shall be joy in heaven upon one sinner that doth penance more than upon ninety-nine just who need not penance." (Luke xv. 4.)

Did not our Lord compare himself to a shepherd?
He did, saying, "I am the good shepherd. The good shepherd giveth his life for his sheep, but the

hireling and he that is not the shepherd, whose own the sheep are not, seeth the wolf coming, and leaveth the sheep and fleeth; and the wolf catcheth and scattereth the sheep; and the hireling fleeth because he is a hireling, and he hath no care for the sheep. I am the good shepherd, and I know mine and mine know me." (John x. 2.)

Was our Lord announced by any of the prophets under the figure of a shepherd?
He was, by the prophets Isaias and Ezekiel; the latter said "And I will set up one shepherd over them," (Ez. xxxiv. 23;) the former, "He shall feed his flock like a shepherd, he shall gather together the lambs with his arm, and shall take them up in his bosom." (Is. xl. 11.)

Repeat the parable of the prodigal son?
"A certain man had two sons, and the younger of them said to his father; father give me the portion of substance that falleth to me; and he divided unto them his substance. And not many days after, the younger son, gathering all together, went abroad into a far country, and there wasted his substance, living riotously.

After he had spent all, what happened?
"And after he had spent all, there came a mighty famine in that country, and he began to be in want, and he went and cleaved to one of the citizens of that country, and he sent him into his farm to feed swine. And he would fain have filled his belly with the husks the swine did eat, and no man gave unto him.

What did he say?
"And returning to himself he said; how many hired servants in my father's house abound with bread, and I here perish with hunger. I will arise, and will go to my father and say to him: father I have sinned against heaven and before thee, I am not now

worthy to be called thy son, make me as one of thy hired servants.

And rising up, what did he do?
"And rising up, he came to his father; and when he was yet a great way off, his father saw him, and was moved with compassion, and running to him fell upon his neck and kissed him. And the son said to him; father I have sinned against heaven and before thee, I am not now worthy to be called thy son.

What did the father say?
"And the father said to his servants, Bring forth quickly the first robe and put it on him, and put a ring on his hand and shoes on his feet; and bring hither the fatted calf and kill it; and let us eat and make merry, because this my son was dead and is come to life again, was lost and is found." (Luke xv.)

What may we learn from this parable?
That whenever we are so unhappy as to stray away from our Heavenly Father by sin, we ought to enter into ourselves and return speedily with the sentiments of humility and contrition evinced by the prodigal, and then we may humbly hope for a similar reception.

CHAPTER XXXI.

PARABLE OF THE TEN TALENTS.

What parable did our Lord speak to show the necessity of diligently co-operating with the designs of God, and being ever ready to render an account of the gifts received?
"A man going into a far country called his servants, and delivered to them his goods; and to one he gave five talents, and to another two, and to another one; to every one according to his proper ability, and im-

mediately he took his journey. And he that had received the five talents, went his way, and traded with the same and gained other five; and in like manner he that had received two, gained other two: but he that had received the one, going his way, digged into the earth and hid his lord's money.

After a long time, what happened?
"But after a long time, the lord of these servants came and reckoned with them, and he that had received the five talents, coming, brought other five talents, saying, Lord thou didst deliver to me five talents, behold I have gained other five over and above.

What did the lord say to the servant that received five talents, and to him that received two?
"His lord said to him; well done good and faithful servant, because thou hast been faithful over a few things, I will place thee over many, enter thou into the joy of thy lord. And he that had received the two talents, came and said, Lord, thou deliveredst to me two talents, behold I have gained other two. His lord said to him: Well done, good and faithful servant, because thou hast been faithful over a few things, I will place thee over many, enter thou into the joy of thy Lord.

What did the servant, who hid his talent say, and what was the lord's answer?
"But he that had received the one talent, came and said: Lord, I know that thou art a hard man, that thou reapest where thou hast not sworn, and gatherest where thou hast not strewed; and being afraid, I went and hid thy talent in the earth, behold, here thou hast that which is thine. And his lord answering, said; wicked and slothful servant, thou knowest that I reap where I sow not, and gather where I have not strewed; thou oughtest therefore to have

committed my money to the bankers, and at my coming I should have received my own with usury. Take ye therefore the talent from him and give it to him that hath ten talents, for, to every one that hath, shall be given and he shall abound: but from him that hath not, that also which he seemeth to have shall be taken away, and the unprofitable servant cast ye out into the exterior darkness; there shall be weeping and gnashing of teeth." (Matt xxv. 14.)

CHAPTER XXXII.

MIRACULOUS CURE OF THE TEN LEPERS.—LAZARUS RAISED TO LIFE.

Relate the particulars of the miracle performed on the ten lepers?
"As he was going to Jerusalem, he passed through the midst of Samaria and Galilee; and as he entered into a certain town, there met him ten men that were lepers, who stood afar off and lifted up their voice saying: Jesus, master, have mercy on us. When he saw them he said; go show yourselves to the priests. And it came to pass, as they went, they were made clean.

What is related of one of them?
"And one of them, when he saw that he was made clean, went back with a loud voice glorifying God, and he fell on his face before his feet giving thanks, and this was a Samaritan. And Jesus answering, said, were not ten made clean, and where are the nine, there is no one found to return to give glory to God but this stranger." (Luke xvii. 11.)

What do the holy Fathers say of the duty of manifesting gratitude to God?
That no favor from God ought to be received without the deepest sense of gratitude; gratitude in re-

turn for one favor is the surest way to receive a second. Gratitude is a part of Christian duty, it is a pleasing virtue and the characteristic of a good heart. And we read in the book of Wisdom, (xvi. 29,) "The hope of the unthankful shall melt away as the winter's ice, and shall run off as unprofitable water."

Relate the miracle of raising Lazarus to life?

"There was a certain man sick, named Lazarus, of Bethania, of the town of Mary, and Martha, her sister; (and Mary was she that anointed the Lord with ointment and wiped his feet with her hair, whose brother Lazarus was sick.) His sisters therefore sent to him, saying: Lord behold he whom thou lovest is sick. And Jesus hearing it, said to them: This sickness is not unto death, but for the glory of God, that the Son of God may be glorified by it."

What did Jesus then do?

"Now Jesus loved Martha and her sister Mary and Lazarus. When he had heard, therefore, that he was sick, he still remained in the same place two days. Then after that he saith to his disciples: Let us go into Judea again. The disciples say to him: Rabbi, the Jews but now sought to stone thee, and goest thou thither again?"

How did Jesus answer them?

"Jesus answered: Are there not twelve hours of the day? If a man walk in the day he stumbleth not, because he seeth the light of this world. These things he said, and after that he said to them; Lazarus, our friend sleepeth, but I go that I may awake him out of his sleep. His disciples therefore said: Lord if he sleep, he shall do well; but Jesus spoke of his death, and they thought that he spoke of the repose of sleep. Then therefore Jesus said to them plainly, Lazarus is dead; and I am glad for your sake that I was not there, that you may believe, but let us go to him."

What did Thomas say?

" Thomas, therefore, who is called Didymus, said to his fellow-disciples: Let us also go, that we may die with him. Jesus therefore came, and found that he had been four days already in the grave."

Where was Bethania?

" Now Bethania was near Jerusalem, about fifteen furlongs off. And many of the Jews were come to Martha and Mary to comfort them concerning their brother."

What is said of Martha and Mary?

" Martha, therefore, as soon as she heard that Jesus was come, went to meet him, but Mary sat at home. Martha therefore said to Jesus: Lord, if thou hadst been here, my brother had not died; but now, also, I know that whatsoever thou wilt ask of God, God will give it thee."

What was the remainder of the dialogue between Jesus and Martha?

"Jesus saith to her: Thy brother shall rise again. Martha saith to him: I know that he shall rise again in the resurrection at the last day. Jesus said to her, I am the resurrection and the life. He that believeth in me, although he be dead, shall live, and every one that liveth and believeth in me shall not die for ever. Believest thou this? She saith to him: Yea, Lord, I have believed that thou art Christ the Son of the living God, who art come into this world."

When she had said these things, what did Martha do?

"And when she had said these things, she went and called her sister Mary secretly, saying. The master is come and calleth for thee. She, as soon as she heard this, riseth quickly, and cometh to him; for Jesus was not yet come into the town, but he was still in that place where Martha had met him."

What is said of the Jews?
"The Jews, therefore, who were with her in the house and comforted her, when they saw Mary that she rose up speedily, and went out, followed her, saying: She goeth to the grave to weep there."

What is said of Mary?
"When Mary, therefore, was come where Jesus was, seeing him, she fell down at his feet, and saith to him: Lord, if thou hadst been here, my brother had not died."

What did Jesus do?
"Jesus, therefore, when he saw her weeping, and the Jews that were come with her, weeping, groaned in the spirit, and troubled himself, and said: Where have you laid him? They said to him: Lord, come and see; and Jesus wept."

What did the Jews say?
"The Jews therefore said: Behold how he loved him; but some of them said; Could not he that opened the eyes of the man born blind have caused that this man should not die?"

What followed?
"Jesus, therefore, again groaning in himself, cometh to the sepulchre. Now it was a cave, and a stone was laid over it. Jesus saith: Take away the stone Martha, the sister of him that was dead, saith to him, Lord, by this time he stinketh, for he is now of four days. Jesus saith to her: Did not I say to thee that if thou believe, thou shalt see the glory of God. They, took, therefore, the stone away, and Jesus lifting up his eyes, said: Father, I give thee thanks that thou hast heard me; and I knew that thou hearest me always, but because of the people who stand about have I said it, that they may believe that thou hast sent me. When he had said these

things, he cried with a loud voice: Lazarus, come forth."

What happened when he had repeated these words?
"And presently he that had been dead came forth; bound feet and hands, with winding bands, and his face was bound about with a napkin. Jesus said to them: Loose him and let him go. Many, therefore, of the Jews, who were come to Mary and Martha, and had seen the things that Jesus did, believed in him." (John xi.)

Did these great miracles seem to allay the animosity of the Jews against our Divine Lord, and make them relent in their evil designs?
No; on the contrary, they more earnestly sought his death, and Caiphas, the High Priest of that year, advised his being put to death.

CHAPTER XXXIII.

ST. MARY MAGDALEN'S FORGIVENESS PRONOUNCED BY OUR LORD.

Relate the circumstances at length that are alluded to above of Mary's anointing our Lord's feet?
Our Lord being invited to the house of a Pharisee was at table with him when a woman, a sinner, hearing it, came in, bringing an alabaster box of precious ointment, and standing behind at his feet, she washed them with her tears, and wiped them with her hair, and anointed them with the ointment, the perfume of which filled the whole house.

What is said of the Pharisee?
On seeing this, the Pharisee, who had invited him, said within himself: If this man were a prophet, he would know surely who, and what kind of woman this is.

How did our Lord reply?
Our Lord replying to this thought, said: Simon, 1

have somewhat to say to thee. A certain creditor had two debtors, the one owed five hundred pence, and the other fifty; and whereas, they had not wherewith to pay, he forgave them both; which, therefore, of the two loveth him most?

What did Simon answer?
Simon replied that he supposed it was he to whom most was forgiven.

What did our Lord tell him?
Our Lord told him he had answered correctly, and turning to the woman, he said to Simon: Dost thou see this woman? I entered into thy house. Thou gavest me no water for my feet; but she with tears hath washed my feet, and with her hair hath wiped them. Thou gavest me no kiss, but she, since she came in, hath not ceased to kiss my feet. My head with oil thou didst not anoint, but she with ointment hath anointed my feet. Wherefore I say to thee many sins are forgiven her, because she hath loved much; but to whom less is forgiven, he loveth less. And he said to her: Thy sins are forgiven thee." (Luke vii.)

What did Judas Iscariot say when he saw Mary Magdalen pour out the precious ointment on our Lord's feet?
Why was this waste of the ointment? Why was it not sold for three hundred pence, and given to the poor? which he said not, because he cared for the poor, but because he carried the purse, and was a thief. But our Lord himself undertook her defence, desiring her not to be molested, saying the poor were always among them, and when they wished they might serve them; but him they had not always. He concluded by foretelling that wherever the gospel should be preached in the whole world, what she had done should be told in memory of her.

What did those at table say within themselves when they heard our Lord pronounce St. Mary Magdalen's forgiveness?
"Who is this that forgiveth sins also?"

What miracle did our Lord perform on a former occasion, to prove, to those who questioned it, that he had power to forgive sin?
He cured a man afflicted with palsy, who was let down in a bed through the roof of the house in which he was giving instructions, for those who carried the patient could not get in at the door on account of the crowd. When our Lord saw their faith, he said, "Man, thy sins are forgiven thee."

What did the Scribes think?
The Scribes and Pharisees hearing these words, began to think: "Who is this that speaketh blasphemies? Who can forgive sins but God alone?"

What did our Lord reply and do?
Our Lord answering their thoughts, replied: "Which is easier to say, thy sins are forgiven thee; or to say, arise and walk. But that you may know that the Son of Man hath power on earth to forgive sins, (He saith to the sick of the palsy,) I say to thee, arise, take up thy bed, and go into thy house." And immediately rising up before them, he took up the bed on which he lay, and went away to his own house glorifying God.

What did our Lord say, when, notwithstanding the many miracles he wrought, the Jews persisted in their unbelief, and even sought to take his life when he declared himself to be the Son of God?
That their obstinacy and hatred were inexcusable, inasmuch as they had not only heard his doctrine, but witnessed his miracles, the like of which had never been done before. And that they had fulfilled the prophecy, "They hated me without cause." (Ps. xxiv. 19.)

CHAPTER XXXIV.

ON THE SIGNS THAT ARE TO PRECEDE THE END OF THE WORLD.

What did our Lord say would be the signs of the approaching end of the world?
That there would be wars and rumors of wars, that nation would rise against nation, and kingdom against kingdom, and in many places earthquakes and famines, and such tribulation as there was not the like from the beginning of the world; after which, the sun and moon would be darkened, and the stars fall from heaven.

In what way did our Lord say he would come at the end of the world?
"Then shall appear the sign of the Son of Man in heaven, and then shall all tribes of the earth mourn, and they shall see the Son of Man coming in the clouds of heaven with much power and majesty. And he shall send his angels with a trumpet and a great voice, and they shall gather together his elect from the four winds, from the farthest parts of the heavens to the utmost bounds of them." (Matt. xxiv. 30, 31.)

What did our Lord foretell would be the employment of the people at the end of the world?
The same as at the time of the Deluge.

In what manner did our Lord foretell he would address the just on his second coming?
"Come, ye blessed of my father, possess the kingdom prepared for you from the foundation of the world; for I was hungry, and you gave me to eat; I was thirsty, and you gave me to drink; I was a stranger and you took me in; naked and you covered me; sick and you visited me; I was in prison and you came to me.

What then will the just answer?
"Then shall the just answer, saying: Lord when did we see thee hungry and fed thee; thirsty, and gave thee drink: and when did we see thee a stranger and took thee in; or naked and covered thee; or when did we see thee sick or in prison and came to thee? And the king answering shall say to them: Amen I say to you, as long as you did it to one of these my least brethren, you did it to me."

What will our Lord say to the wicked at the last day?
"Depart from me ye cursed into everlasting fire which was prepared for the devil and his angels. For I was hungry and you gave me not to eat; I was thirsty and you gave me not to drink; I was a stranger and you took me not in; naked and you covered me not; sick and in prison and you did not visit me.

What shall they answer?
"Then they also shall answer him, saying, Lord when did we see thee hungry or thirsty, or a stranger, or naked, or sick, or in prison, and did not minister to thee? Then he shall answer them saying, Amen I say to you, as long as you did it not to one of these least, neither did you do it to me." (Matt. xxv.)

CHAPTER XXXV.

OUR LORD FORETELLS HIS APPROACHING PASSION.—HIS REPLY WHEN CALLED ON FOR A SIGN SIMILAR TO THE MANNA.

What did our Lord foretell his disciples when he had finished his instructions concerning their preparation for the last judgment?
He said to them, "You know that after two days shall be the Pasch, and the Son of Man shall be delivered up to be crucified." (Matt. xxvi. 2.

In what manner did our Lord enter Jerusalem a few days previous to the Pasch?
Riding on a young ass, on which his disciples had laid their garments: many also spread their garments in the way, and others cut down boughs from the trees; and all with one voice proclaimed: "Hosanna to the Son of David, blessed is he that cometh in the name of the Lord; Hosanna in the highest."

What prophecy was fulfilled by our Lord's entering Jerusalem in that manner?
That of Zacharias: "*Rejoice greatly O daughter of Sion; shout for joy O daughter of Jerusalem, Behold thy King will come to thee, the Just and Saviour, he is poor, and riding upon an ass, and upon a colt, the foal of an ass.*" (Zach. ix. 9.)

On what day does the Church celebrate this triumphant entry of our Lord into Jerusalem?
On Palm Sunday, when branches of palms or other evergreens are blessed and distributed among the faithful, who hold them in their hands during the reading of the Passion on that day, in commemoration of the event.

Did the Jews long retain the sentiments they expressed on the day our Lord entered Jerusalem amidst their acclamations?
No, in a few days after, they joined the chief priests and ancients in demanding of Pilate to put him to death; and to overrule Pilate's objection to condemn a just person, cried out, "His blood be upon us and upon our children."

How did the chief priests and ancients get our Lord into their power?
He was betrayed to them for thirty pieces of silver by Judas Iscariot, one of the twelve apostles. The chief priests had long sought his death, but feared the people to arrest him publicly, and therefore gladly availed themselves of the treachery of Judas.

What did our Lord reply when the Jews said to him. What sign dost thou show that we may see and may believe thee; what dost thou work; our fathers did eat manna in the desert, as it is written, he gave them bread from heaven to eat?
He replied: "Amen, amen I say to you, Moses gave you not bread from heaven, but my father giveth you the true bread from heaven: for the bread of God is that which cometh down from heaven, and giveth life to the world.........I am the bread of life, he that cometh to me shall not hunger, and he that believeth in me shall never thirst..........And this is the will of my father that sent me, that every one who seeth the Son, and believeth in him, may have life everlasting, and I will raise him up in the last day." (John vi. 32.)

What part of this did the Jews murmur at?
At his saying, "I am the living bread which came down from heaven."

What did our Lord answer to their murmurs?
He repeated what he had said, adding, "If any man eat of this bread he shall live for ever; and the bread that I will give is my flesh for the life of the world."

What fresh objection did the Jews raise?
They said, "How can this man give us his flesh to eat."

What did our Lord reply to that?
"Amen, amen I say unto you, except you eat the flesh of the Son of Man and drink his blood you shall not have life in you; he that eateth my flesh and drinketh my blood hath everlasting life, and I will raise him up in the last day; for my flesh is meat indeed, and my blood is drink indeed; he that eateth my flesh and drinketh my blood, abideth in me and I in him. As the living Father hath sent me, and I live by the father, so he that eateth me,

the same also shall live by me. This is the bread that came down from heaven; not as your fathers did eat manna, and are dead. He that eateth this bread shall live for ever." (John vi. 54 to 59.)

What did our Lord say to his disciples when he found that many of them also murmured at what he said?

"Doth this scandalize you; if then you see the Son of Man ascend up where he was before? It is the spirit that quickeneth; the flesh profiteth nothing; the words that I have spoken to you are spirit and life; but there are some of you that believe not. For Jesus knew from the beginning who they were that did not believe, and who he was that would betray him. And he said, therefore did I say to you that no man can come to me unless it be given him by my father."

What effect had these words of our Lord on his disciples?
Many of them deserted him.

What did our Lord say to the twelve when he saw the others leave him?

"Will you also go away?" to which Simon Peter replied, "Lord to whom shall we go? Thou hast the words of eternal life; and we have believed and have known that thou art the Christ the Son of God." (John vi. 68 to 70.)

CHAPTER XXXVI.

OUR LORD DIRECTS HIS APOSTLES TO PREPARE THE PASCH.—HE INSTITUTES THE BLESSED SACRAMENT.

What directions did our Lord give his disciples about preparing the Pasch?
He desired Peter and John to go into the city, and follow a man whom they should meet carrying a

pitcher of water, and ask the master of the house into which he should enter for a room in which to prepare the Pasch, telling them he would show them a large dining-room furnished. They did as our Lord directed, and found every thing as he had said, and made ready the Pasch, to which he with the twelve apostles came at the appointed hour in the evening.

What did our Lord say to his apostles when they were about to eat the Pasch?
"With desire, I have desired to eat this Pasch with you before I suffer, for I say to you that from this time I will not eat it, till it be fulfilled in the kingdom of God."

What remarkable act of humility did our Lord perform on that occasion?
He arose from table, laid aside his garments, and having girded himself with a towel, poured water into a basin and washed the feet of his apostles.

What did St. Peter say when he saw his Divine Master approach to wash his feet?
"Lord dost thou wash my feet? Thou shalt never wash my feet." But on our Lord's saying: "If I wash thee not thou shalt have no part with me." St. Peter replied: "Lord, not only my feet, but also my hands and my head."

What did our Lord say when he sat down to table again after washing his disciples' feet?
"Know ye what I have done to you? You call me Master and Lord, and you say well for so I am: if then I being your Lord and Master have washed your feet, you ought also to wash one another's feet; for I have given you an example, that as I have done to you so you do also."

What did our Lord foretell his apostles on that occasion as a further proof of his being the Messias?
That one of them was about to betray him; and the

Scripture would be fulfilled which says: "*He that eateth bread with me shall lift up his heel against me.* The Son of Man indeed goeth as it is written of him; but wo to that man by whom the Son of Man shall be betrayed; it were better for him if that man had not been born."

What did the apostles say?
Being very much troubled each asked, "Is it I, Lord?" And even Judas, who betrayed him, said: "Is it I, Rabbi?" To whom our Lord replied: "Thou hast said it."

What did our Lord when he and his apostles had eaten the Pasch and fully accomplished the ceremonies prescribed by the old law?
"Taking bread he gave thanks, and brake; and gave to them, saying, This is my body which is given for you, do this for a commemoration of me. In like manner the chalice also, after he had supped, saying: This is the chalice, the new testament in my blood which shall be shed for you."

Does any other apostle allude to the Last Supper of our Lord?
Yes; St Paul, in his First Epistle to the Corinthians, eleventh chapter, says: "I have received of the Lord that which also I have delivered unto you, that the Lord Jesus the same night in which he was betrayed took bread, and giving thanks, broke and said: Take ye and eat, this is my body which shall be delivered for you; this do for the commemoration of me. In like manner also the chalice, after he had supped, saying: This chalice is the new testament in my blood; this do ye as often as you shall drink for the commemoration of me. For as often as you shall eat this bread and drink the chalice you shall show the death of the Lord until he come. Therefore whosoever shall eat this bread or drink the chalice of the Lord unworthily, shall be guilty of the body

and of the blood of the Lord. But let a man prove himself, and so let him eat of that bread and drink of the chalice. For he that eateth and drinketh unworthily, eateth and drinketh judgment to himself not discerning the body of the Lord."

What commandment did our Lord give his apostles, and by pre-eminence call his own, when he had instituted the blessed Eucharist?
To love one another as he had loved them. He on that occasion foretold them the sufferings they should meet for his sake, exhorted them to constancy, and comforted them in the grief they felt at hearing he was soon to be taken from them, by telling them that he was going to prepare a place for them; as where he was they should be, and that he would send them the Paraclete, the Spirit of Truth, to instruct and guide them.

CHAPTER XXXVII.

OUR LORD'S AGONY IN THE GARDEN—THE TREACHERY OF JUDAS—ST. PETER'S DENIAL.

Whither did our Lord lead his disciples when he had finished his last instructions, and had prayed for them?
Across the brook Kedron to the garden of Gethsemani.

What did our Lord say to his disciples while on their way to Gethsemani?
"All you shall be scandalized in me this night; for it is written: *I will strike the shepherd, and the sheep of the flock shall be dispersed.* But after I shall be risen again, I will go before you into Galilee."

What did St. Peter reply?
"Although all shall be scandalized in thee, I will

never be scandalized; yea, though I should die with thee, I will not deny thee."

What did our Lord say to St. Peter?
"Amen, I say to thee that in this night before the cock crow, thou wilt deny me thrice."

What did our Lord when he reached Gethsemani?
Leaving the disciples at some distance, except Peter, James, and John, formerly witnesses of his Transfiguration, now chosen to witness his agony; he told them that his soul was sorrowful even unto death, and desired them to stay and watch with him. Then going forward a little and falling on his face, he prayed, saying: "My father, if it be possible, let this chalice pass from me; nevertheless not as I will but as thou wilt."

When our Lord returned to his three chosen disciples, how did he find them?
He found them asleep, and said to Peter: "What, could you not watch one hour with me? Watch ye and pray, that ye enter not into temptation; the spirit, indeed is willing, but the flesh is weak."

Did they watch during the remainder of the time?
No; for when our Lord returned to them during his prayer a second and third time they were also asleep.

How was our Lord affected during his prayer in the garden?
His mental suffering was so intense, that it produced a bloody sweat, which trickled down over his body in great drops to the ground; during it an angel from heaven came to comfort him.

What occurred at the close of our Lord's prayer and agony in the garden?
Judas, one of the twelve, came, accompanied by an armed multitude sent by the chief priests and ancients to apprehend our Lord. And lest he might escape in the darkness, or some one else be apprehended in mistake, Judas had given them a sign, that the

person whom he should kiss was he, and immediately going to our Lord, he said: "Hail Rabbi," and kissed him.

Did our Lord resent the treachery and reproach Judas for it?
No: he meekly said: Friend, whereto art thou come.... Judas, dost thou betray the Son of Man with a kiss?

How did the rest of the disciples act?
At first they made a faint resistance, and St. Peter, drawing a sword, cut off the right ear of Malchus, servant to the high priest; but our Lord desired them to desist, and touching the servant's ear, healed it. Then the disciples leaving him all fled away, and our Lord was led prisoner to the high priest's house, where the ancients were assembled, determined to condemn him.

Did any of the disciples follow our Lord to the high priest's?
Yes; one whose name is not mentioned, and St. Peter, who followed at a distance, and entering, stood with the officers and servants at a fire, waiting the result of the trial.

What occurred whilst St. Peter was at the fire?
The portress accused him of having been with our Lord; but St. Peter denied it, saying: "Woman, I know him not." A little while after, another repeated the charge, and again St. Peter denied. About an hour after, some others affirmed the same, and amongst them a kinsman of Malchus; but St. Peter repeated the denial, and immediately the cock crew: then remembering the word our Lord had spoken: "Before the cock crow, thou wilt deny me thrice." He went out and wept bitterly.

CHAPTER XXXVIII.

CHRIST BEFORE THE HIGH PRIEST AND COUNCIL.—THE DESPAIR OF JUDAS.

How did the High Priest and council treat our Lord?
To give some show of justice to their proceedings, they summoned a great many witnesses to give testimony against him; but their evidence was so contradictory, that the judges, though anxious, could not condemn him. At length the High Priest observing that our Lord maintained profound silence, rising up, said: "I adjure thee, by the living God, that thou tell us if thou be the Christ the Son of God."

How did our Lord answer, and what did the High Priest say?
Our Lord replied in the affirmative, adding: "Hereafter you shall see the Son of Man sitting on the right hand of the power of God, and coming in the clouds of heaven." Then the High Priest rent his garments, saying, "He hath blasphemed, what further need have we of witnesses? Behold now you have heard the blasphemy. What think you?" they answered, "He is guilty of death."

How did the attendants then treat our Lord?
Most injuriously and cruelly. They blindfolded and buffeted him. Some spat in his face, and others struck him in the face, saying, "Prophesy unto us, O Christ, who is he that struck thee?" Which cruel mockery it is supposed they continued until morning, when the High Priest and ancients re-assembled, and delivered our Lord to the Roman governor to be executed.

Why did they not put him to death themselves, as they were so desirous of it?
The death prescribed by the Jewish law was by

stoning; and it would appear that power over life was no longer possessed by the Jewish nation, for when the priests and ancients accused our Lord to Pilate, he desired them to judge him according to their law, to which they replied: "It is not lawful for us to put any man to death."

What does St. John add, &c.?
And St. John adds, "That the word of Jesus might be fulfilled, which he said signifying what death he should die." For our Lord had foretold his disciples that he would be betrayed to the chief priests who would condemn him to death, and deliver him to the gentiles to be mocked and scourged and crucified.

How did Judas act when he found that the chief priests had condemned our Lord and delivered him to Pontius Pilate?
Full of remorse, he brought back the thirty pieces of silver, saying to the chief priests and ancients: "I have sinned in betraying innocent blood." But these unfeeling wicked men replying: "What is that to us, look thou to it." The unfortunate Judas went and hanged himself in despair.

What use did the chief priests make of the thirty pieces of silver which Judas returned?
They bought with them the potter's field to be a burying place for strangers, for which reason it was called Haceldama, that is, the field of blood. Then was the prophecy fulfilled which says, "They took the thirty pieces of silver," &c.

CHAPTER XXXIX.

CHRIST IS DELIVERED TO PILATE, WHO CONDEMNS HIM TO BE CRUCIFIED.

How did our Lord act while the chief priests and ancients clamorously accused him to Pilate?
He maintained a profound silence, not saying so

much as one word to clear himself of any of the false imputations they alleged, fulfilling that of the prophet: "He shall be led as a sheep to the slaughter, and shall be dumb as a lamb before his shearer, and he shall not open his mouth."

Did Pilate make any effort to rescue our Divine Lord?
He did, but he acted so weakly and irresolutely, that he only increased our Lord's sufferings. Seeing the inveterate malice of our Lord's enemies, and their inability to prove anything against him, he expostulated, saying he found no cause in him, and that he would chastise him, and let him go, particularly as Herod, to whom he had sent our Lord, had not condemned, but only mocked and derided him.

What did Pilate order?
Pilate accordingly ordered him to be scourged, which was most cruelly done, and the soldiers adding insult to cruelty, platted a crown of thorns, which they pressed on his sacred head, and clothing him in a purple garment as a mock king with a reed for his sceptre, scornfully bent the knee before him, saying: "Hail King of the Jews!"

What did the Jews say when Pilate brought forth our Lord to them in this sorrowful condition?
They cried out: "Crucify him, crucify him;" but Pilate being still anxious to save him, and knowing that the chief priests had delivered him up out of envy, proposed to the people to choose whether they would have him or Barrabbas, a notorious robber, released. They, at the instigation of the chief priests and elders, chose Barrabbas, and with loud voices demanded the crucifixion of our Lord. Their voices prevailed over Pilate, and he gave our Lord up to their will, whom they led forth with his cross laid on his mangled shoulders.

Whom did the Jews oblige to assist our Lord in carrying his cross?
Simon of Cyrene, father of Alexander and Rufus, who happened at the time to be coming from the country.

Were any malefactors crucified with our Lord?
Yes, two thieves, who were placed one at each side, by which the prophecy was fulfilled: "He was reputed with the wicked."

What inscription did Pilate place on our Lord's cross?
"Jesus of Nazareth, King of the Jews." It was written in Hebrew, Greek and Latin; and gave offence to the chief priests, who expostulated with Pilate, but could not induce him to alter it.

How long did our Lord hang on the cross before he expired?
Three hours, during which his blessed mother and beloved disciple stood by, sorrowfully witnessing his sufferings, and listening to the scoffs and insults of the wicked multitude.

What did the soldiers with his clothes?
They divided them among them and cast lots for his coat, which was without seam; by which was fulfilled the prophecy: "*They divided my garments,*" &c.

CHAPTER XL.

CHRIST'S LAST WORDS AND DEATH.

Did our Lord speak during his three hours' agony on the cross?
He did; the evangelists record his having spoken seven words.

Which was the first word?
It was a prayer for his enemies. "Father forgive them, for they know not what they do."

What was the second word?
The second was addressed to the penitent thief, who was crucified with him: "This day thou shalt be with me in Paradise."

Repeat the third word?
"Woman, behold thy Son;" which he addressed to his blessed mother on seeing her and his beloved disciple standing by his cross; thus recommending us all in the person of St. John to her maternal solitude. Then addressing his beloved disciple, he said: "Behold thy mother;" and he from that hour took her to his own home.

What was the fourth word?
"Eloi, Eloi, lamma sabacthani," the interpretation of which is, "My God, my God, why hast thou forsaken me?" This is a quotation from the Twenty-first Psalm, and if the Jews even then reflected, they would see that they were fulfilling what was foretold in that Psalm. But those who were present imagining that our Lord invoked Elias, said: "Stay, let us see if Elias will come to him."

What was the fifth word?
"I thirst;" by which he proclaimed not only his corporal thirst, but his spiritual thirst for the salvation of souls, yet little relief was offered him in either; for the first, he was presented with vinegar and gall; and for the second, notwithstanding all his sufferings, how many live at variance with his divine maxims.

What did our Lord say when he had tasted the vinegar?
"It is consummated," for by it was fulfilled the prophecy, "In my thirst they gave me vinegar," &c., which was the immediate prelude to his death.

What were our Divine Lord's last words?
"Father into thy hands I commend my spirit," which

having said in a loud voice, bowing his sacred head, he gave up the Ghost.

On what day does the Church commemorate the death of our Divine Lord ?
On Good Friday, when the churches are hung in mourning.

Why do you call that day good on which Christ suffered such a painful and ignominious death ?
Because on that day, by dying on the cross, he showed the excess of his love and purchased every blessing for us.

Did any phenomena occur at the death of Christ ?
There was darkness over the earth from the sixth to the ninth hour: at the ninth hour, when our Lord expired, the veil of the temple was rent from the top to the bottom; the earth trembled, and many of the dead arose.

What did the centurion and those who were with him say, when they witnessed the earthquake and the things that were done ?
They were greatly terrified and said: "Indeed this was the Son of God."

Did the malefactors crucified with our Lord expire as soon as he?
No; for which reason their legs were broken, as the Jews objected to their remaining on the cross on the Sabbath; but when they saw that our Lord was already dead, they did not break his legs, but a soldier pierced his side with a spear, and blood and water issued from the wound.

What prophecies were fulfilled by this?
One that said, "You shall not break a bone of him;" and another: "They shall look on him whom they have pierced"

CHAPTER XLI

OUR LORD'S BURIAL AND RESURRECTION.

Who took charge of our Lord's burial?
Joseph of Arimathea, assisted by Nicodemus, who brought a mixture of myrrh and aloes, about a hundred pounds weight, which they wrapped with our Lord's body in fine linen.

Where did they bury our Lord?
In a new sepulchre belonging to Joseph of Arimathea, in which no one had ever been laid. It was hewed out of a rock, and was in a garden in the vicinity.

What request did the chief priests and Pharisees make to Pilate when our Lord was buried?
To have the sepulchre guarded until the third day, lest the disciples should steal the body, and then pretend that our Lord had risen according to his prediction.

Did Pilate grant this request?
He did, giving them a guard and full authority to take all the precautions they should deem necessary. So they made the sepulchre sure, sealing the great stone in front, and setting guards.

What effect was produced by all these precautions of the chief priests?
They only made the miracle of the resurrection incontestible, and those who endeavored to conceal it inexcusable. For about dawn on the morning of the third day, an angel descending from heaven rolled back the stone and sat upon it. His countenance was as lightning, and his raiment as snow, and for fear of him the guards being struck with terror became as dead men.

What did the angel say to the women?

But turning to the holy women, among whom was Mary Magdalen, who had just arrived at the sepulchre with spices to anoint the body of our Lord, the angel said to them: "Fear not you, for I know that you seek Jesus who was crucified. He is not here, for he is risen as he said. Come and see the place where the Lord was laid; and going quickly, tell ye his disciples that he is risen, and behold he will go before you into Galilee. There you shall see him. Lo I have foretold it to you."

How did the guards act when they recovered from the first effects of their panic?
They fled away. Some of them went into the city, and told the chief priests all that had been done, who being assembled with the ancients consulted together, and gave the soldiers a great sum of money, desiring them to say, that while they slept, his disciples came by night and stole him away. To which the soldiers agreed, on condition that the priests and ancients should secure them from blame if the governor should hear the report and call them to account.

How did St. Mary Magdalen act, when she perceived the sepulchre open, and that our Lord was not there?
Apparently insensible and indifferent to the vision of the angel, as soon as she saw that our Lord was not in the sepulchre, she ran back to St. Peter and John, saying: "They have taken away the Lord out of the sepulchre, and we know not where they have laid him." Then returning immediately, she remained at the sepulchre weeping.

What did St. Peter and St. John on hearing St. Mary Magdalen's announcement?
They at once ran to the sepulchre, which St. John reached first, yet went not in; but St. Peter, on arriving, entered; St. John followed, and both saw the

linen cloths lying, and the napkin that had been about his head, not lying with the linen cloths but apart, and they believed, though the evangelist adds, "They as yet knew not the Scripture that he must rise again from the dead."

CHAPTER XLII.

APPARITION OF OUR DIVINE LORD TO ST. MARY MAGDALEN AND HIS APOSTLES ON THE DAY OF HIS RESURRECTION.

Did Saint Mary Magdalen remain at the sepulchre after St. Peter and St. John returned home?
She did, and while she was still weeping, she stooped down, and looking into the sepulchre saw two angels in white, sitting one at the head and one at the feet where the body of our Lord had been laid. They said to her: "Woman, why weepest thou?" She replied: "Because they have taken away my Lord, and I know not where they have laid him." Then turning back she saw our Lord himself standing but did not know him; he said to her, "Woman, why weepest thou, whom seekest thou?" She, thinking it was the gardener, said, "Sir, if thou hast taken him hence, tell me where thou hast laid him, and I will take him away." Jesus said to her, "Mary;" She immediately recognized him, and in a transport of joy, turning, said, "Rabboni," that is, Master.

What did our Lord say to her?
Our Lord said to her, "Do not touch me, for I am not yet ascended to my Father, but go to my brethren, and say to them, I ascend to my Father and to your Father, to my God and your God."

Did our Lord appear to the other holy women who had accompanied St. Mary Magdalen on her first visit to the sepulchre?
He did, when they were returning from the sepul-

chre with haste to relate to the disciples the happy
tidings communicated to them by the angel, our
Lord met them and addressed them: "All hail;"
they took hold of his feet and adored him. He bid
them fear nothing, and to tell his brethren they
should see him in Galilee.

*Did the apostles believe the report of Saint Mary
Magdalen and the other holy women when they asserted that they had seen our Lord, and repeated
what he had said to them?*
No; they considered what they said as only idle tales.

To whom did our Lord next appear?
To two disciples who were going from Jerusalem to
Emmaus, a town sixty furlongs distant. They were
conversing of our Lord and were joined by him on
the way, but their eyes being held they did not at
first know him.

Relate the particulars?
While the two disciples were talking of what had
been done to our Lord, he himself drew near and
asked: "What are these discourses that you hold
with one another as you walk and are sad." One
of them named Cleophas replied: "Art thou only a
stranger in Jerusalem and hast not known the things
that have been done there in these days?" To whom
he said: "What things?" They replied: "Concerning Jesus of Nazareth, who was a prophet mighty
in work and word before God and all the people, and
how our chief priests delivered him to be condemned
to death and crucified him. But we hoped that it
was he that should have redeemed Israel; and now
besides all this, to-day is the third day since these
things were done. Yea, and certain women also of
our company affrighted us, who, before it was light
were at the sepulchre, and not finding his body,
came, saying, that they had also seen a vision of
angels, who say that he is alive; and some of our

people went to the sepulchre, and found it so as the women had said, but him they found not."

What then did he say to them?
Then he said to them: "O, foolish, and slow of heart, to believe in all things which the prophets have spoken. Ought not Christ to have suffered these things, and so to enter into his glory?" And beginning at Moses and all the prophets, he expounded to them in all the Scriptures the things that were concerning him. And they drew nigh to the town whither they were going, and he made as though he would go further, but they constrained him, saying: Stay with us, because it is towards evening, and the day is now far spent; and he went in with them.

What came to pass while he was at table?
And it came to pass whilst he was at table with them, he took bread and blessed and brake and gave to them. And their eyes were opened, and they knew him, and he vanished out of their sight. And they said one to the other: Was not our heart burning within us whilst he spoke in the way and opened to us the Scriptures? And rising up the same hour, they went back to Jerusalem, and they found the eleven gathered together, and those that were with them, saying: The Lord is risen, indeed, and hath appeared to Simon. (Luke xxiv.)

What other appearance of our Lord is recorded to have taken place on the day of the Resurrection?
On the evening of the day of the Resurrection, while the disciples were assembled together conversing on the various reports they had heard of the resurrection, and listening to the last which was related by the two disciples from Emmaus, our Lord stood in the midst, and said to them: "Peace be to you; it is I, fear not;" but they being troubled and frightened, thought they saw a spirit, and he said to them:

"Why are you troubled, and why do thoughts arise in your hearts? See my hands and my feet that it is I myself; handle and see, for a spirit hath not flesh and bones as you see me to have." And when he had said this, he showed them his hands and feet; but while they yet believed not, and wondered for joy, he said: "Have you here anything to eat?" and they offered him a piece of broiled fish and a honeycomb; and when he had eaten before them, taking the remains, he gave to them.

What did our Lord say to his disciples on this occasion?

He reminded them of what he had before told them, that all things should be fulfilled which were written in the law of Moses, and in the prophets, and in the Psalms concerning him. Then he opened their understanding that they might understand the Scriptures, and he said to them: Thus it is written, and thus it behooved Christ to suffer, and to rise again from the dead the third day; and that penance and remission of sins should be preached in his name unto all nations, beginning at Jerusalem. (Luke xxiv.)

What did he again say to them?

He said to them again: "Peace be to you, as the Father hath sent me, I also send you:" when he had said this, he breathed on them and said: "Receive ye the Holy Ghost, whose sins you shall forgive they are forgiven them, and whose sins you shall retain, they are retained." (John xx. 21.)

CHAPTER XLIII.

OTHER APPARITIONS OF OUR DIVINE LORD.—HE GIVES CHARGE OF HIS FLOCK TO ST. PETER.—HIS ASCENSION INTO HEAVEN.

Were any of the disciples absent on this occasion?

Yes; Thomas, one of the twelve, was absent; and

being told by the rest that they had seen the Lord, he said he would not believe unless he saw in his hands the print of the nails, and put his finger into the place of the nails, and put his hand into his side.

Did our Divine Lord condescend to his disciple's weakness?

He did; on that day week the disciples being assembled and Thomas with them, our Lord came, the doors being shut, and stood in the midst, and said; "Peace be to you." Then turning to St. Thomas, he said: "Put in thy finger hither, and see my hands and bring hither thy hand and put it into my side, and be not faithless but believing:" Then St. Thomas said to him: "My Lord and my God." Our Lord replied: "Because thou hast seen me, Thomas, thou hast believed; blessed are they that have not seen and have believed."

When did our Lord next manifest himself to his disciples?

When they were on the sea of Tiberias, fishing; they had toiled the whole night and had caught nothing. In the morning our Lord accosted them from the shore, asking had they caught any thing. On their replying, no, he desired them to cast the net on the right side; they did so, and immediately the net was filled. St. John, who was of the party, seeing the draught of fishes, said to St. Peter: "It is the Lord;" on hearing which St. Peter threw himself into the sea and swam towards him: the other disciples followed in the ship dragging the net.

When they came ashore, what followed?

As soon as they came ashore they saw hot coals lying and a fish laid thereon and bread. Jesus said to them: "Bring hither of the fishes which you have now caught." St. Peter went and drew the net to land, full of great fishes, one hundred and fifty-three; and although there were so many the net did not break. Jesus said to them: "Come and dine;" and none of them durst ask him: "Who art Thou?" knowing that it was the Lord.

What did our Lord say to St. Peter when dinner was over?
"Simon, son of John, lovest thou me more than these?" He replied: "Yea, Lord, thou knowest that I love thee." Jesus said: "Feed my lambs." Again, he said: "Simon, son of John, lovest thou me?" St. Peter replied as before; and our Lord again said: "Feed my lambs." The third time our Lord asked the same question, at which St. Peter was troubled, and said: "Lord, thou knowest all things, thou knowest that I love thee." Our Lord said: "Feed my sheep." After which he signified to him by what death he should glorify God.

What did our Lord say to the eleven when they repaired to Galilee to meet him on the Mount according to his appointment?
All power is given to me in heaven and in earth. Going therefore, teach ye all nations, baptizing them in the name of the Father, and of the Son, and of the Holy Ghost, teaching them to observe all things whatsoever I have commanded you, and behold I am with you all days, even to the consummation of the world. (Matt. xxviii. 18.)

Did our Lord appear on any other occasion to his disciples before he ascended into heaven?
Yes: St. Paul relates that he appeared to more than five hundred brethren assembled together. (1 Cor. xv. 6.)

On what day does the Church commemorate the Resurrection of our Lord?
On Easter Sunday.

How long did our Lord remain on earth after his Resurrection?

Forty days, to show that he was truly risen from the dead, and to instruct his apostles?

At the end of the forty days whither did our Lord go?
He ascended from Mount Olivet with his body and soul into heaven.

CHAPTER XLIV.
SHORT ACCOUNT OF THE BOOKS OF HOLY SCRIPTURE.

What part of the Bible is called the New Testament, and why is it so called?
The New Testament, so called to distinguish it from the Old, which was compiled by Moses, the prophets, and other inspired writers before the coming of Christ, contains an account of the life of our Lord, the principal events of the first thirty years after his ascension, the epistles of some of the apostles, and the Revelations of St. John, or the Apocalypse.

What is that part called which contains an account of our Lord's life until his Ascensiom?
The Gospel, as also the four Gospels, because written by four evangelists, SS. Matthew, Mark, Luke, and John.

What is that part called which contains an account of the first thirty years of Christianity after our Lord's Ascension?
The Acts of the Apostles.

At what time after our Lord's Ascension did St. Matthew write his gospel?
About six or eight years after. St. Jerom says that he wrote it at the request of those Jews who had embraced Christianity. St. Epiphanius thinks that it was at the desire of the other apostles. He commences by tracing the genealogy of our Lord, according to the flesh, to Abraham, through the family of David and tribe of Juda.

When did St. Mark write his gospel?
About ten years after our Lord's Ascension; and it is generally thought at Rome, at the request of the Romans.

When did St. Luke write his gospel?
About twenty years after our Lord's Ascension. He wrote it in order to counteract the evil likely to arise from some fabulous histories of Christ which were at that time published. St. Luke also wrote the Acts of the Apostles about ten years later than his gospel.

When did St. John write his gospel?
About sixty-three years after our Lord's Ascension. Some of the ancient Fathers say that he wrote it at the earnest request of the brethren, to confute those who denied the Divinity of Christ and his pre-existence before his temporal birth. St. John also wrote three epistles and the Apocalypse.

How are the evangelists considered to be prefigured?
By the four mystical creatures described in the vision of Ezekiel, the same are also described in the Revelations of St. John. St. Augustine makes the lion the symbol of St. Matthew, who explains the royal dignity of Christ. Others ascribe it to St. Mark, and the man is supposed to be the symbol of St. Matthew, who begins his gospel with Christ's human generation. The calf typifies St. Luke, who begins his gospel with the mention of the priesthood, the calf being a victim of sacrifice; and the eagle, St. John, who soars up to the contemplation of the eternal generation of the Word

CHAPTER XLV.

ACTS OF THE APOSTLES.

THE DESCENT OF THE HOLY CROSS.

What does this book treat of?
Of the principal events in the first thirty years after our Lord's Ascension.

What were they?
The election of Matthias. The descent of the Holy Ghost; the assembling and acts of the first council. The increase of the Church by means of the preaching of St. Peter and St. Paul; an account of the conversion of the latter, the martyrdom of St. Stephen, and the sufferings of some of the early Christians under the persecutions that were raised.

How did the apostles act after our Lord's Ascension?
They retired to the upper part of a house in Jerusalem, where, in company with the Mother of our Lord and others of the faithful they persevered in prayer, expecting the fulfilment of our Lord's promise to send the Holy Ghost; and in the meantime they filled the place vacated by the fall of Judas.

Who proposed to them to fill the vacancy?
St. Peter; and they selected two, Joseph, surnamed Justus, and Matthias, and praying that God would manifest his will, they gave them lots; and the lot falling on Matthias, he was numbered with the eleven apostles.

How long after the ascension of our Lord did the Holy Ghost descend on the apostles?
Ten days, and fifty after his Resurrection. The feast is kept by the Church on Whit-Sunday, otherwise called Pentecost

Describe the coming of the Holy Ghost?
" When the days of the Pentecost were accomplished,

they were all together in one place, and suddenly there came a sound from heaven as of a mighty wind coming, and it filled the whole house where they were sitting. And there appeared to them parted tongues as it were of fire, and it sat upon every one of them; and they were all filled with the Holy Ghost, and they began to speak with divers tongues according as the Holy Ghost gave them to speak." (Acts ii. 1.)

What did the people, at that time assembled in Jerusalem, from various nations, say, when they heard the apostles speaking different languages?
Some were astonished, and inquired into the meaning; others mocked, saying they were intoxicated.

Which of the apostles explained the matter to the multitudes?
St. Peter, who informed them that what they then witnessed was what the prophet Joel had foretold: and having quoted the words of the prophecy, he took occasion to preach the coming, death, and Resurrection of our Lord Jesus Christ, and so efficaciously exhorted and admonished them, that about three thousand were converted on the spot and baptized.

CHAPTER XLVI.

MANNERS OF THE FIRST CHRISTIANS AND MIRACLES PERFORMED BY THE APOSTLES.

What kind of life did the early Christians lead?
One of great piety and simplicity; they had all things in common, those who had possessions and goods sold them, and laid the price at the feet of the apostles, who divided it according to the necessities of each.

What two persons unhappily yielded to temptation by pretending to lay the price of the fie they sold at the feet of the apostles like the rest, but fraudulently keeping back a part?

Ananias and his wife Saphira; the former came in first, and, being reprehended by St. Peter, fell down and died. In about three hours after, Saphira, not knowing what had passed, came in, and being questioned by St. Peter, made the same statement as her husband, on which reprehending her for her deceit, he told her that they who had carried out her husband, and who had only just returned from burying him, should also carry her out. Immediately she fell down and died, and they buried her by her husband.

Did the apostles perform great and frequent miracles?

They did. It was by miracles their divine mission was proved, and according to our Lord's promise, they performed as great as he did whilst on earth.

Relate some of them?

St. Peter and St. John going into the Temple by the gate which was called Beautiful, saw a man begging who was lame from his birth, and who used to be daily carried there to ask alms of those who went in. St. Peter looking at him said: "Silver and gold I have none; but what I have I give thee; in the name of Jesus Christ of Nazareth, arise and walk;" and taking him by the hand, he raised him. And the man immediately leaping up, went into the Temple with them, walking and leaping, and praising God.

What did St. Peter say to the multitudes that collected round him and St. John, wondering at the miracle that had been wrought?

That the lame man had been cured through faith, in the name of Jesus Christ, the Son of God, the author of life, whom they and their rulers had put to death, but whom God had raised from the dead. And quoting the prophets, he showed that what they had foretold had been done to Christ. He then earnestly exhorted them to sincere conversion, and great numbers believed.

How did the priests and the Sadducees act when they found the apostles preaching to the people?
They put them in prison for the night, and on the next morning brought them before the council, in which Annas, the High Priest, and Caiphas presided; for they were grieved that the apostles preached in Jesus the Resurrection from the dead, and all knew that they had been with him.

What answer did St. Peter make when called to account before the council?
"Ye princes of the people and ancients hear, if we this day are examined concerning the good deed done to the infirm man, by what means he hath been made whole. Be it known to you all, and to all the people of Israel, that by the name of our Lord Jesus Christ, of Nazareth, whom you crucified whom God hath raised from the dead, even by him, this man standeth here before you whole. This is, *the stone which was rejected by you the builders, which is become the head of the corner;* neither is there salvation in any other. For there is no other name under heaven given to men, whereby we must be saved."

How did the High Priest and council act on hearing St. Peter's defence?
They threatened him and St. John, commanding them to preach no more; but they did not inflict corporal punishment that time for fear of the people. However, not long after they scourged St. Peter, and the other apostles, threatening them and charging them to preach no more, for they were filled with envy at seeing the numerous and manifest miracles they wrought. Among the rest, one by which St. Peter raised to life a pious widow, named Tabitha

CHAPTER XLVII.

MARTYRDOM OF ST. STEPHEN.—ORDINATION OF THE SEVEN DEACONS.—MISSION OF ST. PHILIP.

Who were the first deacons?
Stephen, Philip, Prochorus, Nicanor, Timon, Parmenas, and Nicholas; seven in number, on whom, the apostles praying, imposed hands, and appointed to their office.

Who was the first martyr?
St. Stephen, the first of the seven deacons, a man of extraordinary holiness, and a performer of many and great miracles.

Why did the Jews put St. Stephen to death?
Because when he was dragged by them before the council, he steadfastly maintained what he had before preached, that our Lord Jesus Christ is he whom all the prophets foretold. And as he continued to urge the subject, looking up to heaven he saw the glory of God, and Jesus standing at the right hand of God, which he announced to them, and immediately with one accord, running violently on him, they cast him out of the city and stoned him.

What did St. Stephen say whilst they stoned him?
"Lord Jesus receive my spirit," and falling on his knees he cried with a loud voice, "Lord lay not this sin to their charge."

Is there any person in particular named as being present at, and consenting to St. Stephen's death?
Yes, Saul, a native of Tarsus, then a furious persecutor of the Church, afterwards a zealous apostle.

What was the consequence of the persecution that was raised after St. Peter's martyrdom?
That the faithful were dispersed through the neighboring provinces, and thus made the truth more widely known.

To what part did St. Philip, the second of the deacons go?

To Samaria, were he converted great numbers, and among them a famous magician, named Simon, who had long misled the people; but being baptized, kept close to Philip, wondering at the great miracles he performed. Yet it would appear that his assiduity proceeded from a worldly motive, for when St. Peter and St. John arrived from Jerusalem to confirm the faithful, Simon seeing that the Holy Ghost was conferred by the imposition of the hands of the apostles (for the communication of the Holy Ghost, in confirmation, was at that time often accompanied by miraculous manifestations) offered money to obtain the same power; for which St. Peter reprchended him.

What person of distinction was St. Philip the instrument in converting?

The treasurer of Candace, queen of Ethiopia, a person of great piety, who, being on his return from worshipping in the Temple of Jerusalem, was sitting in his chariot and reading the prophet Isaiah. When near Gaza, the Spirit commanded Philip to go to him. On doing so, he heard him read the following passage: "He was led as a sheep to the slaughter, and like a lamb without voice before his shearer, so openeth he not his mouth. In humility his judgment was taken away. His generation who shall declare, for his life shall be taken from the earth"

What did St. Philip ask?

St. Philip asked, did he understand what he read; the treasurer replied that he could not, unless some one explained it, and he requested St. Philip to do so. During the explanation, his heart was so moved, that on reaching some water, he begged for and received baptism.

CHAPTER XLVIII.

CONVERSION OF ST. PAUL.—BAPTISM OF CORNELIUS.

In the meantime, how was Saul, he that assisted at St. Stephen's martyrdom, employed?
In persecuting the Church to the utmost of his power, and not content with doing so in Jerusalem, he asked letters of the High Priest and ancients to the synagogues in Damascus, that if he discovered any of the faithful there, he might bring them bound to Jerusalem.

What occurred on his way to Damascus when he had nearly reached the city?
A brilliant light suddenly shone round him and his companions, and our Lord called him, saying: "Saul, Saul, why persecutest thou me?" Trembling and astonished, Saul fell prostrate on the ground, and asked: "Who art thou, Lord?" Our Lord replied, "I am Jesus, whom thou persecutest." Saul humbly answered: "Lord, what wilt thou have me do?" "Arise, and go into the city," said our Lord, "and there it shall be told thee what thou must do."

What followed?
On which Saul arose, but being unable to see, was led by his companions into Damascus, where he remained three days and nights without food. After which, a holy man, named Ananias, was sent by God to restore his sight and baptize him. And to the astonishment of all, he who had come to persecute became an apostle, and preached Christianity in the synagogues.

How did the Jews act towards Saul, otherwise St. Paul, on his conversion?
They sought to kill him; but the faithful concealed him, and let him down by a basket by night from

the town wall, by which he escaped, and returned to Jerusalem

How did St. Paul act on reaching Jerusalem?
He thought to join the disciples, but they, not knowing of his conversion, shunned him, fearing that he was insincere, until Barnabas took him to the apostles, and related the circumstances of his conversion. From this time he appeared openly with them, and continued to preach to both Jews and gentiles to the end of his life, which he closed by martyrdom.

Who was the first gentile baptized?
Cornelius, a Roman centurion, residing in Cesarea, a good and charitable man, who with his whole family feared God, and gave great alms to the poor.

Relate the particulars of his conversion?
An angel entering his house, said to him: "Cornelius, thy prayers and thy alms are ascended for a memorial in the sight of God; and now send men to Joppa, and call hither one Simon, who is surnamed Peter. He lodgeth with one Simon, a tanner, whose house is by the sea-side. He will tell thee what thou must do."

What did Cornelius do?
Cornelius immediately did what the angel commanded; and when his messengers drew near Joppa, St. Peter also had a vision, in which he saw the heavens opened, and a great sheet let down, in which was a variety of living creatures; and he heard a voice desiring him to arise, kill, and eat; but he declined, saying, that he had never eaten anything common or unclean, to which the voice replied: "That which God hath cleansed, do not thou call common." This was repeated three times; after which, all were again taken up into heaven; and while St. Peter was pondering the meaning of the vision, the messengers from Cornelius arrived, whom the Spirit commanded him to accompany.

On his arrival in Cesarea, what did St. Peter find?

On St. Peter's arrival in Cesarea, whither he was accompanied by six of the brethren, he found Cornelius with his friends and relations assembled to hear the word of God. While he preached to them, the Holy Ghost descended on them, conferring the gift of tongues as on the apostles at the beginning, at which the disciples were astonished, but St. Peter remembering the word of our Lord: "John indeed baptized with water, but you shall be baptized with the Holy Ghost:" said: "Can any man forbid water that these should not be baptized who have received the Holy Ghost as well as we."

What fault did the Jewish converts in Jerusalem find with St. Peter's conduct on this occasion?

That he had gone into the house of a gentile and had eaten with him, for it was not allowed among the Jews to do so. But St. Peter justified himself alleging the vision he had, and also the descent of the Holy Ghost on Cornelius and his whole house, adding: "If then, God gave them the same grace as to us also who believed in the Lord Jesus Christ, who was I that could withstand God?" which answer satisfied them.

CHAPTER XLIX.

MIRACULOUS DELIVERANCE OF ST. PETER FROM PRISON PREACHING OF ST. PAUL.

Why did Herod imprison St. Peter?

To please the Jews who, he perceived, were gratified by his causing St. James, the brother of St. John, to be beheaded, and he intended also to execute St. Peter. But the night before the appointed day an angel entering the prison awoke St. Peter, who was sleeping amidst his guards, and desired him arise and follow him. He did so, for his fetters fell off but still he thought it was only a dream, until entering the city gate which opened of itself, and following on through one street the angel disappeared, when he came to himself, and returned thanks to God for his deliverance.

To what place did St. Peter go on his deliverance?
To the house of Mary, the mother of John and Mark, where many of the brethren were assembled in prayer. When he knocked, a maid, named Rhode, came to the gate, but, on hearing his voice, was so overjoyed that without waiting to open it, she ran back to announce his arrival. The disciples at first could not believe it but thought it was his angel; on being admitted, he related the manner of his miraculous deliverance, desired them to tell the rest of the brethren, for they had all been praying for him; and withdrew for the present to another place.

How did Herod act when he discovered that St. Peter had escaped?
After ineffectual inquiries and searches, he condemned the keepers of the prison to death.

How did Herod end his life?
He was eaten alive by worms, in punishment of his pride; for, on one occasion, being arrayed in royal robes and making an oration, the people cried out, "It is the voice of a god and not of a man;" at which Herod being elated did not give the honor to God, and immediately he was struck by an angel with that incurable and loathsome disease.

How was St. Paul engaged during these occurrences?
Being obliged to fly from Jerusalem, the brethren conveyed him safely to Tarsus, whence, at the request of St. Barnabas, he went to Antioch, where, by their united labors, they converted such multitudes that the disciples at Antioch were first named Christians.

Besides many other places, the two apostles went to Cyprus, where the proconsul Sergius Paulus embraced the faith. From this time, the apostle of the gentiles is no longer named Saul in holy Scripture, but Paul.

What remarkable person in the family of Sergius Paulus withstood the apostles, and endeavored to hinder the proconsul from embracing the faith?

A Jew, named Bariseus, otherwise Elymas, a famous magician; but St. Paul, rebuking him for his deceit, said: "Behold the hand of the Lord is upon thee, and thou shalt be blind, not seeing the sun for a time," upon which Elymas lost his sight, and had to be led about, and the proconsul seeing what was done became a convert.

What miracle did St. Paul perform at Lystra?

He cured a man who had been a cripple from his birth; on which the heathens fancying that the gods had come in human form, and that St. Barnabas was Jupiter, and St. Paul Mercury, because he was chief speaker, would have offered sacrifice to them, and could hardly be prevailed on to desist by all the apostles could say, assuring them that they were like themselves, mortal, but had come to announce to them the one only true God.

How did these very people treat St. Paul a few days after?

Being irritated against him by the slanders of some Jews, they stoned him, leaving off only when they thought he was dead; but when they had gone away, and the brethren only remained, he revived, and soon after, with Barnabas, went to preach the gospel in other places, without being deterred by the persecutions and contradictions he met with.

CHAPTER L.

COUNCIL AT JERUSALEM.—TRAVELS AND LABORS OF ST. PAUL.

When was the first council held, and why was it convened?
It was held at Jerusalem, and consisted of the apostles and ancients, who assembled to consider and decide on a subject of dispute raised by the Jewish converts, some of whom insisted that the gentile converts should be subjected to the observance of the ceremonial law of Moses. The council decided that the converts should not be made to observe the ceremonial, saying, that it appeared good to the Holy Ghost and to them so to decree, which decision was received with joy. This council was held in the year 51.

What countries were principally blessed by St. Paul's apostolic labors?
Several parts of Asia Minor and Greece, through which he travelled with indefatigable zeal from province to province, from one island to another, as the necessities of the infant church required, often at the risk of his life, and everywhere persecuted by the Jews.

For what were St. Paul and his holy companion Silas thrown into prison in Philippi?
Because St. Paul cast a pythonical spirit out of a young woman, her employers, who used to make money by her divining, accused him and Silas to the magistrates, who condemned them to be scourged and imprisoned. At midnight, while the holy prisoners were at their prayers, a sudden earthquake shook the prison, and set the doors open.

What is said of the jailor?
The jailor, seeing the prison open, and fearing to be

called to account for the escape of the prisoners, was going to kill himself, but St. Paul cried out to him that they were all there, and taking that occasion to preach the faith to him, the jailor and all his family embraced it on the spot.

What remarkable conversion did St. Paul effect at Athens?
That of St. Dionysius, the learned Areopagite, with some others. The people of Athens were at that time immersed in idolatry. Among the numerous altars raised to idols throughout their city, one was inscribed, "To the unknown God," from which St. Paul took occasion to instruct them in the knowledge of the one only true God.

What gave rise to a tumult at Ephesus while St. Paul preached there?
A silversmith, named Demetrius, who made a great deal of money by manufacturing little temples of Diana, fearing that his trade would be injured if the apostles were allowed to preach, collected some interested persons, and made a great clamor, until a considerable part of the inhabitants became excited, shouting, "Great is Diana of the Ephesians." At length the authorities succeeded in quelling the tumult and dispersing the people.

What great miracle did St. Paul perform at Troas?
He raised a young man named Eutychus to life, who had fallen from the window of an upper room, being overcome by sleep while St. Paul was preaching.

Note.—That is a member of the Areopagus, an assembly composed of the most learned of the Athenians.

Note.—There was a famous temple of Diana at Ephesus, which was much resorted to, and those who visited it, wishing to take with them a memorial, used to purchase little silver imitations which caused a considerable trade in these articles.

CHAPTER LI.

ST. PAUL'S RETURN TO JERUSALEM, HIS PERSECUTION BY THE JEWS.—HE APPEALS TO CÆSAR AND IS SENT TO ROME.

How was St. Paul received in Jerusalem when he returned after his great and successful apostolic labors?
With great joy by the faithful; but not many days after his arrival while he was in the Temple engaged in religious exercises, some Jews of Asia violently seized him, and dragging him out, raised such an uproar by false accusations, that a multitude collected, and would have killed the holy apostle but for the timely interference of the Roman tribune, who rescued him with much difficulty; and not being able to ascertain of what they accused him, some crying one thing, some another, he ordered the soldiers to take him bound to their quarters, while the people followed and demanded his death.

What request did St. Paul make to the tribune when he had reached a place of safety, being on the stairs leading to the castle?
That he would allow him to speak to the people; which being granted he addressed them in Hebrew, giving them an account of his birth at Tarsus, his education in Jerusalem, his former violence against the Christians, and conversion on the way to Damascus; adding that after it, while he was praying in the Temple in Jerusalem, our Lord appeared unto him and commissioned him to preach to the gentiles. They heard him attentively until he mentioned, "the gentiles," but then raised such a clamor, that the tribune ordered him to be brought in and to be tortured, to make him discover why they clamored, but

desisted when he understood that he was a Roman citizen.

How did the tribune act the next day?
He summoned the priests and all the council that he might know of what they accused the prisoner. But one part being Sadducees, the other Pharisees, St Paul took advantage of their disagreement and professed himself a Pharisee in his belief of the resurrection of the dead. They became immediately divided in their judgment for and against him, and both parties became so violent that the tribune ordered a guard of soldiers to bring St. Paul from among them, lest they might tear him in pieces.

Did the Jews still continue their persecution of St. Paul?
They did, and so implacable was their hatred, that forty of them entered into a conspiracy with the chief priests and ancients to murder him, but his nephew discovered the conspiracy, and gave information of it to the tribune, who sent him in care of a strong guard to Felix, the governor, residing at Cesarea.

How did Felix treat St. Paul?
He immediately dismissed his accusers, seeing that he was innocent, yet hoping to extort money from him kept him a prisoner two years, and left him so when he was succeeded by the new governor Festus, as he was anxious to please the Jews.

What request did the Jews make to the new governor?
To send St. Paul to Jerusalem, intending to assassinate him on the road; but the apostle knowing their intention, and seeing no other way to escape, appealed to Cæsar. Festus admitted the appeal, and promised to send him to Rome.

Note.—The Sadducees denied the resurrection of the body, and the existence of angels and spirits; the Pharisees admitted both.

What illustrious person visited Festus shortly after, and heard St. Paul in defence of the faith?
King Agrippa, who, though educated in Rome; was well read in the law and the prophets, which gave the holy apostle the more confidence in quoting them before him; and he so clearly proved that what was written in Moses and the prophets concerning Christ had been fulfilled, that Agrippa said: "In a little thou persuadest me to become a Christian;" to which St. Paul replied: "I would to God that both in a little, and in much, not only thou, but also all that hear me this day, should become such as I also am, except these bands."

What decision did the king and governor come to on hearing St. Paul's defence?
That he had done nothing deserving of punishment, and might be set at liberty only for his appeal to Cæsar.

What did Festus then do with St. Paul?
He gave him and other prisoners in charge to Julius, a centurion, with orders to conduct him to Rome. Accordingly, they were put on board a ship, but after a long and perilous voyage were shipwrecked on the coast of Malta. The ship was broken to pieces, but Almighty God preserved the lives of all on board (276 persons) for sake of his holy servant.

How did the inhabitants act towards the shipwrecked people?
Most kindly, particularly Publius, the principal person of the place, who entertained them for three days.

Note.—This Agrippa was son to Agrippa the Great, and grandson to Aristobulous, who was put to death by his father Herod, the Idumean. Agrippa the Great spent a long time in Rome, whither he went to bring charges against Herod the Tetrarch; but not succeeding, he remained and cultivated the friendship of some persons of rank, among the rest of Caius Caligula, who, when made, Cæsar conferred the tetrarchate of Philip on Agrippa with the title of king.

Did St. Paul perform any miracles during his stay in Malta?
He did: he cured Publius' father who was in fever, after which all the sick came to him and were cured. St. Paul was delayed three months in Malta, after which he arrived with little delay in Rome.

How was he treated at Rome?
With courtesy, as far as related to the hardships of imprisonment, for he was permitted to live in his own private lodging with only one guard, and there to instruct and preach; but he was kept a prisoner two years.

CHAPTER LII.

THE EPISTLES.

ST. PAUL'S EPISTLES TO THE ROMANS, CORINTHIANS, AND GALATIANS.

How many Epistles are recorded in the New Testament?
Twenty-one; fourteen of which were written by St. Paul; one by St. James; two by St. Peter; three by St. John; and one by St. Jude.

Name those written by St. Paul?
One to the Romans; two to the Corinthians; one to the Galatians; one to the Ephesians; one to the Philippians; one to the Colossians; two to the Thessalonians; two to Timothy; one to Titus; one to Philemon; and one to the Hebrews.

Why is precedence given to the Epistle to the Romans though some of the others were written previously?
On account of the sublimity of the matter contained in it, and the pre-eminence of the place to which it was addressed.

Where did St. Paul write it?
At Cornith, about twenty-four years after our Lord's Ascension, when he was preparing to go to Jerusalem with charitable contributions, collected in Achaia and Macedonia for the relief of the Christians in Judea.

What is the subject of the Epistle to the Romans?
The Apostle commends the faith of the Romans, and contrasts the just who live by faith with the worldly wise, who, puffed up with pride and filled with iniquity, turn away from God, who in turn rejects them.

How does he exhort them?
He exhorts them to be not hearers only, but doers of the law; as such alone whether Jews or Gentiles shall be justified.

Of what does he remind them?
He reminds them that the Jews were the depositaries of the law and heirs of the Fathers to whom the promises were made; yet many were cut off as broken branches, and the gentiles engrafted in their stead; which, nevertheless, should not make them proud, but rather fearful lest he who did not spare the natural branches should also reject them. He corrects the error of those who looked on the outward observance of the works of the law as sufficient for justification.

What does he show and exhort?
He shows that no work is available to justice and salvation, unless done through faith, and proceeding from grace, the necessity and excellence of which he inculcates. He exhorts the strong to support the weak, and to avoid scandalizing them by an imprudent use of the liberty they had by the new law to eat indiscriminately those meats accounted unclean in the old.

How does he caution the weak?
The weak he cautions against rash judging the

others, and also against acting contrary to the dictates of their conscience; telling them that if they believe the meat unclean it becomes so to them and they transgress in using it. In fine, St. Paul exhorts all to lead lives becoming the newness of life to which God had raised them, to put off the works of darkness, and to put on our Lord Jesus Christ.

When did St. Paul write his Epistles to the Corinthians?
About twenty-four years after our Lord's Ascension. The first at Ephesus; the second he sent from some place in Macedonia.

What is the subject of the First Epistle to the Corinthians?
St. Paul reproves them with apostolic authority for their dissensions and lawsuits, and prescribes the excommunication of one of them who had been guilty of a scandalous crime. He instructs them in faith and morals; and the reverence with which they should behave in the Church, introducing for this end the history of the institution of the Eucharist, as follows: "I have received of the Lord that which also I delivered unto you, that the Lord Jesus the same night in which he was betrayed took bread, and giving thanks broke and said, take ye and eat; this is my body, which shall be delivered for you. This do for the commemoration of me. In like manner, also, the chalice, after he had supped, saying, this chalice is the New Testament in my blood. This do ye as often as you shall drink for the commemoration of me; for as often as you shall eat this bread, and drink the chalice, you shall show the death of the Lord until he come. Therefore, whosoever shall eat this bread, or drink the chalice of the Lord unworthily, shall be guilty of the body and of the blood of the Lord; but let a man prove himself, and so let him eat of that bread and drink of

the chalice; for he that eateth and drinketh unworthily, eateth and drinketh judgment to himself, not discerning the body of the Lord."

To what does he earnestly exhort them?
He earnestly exhorts them to cordial mutual charity, and exemplifies the union that ought to exist among them by that which subsists between the members of the body; for as the eye cannot say to the hand, I need not thy help; nor the head to the feet, I have no need of you; but all are careful of one another, so in the Church each performs the part allotted for the good of the whole, forming one body, actuated by one spirit, and each necessary in his own place.

What does he say?
He goes on to say: "If I speak with the tongues of men and angels, and have not charity, I am become as sounding brass, or a tinkling symbol; and if I should have prophecy, and should know all mysteries and all knowledge, and if I should have all faith, so that I could remove mountains and have not charity, I am nothing. And if I should distribute all my goods to feed the poor, and if I should deliver my body to be burned, and have not charity, it profiteth me nothing. Charity is patient, is kind. Charity envieth not, dealeth not perversely; is not puffed up; is not ambitious; seeketh not her own; is not provoked to anger; thinketh no evil; rejoiceth not in iniquity, but rejoiceth with the truth; beareth all things, believeth all things, hopeth all things, endureth all things."

What is the subject of the Second Epistle to the Corinthians?
The apostle comforts those whom his former admonitions had reformed; and forgives him whose excommunication he had in his first epistle prescribed, on his manifesting sorrow and doing penance. He

expresses his affection to the Corinthians and intention of visiting them, hoping it would be with joy and not with reproof and sorrow. He cautions them against false teachers, gives an account of his sufferings, also of the favors God had bestowed on him, and exhorts them to the practice of every Christian virtue.

When did St. Paul write his Epistle to the Galatians?
He wrote it at Ephesus about twenty-three years after our Lord's Ascension; and for the purpose of reclaiming them from errors which some of them had fallen into by the means of false teachers, who inculcated the necessity of observing the rites and ceremonies of the Mosaic law.

CHAPTER LIII.

ST. PAUL'S EPISTLES TO THE EPHESIANS, PHILIPPIANS, COLOSSIANS, AND THESSALONIANS.

When did St. Paul write his Epistle to the Ephesians?
About twenty-nine years after our Lord's Ascension, while he was prisoner in Rome. In it the holy apostle admonishes them not to suffer themselves to be tossed to and fro, and carried about by every wind of doctrine; but being renewed in the spirit of their mind to put on the new man, who, according to God is created in justice and holiness of truth, not overreaching one another or speaking evil, but assisting each other and being kind, and merciful and forgiving.

How does he conclude?
He concludes by instructing husbands and wives, parents and children, masters and servants, in their respective duties, exhorting all to stand on their guard against the attacks of the wicked one.

When did St. Paul write his Epistle to the Philippians?
About twenty-nine years after our Lord's Ascension. In it he expresses great charity for them, and his constant remembrance of them in prayer. Mentions that his imprisonment, far from impeding, tended to the furtherance of the gospel, which was a source of great joy to him, though some of those who preached it were actuated by unworthy motives.

What does he recommend?
He recommends to them unity and humility, proposes to them our Lord's example, who humbled himself, becoming obedient unto death even to the death of the cross; and exhorts them to work out their salvation with fear and trembling, to avoid false teachers, and to persevere in doing as he had instructed them. He concludes by thanking them for the presents they had sent him, and gives them his blessing.

When did St. Paul write his Epistle to the Colossians?
About the same time that he wrote to the Ephesians and Philippians, and while he was still in prison. It is in substance much the same as that to the Ephesians.

When did St. Paul write his Epistles to the Thessalonians?
About nineteen years after our Lord's Ascension, being the earliest in point of time. Thessalonica was the capital of Macedonia, where, on St. Paul's preaching, some Jews and many gentiles were converted; but on a persecution being raised by the unbelieving Jews he was obliged to quit. On his arrival in Athens, he sent Timothy to comfort and encourage the converts in Thessalonica, and proceeded himself to Corinth, whence he wrote these two epistles.

CHAPTER LIV.

ST. PAUL'S EPISTLES TO TIMOTHY, TITUS, PHILEMON, AND THE HEBREWS.

When did St. Paul write his Epistles to his beloved disciple St. Timothy?
He wrote the first about thirty-three years after our Lord's Ascension. It is an instruction to St. Timothy, then Bishop of Ephesus, for his own government and that of his charge. The second epistle appears to have been written during his last imprisonment in Rome, a little before his martyrdom. In it he gives further instructions to Timothy, and tells him to come to him.

When did St. Paul write his Epistle to his disciple St. Titus, the Bishop of Crete?
About thirty-three years after our Lord's Ascension. It contains directions to St. Titus to ordain priests in the different cities where they were wanted, describes the requisite dispositions and qualifications for such, with other instructions for himself and flock.

What is the substance of St. Paul's Epistle to Philemon?
Philemon, who was a noble citizen of Colossa, was robbed by his servant Onesimus, who then fled to Rome, where he had the happiness to meet St. Paul, who was there a prisoner for the first time. The holy apostle converted him to the faith, and sent him back to his master with this epistle, requesting and exhorting him to forgive the past, and to receive the new convert with kindness and affection.

When did St. Paul write his Epistle to the Hebrews, or converted Jews of Palestine?
About twenty-nine years after our Lord's Ascension, and apparently while the apostle was in Italy. He

instructs them in the divinity of our Lord, the preeminence of his priesthood above the Levitical, and of the new law above the old. He extols the efficacy and fruits of faith demonstrated in the patriarchs, and exhorts the faithful to patience, perseverance, and fraternal charity.

CHAPTER LV.

EPISTLE OF ST. JAMES.

To whom did St. James address his Epistle?
To the faithful in general, for which reason it is styled Catholic or universal. He wrote it a little before his martyrdom, and about twenty-eight years after our Lord's Ascension. The writer was St. James the Less, cousin of our Lord, and first bishop of Jerusalem.

What is the subject of the Epistle?
The holy apostle exhorts the faithful to patience and fortitude under temptations, assuring them in the words of holy Job, that when they have been proved they shall receive the crown of life. He counsels them to pray with lively faith, to be doers of the law and not hearers only; to be meek, merciful, and charitable; to observe all the commandments, for they who break one become guilty of all. In fine to manifest their faith by works, not to let it resemble that of the devils who believe and tremble; for even as the body without the spirit is dead, so also faith without works is dead. He conjures them to guard their tongues and hearts, to pay their just debts, and always stand in readiness, not knowing when God may call them; to pray when in affliction, and when sick to have the priests called in to pray for and to anoint them, adding, "The prayer of faith shall save the sick man, and the Lord shall raise him up; and if he be in sins they shall be forgiven him."

CHAPTER LVI.

ST. PETER'S TWO EPISTLES.

When did St. Peter write his first Epistle?
About fifteen years after our Lord's Ascension. He wrote it in Rome, and addressed it to the faithful dispersed through Pontus, Galatia, Cappadocia, Asia, and Bythinia.

What is the subject of it?
The holy apostle exhorts them to act in a manner becoming their vocation as Christians, aspiring to the holiness to which they were called, keeping themselves as pilgrims in this world, and by their edifying conduct bringing the unbelievers to glorify God. He desires them to be subject to every human creature for God's sake; and encourages them to suffer patiently the wrongs done them, for the love of God and in imitation of Jesus Christ, who, when he was reviled, did not revile, when he suffered, threatened not, but delivered himself to him who judged him unjustly.

How does he caution women?
He cautions women against vanity in dress, and desires them rather to adorn their souls with meekness and mildness, which will render them pleasing in the sight of God. In fine, he admonishes all to be prudent, and to watch in prayer, as the end of all is at hand; and their adversary, the devil, goeth about like a roaring lion seeking whom he may devour. The apostle concludes with instructions to both clergy and laity, conjuring all to preserve constant mutual charity.

When did St. Peter write his second Epistle?
A little before his martyrdom, about thirty-five years after our Lord's Ascension. In it, he exhorts the faithful to fly sin and practise virtue and to labor

by good works to make their calling and election
sure.

Against what does he warn them?
He warns them against false teachers, and reminds
them of the awful judgments of God on sinners, first
inflicted on the angels, afterwards on those drowned
in the flood, then on Sodom and Gomorra; and to
deter them still more from sin, and make them keep
their hearts disengaged from the things of this world,
he foretells that it will be destroyed by fire, and the
day of the Lord will come when least expected.

CHAPTER LVII.

ST. JOHN'S THREE EPISTLES.—EPISTLE OF ST. JUDE.—
THE APOCALYPSE.

When did St. John write his first Epistle?
About sixty-six years after our Lord's Ascension.
It is addressed to the faithful in general. The holy
apostle instructs them in the mysteries of the Trinity
and of the Incarnation, in the necessity of keeping
the commandments, and of loving God and the
neighbor, saying that by so doing they shall be
known to be disciples of Christ; but if any hate a
brother, such is a murderer, and cannot have eternal life.

On what does he enlarge?
St. John enlarges much on charity, earnestly and
lovingly entreating, and exhorting all to practise it,
adducing the example of the Eternal Father who
gave his only Son, and of the Son who offered himself a propitiation for us; for which reason we should
not only love him who first loved us, but should assist our neighbor in his necessities, and be ready
even to lay down our lives for him.

To whom did St. John write his second Epistle?
To a pious lady, named Electa and her family whom

he instructs, and warns against holding any communication with the teachers of false doctrine.

To whom did St. John write his third Epistle?
To a Christian, named Gaius, whom he commends for his charity, and promises soon to visit, and to correct the evil practices of one named Diotrephes.

To whom did St. Jude write his Epistle?
To the faithful in general, whom he earnestly exhorts to preserve the faith transmitted to them, and to avoid the doers and teachers of iniquity, whose evil deeds he reminds them were foretold by the apostles. He begs of them to keep themselves in the love of God, waiting for the mercy of our Lord Jesus Christ unto life everlasting.
This epistle appears to have been written, when most of the apostles, or all of them, but St. John, were dead.

When did St. John write the Apocalypse or Book of Revelations?
About sixty-four years after the Ascension of our Lord, while he was exiled by order of the Emperor Domitian, in the island of Patmos.

What is the subject of it?
In the three first chapters are admonitions and instructions which St. John was commanded in a vision, to write to the seven bishops of the churches of Asia. In the remaining chapters are prophecies of what will come to pass in the Church, particularly towards the end of the world.

APPENDIX.

EXTRACTS FROM THE PROPHETS.

PROPHECIES OF THE COMING OF OUR LORD.—OF THE PRINCIPAL EVENTS IN HIS LIFE.—OF HIS DEATH, RESURRECTION, ASCENSION AND OF THE DESCENT OF THE HOLY GHOST.

"All things must needs be fulfilled which are written in the law of Moses, and in the Prophets, and in the Psalms, concerning me."—Luke xxiv. 44.

PREDICTIONS.

A REDEEMER IS PROMISED TO OUR FIRST PARENTS.

"And the Lord God said to the serpent, I will put enemies between thee, and the woman, and thy seed and her seed, she (or it) shall crush thy head." (Gen. iii. 15.)

THE PROMISE RENEWED TO ABRAHAM AND ISAAC.

"The Lord said to Abraham...In thee shall the kindred of the earth be blessed " (Gen. xii. 3.) "Sarah thy wife shall bear thee a son, and thou shalt call his name Isaac, and I will establish my covenant with him for a perpetual covenant, and with his seed after him." (Gen. xvii. 19.) Isaac bequeathed the blessing to Jacob. (Gen. xxvii. 27,) who left it as a rich inheritance to Juda. (Gen. xlix. 10.)

FULFILMENT.

"When the fulness of the time was come, God sent his Son, made of a woman, made under the law: that he might redeem them who were under the law." (Gal. iv. 4.)

"To Abraham were the promises made, and to his seed. He saith not, *and to his seeds*, as of many; but as of one, '*and to thy seed*,' which is Christ." (Gal. iii. 16.) "The God of Abraham, and the God of Isaac, and the God of Jacob, the God of our fathers hath glorified his Son Jesus, whom you indeed delivered up, and denied before the face of Pilate, when he judged he should be released." (Acts iii. 13.) By faith he (Abraham) abode in the land, dwelling in cottages with Isaac and Jacob, the co-heirs of the same promises." (Heb. xi. 9.)

PREDICTIONS.

SIGNS BY WHICH THE TIME OF THE COMING OF THE REDEEMER SHOULD BE MANIFESTED.

"The sceptre shall not be taken away from Juda, nor a ruler from his posterity, till he come that is to be sent, and he shall be the expectation of nations." (Gen. xlix. 10.)

FROM AMONG THE DESCENDANTS OF JUDA, GOD CHOSE THE FAMILY OF DAVID.

"The Lord chose the tribe of Juda.... And he chose David his servant." (Psalms lxxvii. 68, 70.) "And there shall come forth a rod out of the root of Jesse, and a flower shall rise up out of his root, and the Spirit of the Lord shall rest upon him; the spirit of wisdom and of understanding, the spirit of counsel and of fortitude, the spirit of knowledge and of Godliness. And he shall be filled with the spirit of the fear of the Lord." (Isaias xi. 1.) "He appointed to David his servant to raise up of him a most mighty king, and sitting on the throne of glory for ever." (Eccles. xxiv. 34.)

THE LENGTH OF TIME TO THE COMING AND DEATH OF OUR LORD, FORETOLD BY DANIEL.

"From the going forth of the word to build up Jerusalem again, unto Christ the prince, there shall be seven weeks and sixty-two weeks...... And after sixty-two weeks Christ shall be slain, and the people that shall deny him shall not be his." (Dan. ix. 25.)

FULFILMENT.

At the time of our Lord's birth, the sceptre (which seems to signify political power) was partly taken away from the Jews by the great power the Romans then exercised in Judea, and also by the introduction of Herod, who was a foreigner, as king: but it was not until the siege and destruction of Jerusalem under Titus Vespasian, a few years after our Lord's Passion, that this translation of the sceptre was finally completed.

"Of this man's (David's) seed, God, according to his promise, hath raised up to Israel a Saviour Jesus." (Acts xiii. 23.) "The angel Gabriel was sent from God into a city of Galilee, called Nazareth, to a virgin espoused to a man whose name was Joseph, of the house of David, and the virgin's name was Mary, and the angel being come in, said unto her, Hail full of grace, the Lord is with thee, blessed art thou among women .... Behold thou shalt conceive in thy womb, and shalt bring forth a son, and thou shalt call his name Jesus. He shall be great, and shall be called the Son of the Most High, and the Lord God shall give unto him the throne of David his father, and he shall reign in the house of Jacob for ever, and of his kingdom there shall be no end." (Luke i. 26.)

From the twentieth year of the reign of Artaxerxes, in which he issued the decree to rebuild Jerusalem, to the Baptism of our Lord, is computed by chronologists to be four hundred and eighty-three years; the term "weeks," used by Daniel, being universally admitted to mean weeks of years.

EXTRACTS FROM THE PROPHETS.

| PREDICTIONS. | FULFILMENT. |

THE PRECURSOR OF THE REDEEMER PREDICTED BY ISAIAS AND MALACHIAS.

"The voice of one crying in the desert, Prepare ye the way of the Lord." (Isaias xl. 3.) "Behold I send my angel, and he shall prepare the way before my face." (Mal. iii. 1.)

Some of the priests and Levites being deputed to ask St. John Baptist, "Who art thou," he replied, "I am the voice of one crying in the wilderness, make straight the way of the Lord, as said the prophet Isaias," (John i. 23.) Our Blessed Lord himself bore testimony to St. John, saying, "This is he, of whom it is written, Behold I send my angel," &c. (Luke vii. 27.)

ISAIAS FORETOLD THAT OUR BLESSED LORD WOULD BE BORN OF A VIRGIN.

"Behold a virgin shall conceive, and bear a son, and his name shall be called Emanuel." (Isaias vii. 14.) "Emanuel being interpreted is, God with us." (Mat. i. 23.)

"Joseph her husband being a just man, and not willing publicly to expose her, was minded to put her away privately. But while he thought on these things, behold the angel of the Lord appeared to him in his sleep, saying Joseph, son of David, fear not to take unto thee Mary thy wife, for that which is conceived in her is of the Holy Ghost, and she shall bring forth a son, and thou shalt call his name Jesus, for he shall save his people from their sins. Now all this was done that it might be fulfilled which the Lord spoke by the prophet saying, Behold a virgin," &c (Matt. i. 19, 23.)

THE PLACE OF OUR REDEEMER'S BIRTH FORETOLD BY MICHEAS.

"And thou, Bethlehem Ephrata, art a little one among the thousands of Juda; out of thee shall he come forth unto me, that is to be the ruler in Israel, and his coming forth is from the beginning, from the days of eternity." (Micheas v. 2.)

"When Jesus therefore was born in Bethlehem of Juda in the days of king Herod, behold there came wise men from the East to Jerusalem saying, Where is he that is born king of the Jews? For we have seen his star in the East, and are come to adore him. And king Herod hearing this was troubled, and all Jerusalem with him. And assembling together all the chief priests and the scribes of the people, he inquired of them where Christ should be born; but they said to him, in Bethlehem of Juda; for so it is written by the

EXTRACTS FROM THE PROPHETS.

PREDICTIONS.

THE HOUR OF HIS BIRTH.

"While all things were in quiet silence, and the night was in the midst of her course, Thy Almighty Word came down from heaven from Thy royal throne." (Wis. xviii. 14.)

OUR LORD'S PRESENCE IN THE TEMPLE FORETOLD BE AGGEUS AND MALACHIAS.

"Yet one little while, and I will move the heaven and the earth, and the sea, and the dry land, and I will move all nations; and *the desired of all nations shall come;* and I will fill this house with glory, saith the Lord of Hosts." (Aggeus ii. 7.)

"And presently the Lord whom you seek, and the angel of the testament whom you desire shall come to his temple. Behold he cometh, saith the Lord of Hosts." (Mal. iii. 1.)

THAT OUR LORD SHOULD BE ADORED BY EASTERN KINGS SOON AFTER HIS BIRTH.

"Arise, be enlightened O Jerusalem, for thy light is come, and the glory of the Lord is risen upon thee...... And the gentiles shall walk in thy light, and kings in the brightness of thy rising.... all they from Saba shall come, bringing

FULFILMENT.

prophet. And thou Bethlehem, &c. (Matt. ii. 1—6.)

"And there were in the same country shepherds watching and keeping the night watches over their flocks.... And behold an angel of the Lord stood by them, and the brightness of God shone round about them, and they feared with a great fear. And the angel said to them, Fear not, for behold I bring you good tidings of great joy that shall be to all the people for this day is born to you a Saviour, who is Christ the Lord, in the city of David." (Luke ii. 8.)

"And behold there was a man in Jerusalem, named Simeon, and this man was just and devout, waiting for the consolation of Israel, and the Holy Ghost was in him. And he had received an answer from the Holy Ghost that he should not see death before he had seen the Christ of the Lord. And he came by the Spirit into the Temple. And when his parents brought in the child Jesus, to do for him according to the custom of the law, he also took him into his arms, and blessed God and said, Now, Thou dost dismiss thy servant O Lord according to thy word in peace; because my eyes have seen thy salvation which thou hast prepared before the face of all people; a light to the revelation of the Gentiles, and the glory of thy people Israel." (Luke ii.)

"In the days of king Herod, behold there came wise men from the East to Jerusalem, saying where is he that is born king of the Jews? For we have seen his star in the East, and are come to adore him.... Then Herod as

EXTRACTS FROM THE PROPHETS.

PREDICTIONS.	FULFILMENT.
gold and frankincense, and showing forth praise to the Lord." (Isaias lx. 1.) "The kings of Tharsis and the islands shall offer presents, the kings of the Arabians and of Saba shall bring gifts, and all kings of the earth shall adore him." (Psm. lxxi. 10.)	vately calling the wise men learned diligently of them the time of the star which appeared to them; and sending them into Bethlehem, said, Go, and diligently inquire after the child, and when you have found him, bring me word again, that I also may come and adore him.... and behold the star which they had seen in the East went before them, until it came and stood over where the child was; and seeing the star they rejoiced with exceeding great joy; and entering into the house they found the child with Mary his mother, and falling down they adored him, and opening their treasures they offered him gifts, gold, frankincense, and myrrh." (Matt. ii.)
HIS FLIGHT INTO EGYPT. "Behold the Lord will ascend upon a swift cloud, and will enter into Egypt, and the idols of Egypt shall be moved at his presence." (Isaias xix. 1.)	"Behold an angel of the Lord appeared in sleep to Joseph, saying, Arise, take the child and his mother and fly into Egypt, and be there until I shall tell thee; for it will come to pass that Herod will seek the child to destroy him. Who arose, and took the child and his mother by night, and retired into Egypt. (Matt. ii. 13.)
THE MASSACRE OF THE INNOCENTS FORETOLD BY JEREMIAS. "A voice was heard on high of lamentation of mourning and weeping, of Rachel weeping for her children, and refusing to be comforted, for them, because they are not." (Jer. xxxi. 15.) The tomb of Rachel was at Bethlehem.	"The wise men having received an answer in sleep that they should not return to Herod, they went back another way into their own country.... Then Herod perceiving that he was deluded by the wise men, was exceedingly angry; and sending, killed all the men-children that were in Bethlehem, and in all the borders thereof from two years old and under.... Then was fulfilled that which was spoken by Jeremias, the prophet, saying, A voice was heard," &c. (Matt. ii.)
THE RETURN OF OUR LORD FROM EGYPT FORETOLD BY OSEE. "I called my Son out of Egypt." (Osee xi. 1.)	"When Herod was dead, behold an angel of the Lord appeared

EXTRACTS FROM THE PROPHETS.

PREDICTIONS	FULFILMENT.
	in sleep to Joseph in Egypt, saying, Arise, take the child and his mother, and go into the land of Israel; for they are dead that sought the life of the child. Who arose, and took the child and his mother, and came into the land of Israel.... That it might be fulfilled which the Lord spoke by the prophet saying, Out of Egypt have I called my Son." (Matt. ii.)
OUR BLESSED LORD PREFIGURED BY MOSES. "The Lord thy God will raise up to thee a prophet of thy nation, and of thy brethren like unto me, him thou shalt hear." (Deut.) "I (Moses) was the mediator, and stood between the Lord and you at that time." (Deut.) "I will raise them up a prophet out of the midst of their brethren like to thee; and I will put my words in his mouth, and he shall speak to them all that I shall command him." (Deut. xviii. 5.)	"The law was given by Moses, grace and truth came by Jesus Christ." (John i. 17.) "He (the Lord Jesus) is the mediator of the New Testament." (Heb. ix. 15.) "Jesus taketh unto him Peter and James, and John his brother, and bringeth them up into a high mountain apart......and lo! a voice out of the cloud, saying, This is my beloved Son, in whom I am well pleased, hear ye him." (Matt. xvii. 1.)
OUR BLESSED LORD DESIGNATED AS A RULER AND TEACHER. "All thy children shall be taught of the Lord." (Isaias liv. 13.) "And you, oh children of Sion, rejoice and be joyful in the Lord your God, because he hath given you a teacher of justice." (Joel ii. 23.) "For the lawgiver shall give a blessing, the God of gods shall be seen in Sion." (Ps. lxxxiii.) "For he that made thee shall rule over thee; the Lord of Hosts is his name. And thy Redeemer, the holy one of Israel, shall be called the God of all the earth." (Isaias liv. 5.)	"God, who at sundry times, and in divers manners spoke in times past to the Fathers by the prophets, last of all in these days hath spoken to us by his Son, whom he hath appointed heir of all things, by whom also he made the world." (Heb. i. 1.) "And he was teaching daily in the Temple." (Luke xix.) "The woman saith to him, I know that the Messias cometh who is called Christ, therefore when he is come, he will tell us all things. Jesus saith to her, I am he who am speaking with thee." (John. iv. 25.)
THAT THE REDEEMER WOULD BE SON OF GOD. "The Lord hath said to me, Thou art my Son: this day have I begotten thee. Ask of me and I will give thee the gentiles for thy inheritance, and the utmost parts of the earth for thy possession."	"The *Word* was made flesh, and dwelt among us, (and we saw his glory, the glory as it were of the only begotten of the Father,) full of grace and truth." (John i. 14.)

PREDICTIONS.

(Ps. ii. 7.) "And the gentiles shall fear thy name, O Lord, and all the kings of the earth thy glory." (Ps. ci. 17.) "The Lord said to my Lord, sit thou on my right hand until I make thy enemies thy footstool." (Ps. cix. 1.) "Adore him, all you his angels." (Ps. xcvi. 7.) "Thy throne, O God, is for ever and ever. The sceptre of thy kingdom is a sceptre of uprightness. Thou hast loved justice and hatedst iniquity; therefore God, thy God hath anointed thee with the oil of gladness above thy fellows." (Ps. xliv. 7.) "In the beginning, O, Lord, thou foundedst the earth, and the heavens are the works of thy hands. They shall perish, but Thou remainest, and all of them shall grow old like a garment, and as a vesture Thou shalt change them, and they shall be changed; but Thou art always the self-same, and thy years shall not fail." (Ps. ci. 26.)

FULFILMENT.

"The Pharisees being gathered together, Jesus asked them, saying, What think ye of Christ? Whose son is he? They say to him, David's. He saith to them, How then doth David in spirit call him Lord, saying, The Lord said to my Lord," &c. If David then call him Lord, how is he his son? And no man was able to answer him." (Matt. xxii. 41.)

"God, who at sundry times, and in divers manners spoke, in times past to the fathers by the prophets, last of all in these days hath spoken to us by his Son, whom he hath appointed heir of all things by whom also he made the world. Who being the brightness of his glory, and the figure of his substance, and upholding all things by the word of his power, making purgation of sins, sitteth on the right hand of the Majesty on high . . . to which of the angels hath he said at any time, *Thou art my son*, &c. And again, when he bringeth in the first begotten into the world, he saith, *And let all the angels of God adore him*. And to the angels indeed he saith, *He that maketh his angels spirits, and his ministers a flame of fire*. But to the Son, *Thy throne, O God*, &c. And *Thou in the beginning, O Lord, didst found the earth*, &c. But to which of the angels said he at any time, *Sit on my right hand*," &c. (Heb. 1.)

OUR BLESSED LORD PREFIGURED BY MELCHISEDECH, AND DESIGNATED 'PRIEST FOR EVER,' ACCORDING TO HIS ORDER, BY THE ROYAL PROPHET.

"Melchisedech, the king of Salem, bringing forth bread and wine, for he was the priest of the Most High God, blessed him and said, Blessed be Abram by you; the Most High God, who created heaven and earth, and blessed be the Most High God, by whose protection the enemies are in thy hands."

"The Lord Jesus, the same night in which he was betrayed, took bread and giving thanks, broke and said, This is my Body which shall be delivered for you, this do for the commemoration of me. In like manner also the chalice, after he had supped, saying, This chalice is the New Testament

PREDICTIONS.	FULFILMENT.
And he gave him tithes of all." (Gen. xiv. 18.)	in my blood. This do ye, as often as you shall drink for the commemoration of me." (1 Cor. xi. 23.)
"The Lord hath sworn, and he will not repent, Thou art a priest for ever, according to the order of Melchisedech." (Ps. cix. 9.)	"If then perfection was by the Levitical priesthood, (for under it the people received the law) what further need was there that another priest should rise according to the order of Melchisedech, and not be called according to the order of Aaron.... For he of whom these things are spoken, is of another tribe, of which no one attended at the altar. For it is evident that our Lord sprung out of Juda, in which tribe Moses spoke nothing concerning priests. And it is yet far more evident, if, according to the similitude of Melchisedech, there ariseth another priest." - (Heb. vii. 11.)

HIS DOCTRINE TO BE PREACHED TO THE POOR.

"The Spirit of the Lord is upon me, because the Lord hath anointed me. He hath sent me to preach to the meek, to heal the contrite of heart, and to preach a release to the captives, and deliverance to them that are shut up. To proclaim the acceptable year of the Lord, and the day of vengeance of our God; to comfort all that mourn." (Isaias lxi. 1.)	"And the book of Isaias the prophet was delivered unto him, and as he unfolded the book, he found the place where it was written, *The spirit of the Lord,* &c. And he began to say to them, This day is fulfilled this scripture in your ears. And all gave testimony to him, and they wondered at the grace that proceeded from his mouth." (Luke iv. 17.)

HIS MIRACLES.

"God himself will come and will save you, then shall the eyes of the blind be opened, and the ears of the deaf shall be unstopped, then shall the lame man leap as a hart, and the tongue of the dumb shall be free." (Isaias xxxv. 5.)	"Now when John had heard in prison the works of Christ, sending two of his disciples he said to him, Art thou he that art to come, or look we for another? And Jesus making answer said to them Go, and relate to John what you have heard and seen; the blind see, the lame walk, the lepers are cleansed, the deaf hear, the dead rise again, the poor have the gospel preached to them." (Matt. xi. 2, and Luke vii. 19.)

HIS MEEKNESS.

"Behold my servant, I will uphold him, my elect, my soul delighteth in him, I have given my Spirit upon him, he shall bring	"At that time Jesus answered and said, I confess to thee O Father, Lord of heaven and earth, because thou hast hid these things

PREDICTIONS.

forth judgment to the gentiles. He shall not cry, nor have respect to persons, neither shall his voice be heard abroad. The bruised reed he shall not break and the smoking flax he shall not quench: He shall bring forth judgment unto truth, he shall not be sad nor troublesome." (Isaias xlii. 1.)

HIS ZEAL.

"The zeal of thy house hath eaten me up." (Ps. lxviii. 10.)

CHRIST'S ENTRY INTO JERUSALEM.

"Rejoice greatly, O daughter of Sion, shout for joy O daughter of Jerusalem, Behold thy king will come to thee, the just and Saviour; he is poor and riding upon an ass, and upon a colt the foal of an ass." (Zac. ix. 9.)

"Blessed be he that cometh in the name of the Lord." (Ps. cxvii. 95.)

"Behold the Lord hath made it to be heard in the ends of the earth, tell the daughter of Sion behold thy Saviour cometh."— (Isaias lxii. 11.)

FULFILMENT.

from the wise and prudent, and hast revealed them to little ones. Yea Father; for so hath it seemed good in thy sight. All things are delivered to me by my Father and no one knoweth the Son but the Father; neither doth any one know the Father but the Son; and he to whom it shall please the Son to reveal him. Come to me all you that labor, and are burdened, and I will refresh you. Take up my yoke upon you, and learn of me, because I am meek and humble of heart, and you shall find rest to your souls." (Matt. xi. 25.)

"And he found in the temple them that sold oxen, and sheep, and doves, and the changers of money sitting.... and when he had made as it were a scourge of little cords, he drove them all out of the temple, the sheep also, and the oxen; and the money of the changers he poured out; and the tables he overthrew; and to them that sold doves he said, Take these things hence, and make not the House of my Father a house of traffic. And his disciples remembered that it was written, "*The zeal of thy house*," &c. (John ii. 14.)

"And when they were drawing near to Jerusalem and to Bothania, at the Mount of Olives, he sendeth two of his disciples, and saith to them, Go into the village that is over against you, and immediately at your coming in thither you shall find a colt tied, upon which no man yet hath set: loose him, and bring him: and if any man shall say to you, What are you doing? say ye that the Lord hath need of him: and immediately he will let him come hither.... And they brought the colt to Jesus, and they laid their garments on him, and he sat upon him. And many spread their garments in the way; and others cut down boughs from the trees, and strewed them

PREDICTIONS.

BY WHOM BETRAYED.

"For even the man of my peace in whom I trusted, who eat my bread hath greatly supplanted me." (Ps. xl. 10.)

FOR WHAT PRICE.

"And they weighed for my wages thirty pieces of silver, and the Lord said to me, cast it to the statuary, a handsome price that I was prized at by them. And I took the thirty pieces of silver, and I cast them into the house of the Lord to the statuary." (Zach. xi. 12.)

THE FOLLOWING, QUOTED BY ST. MATTHEW FROM JEREMIAS, IS NO LONGER FOUND IN THE ORIGINAL, BEING LOST, TOGETHER WITH OTHER PORTIONS OF THE HOLY SCRIPTURE.

"And they took the thirty pieces of silver, the price of him that was prised, whom they prized of the children of Israel, and they gave them into the potters' field as the Lord appointed to me."* (Matt. xxvii. 9.)

FULFILMENT.

in the way. And they that went before, and they that followed, cried, saying, *Hosannah, blessed is he that cometh in the name of the Lord.*.And he entered into Jerusalem....(Mark xi.) Now all this was done that it might be fulfilled which was spoken by the prophet saying, *Tell ye the daughter of Sion: Behold thy King cometh to thee,*" &c. (Matt. xxi. 4.)

"And Judas Iscariot, one of the twelve went to the chief priests to betray him to them....And when they were at table, and eating, Jesus saith, Amen, I say unto you, one of you that eateth with me shall betray me. But they began to be sorrowful, and to say to him one by one, Is it I? who saith to them, one of the twelve who dippeth with me his hand in the dish." (Mark xiv. 10.)

"Then went one of the twelve who was called Judas Iscariot, to the chief priests, and said to them What will you give me, and I will deliver him unto you? But they appointed him thirty pieces of silver." (Matt. xxvi. 14.)

"Then Judas, who betrayed him, seeing that he was condemned, repenting himself, brought back the thirty pieces of silver to the chief priests and ancients, saying, I have sinned in betraying innocent blood. But they said, What is that to us, look thou to it. And casting down the pieces of silver in the Temple, he departed and went and hanged himself with a

---

* St. Jerom says that he saw the above text in a Hebrew copy of Jeremias, which was shown to him by a Jew

PREDICTIONS.

OF THE ENVY OF CHRIST'S ENEMIES, AND THEIR MALICIOUS DESIGNS AGAINST HIM.

"Let us therefore lie in wait for the Just, because he is not for our turn, and he is contrary to our doings, and upbraideth us with transgressions of the law, and divulgeth against us the sins of our way of life. He boasteth that he hath the knowledge of God, and calleth himself the Son of God. He is become a censurer of our thoughts. He is grievous unto us even to behold; for his life is not like other men's, and his ways are very different. We are esteemed by him as trifles, and he abstaineth from our ways as from filthiness, and he preferreth the latter end of the just, and glorieth that he hath God for his father. Let us see then if his words be true, and let us prove what shall happen to him, and we shall know what his end shall be. For if he be the true Son of God, he will defend him, and will deliver him from the hands of his enemies. Let us examine him by outrages and tortures, that we may know his meekness and try his patience. Let us condemn him to a most shameful death, for there shall be respect had unto him by his words. These things they thought, and were deceived, for their own malice blinded them." (Wis. ii. 12.)

FULFILMENT.

halter. But the chief priests having taken the pieces of silver, said, It is not lawful to put them into the corbona, because it is the price of blood; and after they had consulted together, they bought with them the potters' field to be a burying place for strangers." (Matt. xxvii. 3.)

"The chief priests, therefore, and the Pharisees gathered a council, and said, What do we, for this man doth many miracles? If we let him alone so, all will believe in him, and the Romans will come and take away our place and nation. But one of them, named Caiphas, being the High Priest that year, said to them, You know nothing; neither do you consider that it is expedient for you that one man should die for the people, and that the whole nation perish not.... From that day, therefore, they devised to put him to death." (John xi. 47.) "When the chief priests, therefore, and the servants had seen him, they cried out, saying, Crucify him, crucify him. Pilate saith to them, Take him you and crucify him, for I find no cause in him. The Jews answered him, We have a law, and according to that law he ought to die, because he made himself the Son of God." (John xix.)

"And they that passed, blasphemed him, wagging their heads, and saying, Vah, thou that destroyed the temple of God, and in three days dost rebuild it, save thy own self; if thou be the Son of God come down from the cross. In like manner also, the chief priests, with the scribes and ancients, mocking, said, He saved others, himself he cannot save; if he be the King of Israel, let him now come down from the cross, and we will believe him. He trusted in God, let him now deliver him, if he will have him; for he said I am the Son of God." (Matt. xxvii. 39.)

PREDICTIONS.

HIS SEIZURE.

"The breath of our mouth, Christ the Lord is taken in our sins." (Lam. iv. 20.)

"They have opened their mouths against me as a lion ravening and roaring...... many dogs have encompassed me, the council of the malignant hath besieged me." (Ps. xxi. 14.)

THE FLIGHT OF THE APOSTLES.

"Awake, O sword, against my shepherd, and against the man that cleaveth to me, saith the Lord of Hosts: strike the shepherd and the sheep shall be scattered." (Zac. xiii. 7.)

"And I looked for one that would grieve together with me, but there was none, and for one that would comfort me, and I found none." (Ps. lviii. 21.)

THE SCOURGING OF OUR DIVINE LORD.

"I have given my body to the strikers, and my cheeks to them that plucked them, I have not turned away my face from them that rebuked me and spit upon me." "He was wounded for our iniquities, he was bruised for our sins, the chastisement of our peace was upon him, and by his bruises we are healed." (Is. l. 6; and liii. 5.)

HIS PATIENCE UNDER SUFFERINGS.

"He shall be led as a sheep to the slaughter, and shall be dumb as a lamb before his shearer, and he shall not open his mouth." (Isaias liii. 7.)

FULFILMENT.

"Judas therefore having received a band of soldiers and servants from the chief priests, and the Pharisees, cometh thither with lanterns, and torches, and weapons...... Then the band, and the tribune, and the servants of the Jews took Jesus, and bound him, and they led him away to Annas, first, for he was father-in-law to Caiphas, who was the High Priest of that year. Now Caiphas was he, who had given the counsel to the Jews, that it was expedient that one man should die for the people." (John xviii. 3.)

"Then his disciples leaving him, all fled away." (Mark xiv. 50.)

"Then therefore Pilate took Jesus and scourged him, and the soldiers platting a crown of thorns, put it upon his head, and they put on him a purple garment, and they came to him and said, Hail King of the Jews, and they gave him blows." (John xix. 1.)

"And spitting upon him, they took the reed and struck his head." (Matt. xxvii. 30.)

"And the men that held him mocked him, and struck him." (Luke xxii. 63.)

"And when he was accused by the chief priests and ancients he answered nothing." (Matt. xxvii. 12.)

"And bearing his own cross he went forth to that place which is

EXTRACTS FROM THE PROPHETS.

PREDICTIONS.	FULFILMENT.

THE INJURY HE SUFFERED IN REPUTATION.

"He was reputed with the wicked." (Is. liii. 12.)

"Despised and the most abject of men, a man of sorrows, and acquainted with infirmity; and his look was as it were hidden and despised, whereupon we esteemed him not.... And we have thought him as it were a leper, and as one struck by God and afflicted. (Is. liii. 3.)

...called Calvary, but in Hebrew Golgotha." (John xix. 17.)

"Many bore false witness against him." (Mark xiv. 56.)

"And they began to accuse him saying, We have found this man perverting our nation, and forbidding to give tribute to Cæsar, and saying that he is Christ the King ....Herod with his army set him at nought, and mocked him, putting on him a white garment." (Luke xxiii. 2.)

"And with him they crucify two thieves, the one on his right hand, and the other on his left; and the Scripture was fulfilled which saith, *And with the wicked he was reputed.*" (Mark xv. 27.)

THE WOUNDS ON HIS HANDS AND FEET.

"They have dug my hands and feet." (Psalms xxi. 17.)

"And they shall say to him, What are these wounds in the midst of thy hands. And he shall say, With these I was wounded in the house of them that loved me." (Zac. xiii. 6.)

"And when they were come to the place which is called Calvary, they crucified him there." (Luke xxiii. 33.)

Nailing his hands and feet with gross nails to the wood of the cross.

OUR BLESSED LORD'S PRAYING FOR HIS EXECUTIONERS.

"—— He hath delivered his soul unto death, and was reputed with the wicked; and he hath borne the sins of many, and hath prayed for the transgressors."— (Isaias liii. 12.)

"And when they were come to the place which is called Calvary, they crucified him there; and the robbers, one on the right hand, and the other on the left. And Jesus said, Father forgive them, for they know not what they do." (Luke xxiii. 33.)

THE VINEGAR AND GALL GIVEN HIM ON THE CROSS.

"And they gave me gall for my food, and in my thirst they gave me vinegar to drink." (Ps. lviii. 22.)

"And they gave him wine to drink mingled with gall." (Matt. xxvii. 34.)

Jesus knowing that all things were now accomplished, that the Scripture might be fulfilled, said, I thirst. Now there was a vessel set there full of vinegar; and they putting a sponge full of vinegar

PREDICTIONS.	FULFILMENT.
	about hyssop, put it to his mouth." (John xix. 28.)
HIS CRUCIFIXION PREFIGURED BY THE BRAZEN SERPENT. "As Moses lifted up the serpent in the desert, so must the Son of Man be lifted up." (John iii. 14.)	"They crucified him.....and Pilate wrote a title also, and he put it upon the cross, and the writing was, Jesus of Nazareth the King of the Jews." (John xix. 18.)
THE DIVISION OF HIS GARMENTS. "They parted my garments amongst them, and upon my vesture they cast lots." (Ps. xxi. 19.)	"The soldiers therefore when they had crucified him took his garments, and they made four parts, to every soldier a part, and also his coat. Now the coat was without seam, woven from the top throughout. They said then to one another, Let us not cut it, but let us cast lots for it whose it shall be; that the Scripture might be fulfilled, saying, *They have parted my garments,*" &c. (John xix. 23.)
THE PIERCING OF OUR LORD'S SIDE. "They shall look upon me whom they have pierced." (Zac. xii. 10.)	"They broke the legs of the first, and of the other that was crucified with him; but after they were come to Jesus when they saw that he was already dead, they did not break his legs; but one of the soldiers with a spear opened his side, and immediately there came out blood and water. ....For these things were done that the Scripture might be fulfilled, *You shall not break a bone of him;* and again, another Scripture saith, *They shall look on him whom they pierced.*" (John xix. 32 to 37.)
SUDDEN DARKNESS AT HIS DEATH. "And it shall come to pass in that day, saith the Lord God, that the sun shall go down at mid-day, and I will make the earth dark in the day of light." (Amos viii. 9.)	"And it was almost the sixth hour; and there was darkness over all the earth until the ninth hour. And the sun was darkened, and the veil of the temple was rent in the midst. And Jesus crying with a loud voice, said, Father into thy hands I commend my spirit. And saying this he gave up the ghost." (Luke xxiii. 44.)

PREDICTIONS.

OUR BLESSED LORD'S BURIAL AND RESURRECTION PREFIGURED BY JONAS.

"An evil and adulterous generation seeketh a sign; and a sign shall not be given it, but the sign of Jonas the prophet. For as Jonas was in the whale's belly three days and three nights, so shall the Son of Man be in the heart of the earth three days and three nights." (Matt. xii. 39, and Jonas i.)

OUR BLESSED LORD'S ASCENSION.

"Thou hast ascended on high, Thou hast led captivity captive, Thou hast received gifts in men ....sing ye to God who mounteth above the heaven of heavens, to the east." (Psalm lxvii. 19.)
"God is ascended with jubilee and the Lord with the sound of trumpet." (Ps. xlvi. 6.)

THE DESCENT OF THE HOLY GHOST.

"It shall come to pass after this, that I will pour out my Spirit upon all flesh; and your sons and your daughters shall prophesy; your old men shall dream dreams, and your young men shall see visions. Moreover upon my servants and handmaids in those days I will pour forth my Spirit. (Joel ii. 28.)

FULFILMENT.

"Why seek you the living with the dead, he is not here, but is risen. Remember how he spoke unto you, when he was yet in Galilee, saying, The Son of Man must be delivered into the hands of sinful men, and be crucified, and the third day rise again: and they remembered his words; and going back from the sepulchre, they told all these things to the eleven and to all the rest." (Luke xxiv. 5.)

"While they looked on he was raised up, and a cloud received him out of their sight. And while they were beholding him go up to heaven, behold two men stood by them in white garments, who also said, Ye men of Galilee why stand you looking up to heaven? This Jesus who is taken up from you into heaven, shall so come as you have seen him going into heaven." (Acts i. 9.)

"And when the days of the Pentecost were accomplished, they were altogether in one place; and suddenly there came a sound from heaven as of a mighty wind coming, and it filled the whole house where they were sitting. And there appeared to them parted tongues as it were of fire, and it sat upon every one of them: and they were all filled with the Holy Ghost, and they began to speak with divers tongues, according as the Holy Ghost gave them to speak....This is that which was spoken by the prophet Joel: *And it shall come to pass,*" &c. (Acts ii. 1.)

"And beginning at Moses, and all the prophets, he expounded to them in all the Scriptures the things that were concerning him."— (Luke xxiv. 27.)

"We have found him of whom Moses in the law, and the prophets did write, Jesus, the son of Joseph of Nazareth.—(John i. 45.)

SCRIPTURE TEXTS

INFALLIBILITY OF THE CHURCH.

"Going therefore teach ye all nations......And behold I am with you all days, even to the consummation of the world." (Matt. xxviii. 19, 20.) The Church is "the pillar and ground of truth." (1 Tim. iii. 15.)

THE AUTHORITY OF THE CHURCH.

"Go ye into the whole world, and preach the gospel to every creature." (Mark xvi. 15.) "He that heareth you heareth me; and he that despiseth you, despiseth me; and he that despiseth me, despiseth him that sent me." (Luke x. 16.) "If he will not hear them, tell the Church; and if he will not hear the Church, let him be to thee as the heathen and the publican." (Matt. xviii. 17.)

FAITH NECESSARY TO SALVATION.

"He that believeth and is baptized shall be saved; but he that believeth not shall be condemned." (Mark xvi. 16.) "Without faith it is impossible to please God." (Heb. xi. 6.)

FAITH NOT SUFFICIENT WITHOUT WORKS.

"If thou wilt enter into life keep the commandments." (Matt. xix. 17.) "So let your light shine before men that they may see your good works and glorify your Father who is in heaven." (Matt. v. 16.) "If I should have all faith, so that I could remove mountains, and have not charity, I am nothing." (1 Cor. xiii. 2.) "As a body without the spirit is dead; so also faith without works is dead." (James ii. 26.)

BAPTISM.

"Going therefore teach ye all nations, baptizing them in the name of the Father and of the Son and of the Holy Ghost." (Matt. xxviii. 19.) "Except a man be born again of water and the Holy Ghost, he cannot enter the kingdom of God." (John iii. 5.) "Be baptized every one of you." (Acts ii. 38.)

CONFIRMATION.

"Now when the Apostles that were in Jerusalem had heard that Samaria had received the word of God, they sent to them Peter and John, who, when they were come, prayed for them that they might receive the Holy Ghost. Then they laid their hands upon them, and they received the Holy Ghost." (Acts viii. 14, 15, 17.) "And when Paul had imposed his hands upon them, the Holy Ghost came upon them." (Acts xix. 6.)

THE BLESSED EUCHARIST.

"While they were at supper Jesus took bread and blessed and broke, and gave to his disciples and said, Take ye and eat, this is my body; and taking the chalice he gave thanks and gave to them saying, Drink ye all of this, for this is my blood of the New Testament which shall be shed for many unto remission of sins." (Matt. xxvi. 26—28.) See also Mark xiv. 22—24, and Luke xxii. 19, 20.

COMMUNION UNDER ONE KIND.

"If any man eat of this bread, he shall live for ever." (John vi. 52.) "Therefore, whosoever shall eat this bread or drink the chalice of the Lord unworthily shall be guilty of the body and of the blood of the Lord." (1 Cor. xi. 27.) Observe the word *or*, in the first part of the sentence, ["eat or drink"] and the word *and* in the second ["the body and blood."]

SACRIFICE OF THE MASS.

"I have no pleasure in you, saith the Lord of Hosts, and I will not receive a gift of your hand: for from the rising of the sun even to the going down, my name is great among the gentiles, and in every place there is sacrifice, and there is offered to my name a clean oblation." (Mal. i. 10, 11.) "Melchisedech, the king of Salem, bringing forth bread and wine, for he was the priest of the Most High God." (Gen. xiv. 18.) "The Lord hath sworn and he will not repent, Thou art a priest for ever according to the order of Melchisedech." (Psm. cix. 4.) St. Paul dwells strongly on Christ's priesthood according to the order of Melchisedech in the fifth and seventh chapter of his Epistle to the Hebrews. "And taking bread he gave thanks and brake, and gave to them saying, This is my body which is given for you. Do this for a commemoration of me. In like manner the chalice also after he had supped saying: This is the chalice the New Testament in my blood, which shall be shed for you." (Luke xxii. 19, 20.)

PENANCE.

"Amen I say to you, whatsoever you shall bind upon earth shall be bound also in heaven: and whatsoever you shall loose upon earth, shall be loosed also in heaven." (Matt. xviii. 18.) "He breathed on them and he said to them, Receive ye the Holy Ghost; whose sins you shall forgive, they are forgiven them; and whose sins you shall retain, they are retained." (John xx. 22, 23.)

EXTREME UNCTION.

"Is any man sick amongst you? Let him bring in the priests of the Church, and let them pray over him, anointing him with oil in the name of the Lord, and the prayer of faith shall save the sick man; and the Lord shall raise him up, and if he be in sins they shall be forgiven him." (James v. 14, 15.)

HOLY ORDERS.

"I admonish thee that thou stir up the grace of God, which is in thee by the imposition of my hands." (2 Tim. i. 6.) "These, they set before the apostles, and they, praying, imposed hands upon them." (Acts vi. 6.) "They fasting and praying, and imposing their hands on them, sent them away." (Acts xiii. 3.)

MATRIMONY.

"What therefore God hath joined together let not man put asunder." (Mark x. 9.) "For this cause shall a man leave his father and his mother, and shall cleave to his wife, and they shall be two in one flesh. This is a great sacrament, but I speak in Christ and in the Church." (Ephes. v. 31, 32.)

APOSTOLIC TRADITION.

"Go ye into the whole world, and preach the Gospel to every creature." (Mark xvi. 15.) "Hold the form of sound words which thou hast heard of me in faith." (2 Tim. 1. 13.) "And we charge you, brethren, in the name of our Lord Jesus Christ, that you withdraw yourselves from every brother walking disorderly, and not according to the tradition which they have received of us." (2 Thes. iii. 6.) "The things which thou hast heard of me by many witnesses, the same commend to faithful men, who shall be fit to teach others also." (2 Tim. ii. 2.)

APPENDIX.

RELICS.

"And God wrought by the hand of Paul more than common miracles, so that even there were brought from his body to the sick, handkerchiefs, and aprons, and the diseases departed from them. And the wicked spirits went out of them." (Acts xix. 11, 12.)

INDULGENCES.

"Amen, I say to you, whatsoever you shall bind on earth shall be bound also in heaven; and whatsoever you shall loose on earth, shall be loosed also in heaven." (Matt. xviii. 18.) "Wherefore, I beseech you that you would confirm your charity towards him, ... for what I forgive . . . . I have done it in the person of Christ." (2 Cor. ii. 8, 10.)

PURGATORY AND PRAYERS FOR THE DEAD.

"Judas, the valiant commander, having made a gathering, sent 1,200 drachms of silver to Jerusalem for sacrifice, to be offered for the sins of the dead, thinking well and religiously concerning the resurrection. . . . . It is therefore a holy and wholesome thought to pray for the dead, that they may be loosed from sins." (2 Mac. xii. 43, 46.)

COMMUNION OF SAINTS.

"There shall be joy before the angels of God, upon one sinner doing penance." (Luke xv. 10.) The angel Raphael said to Tobias, "When thou didst pray with tears and didst bury the dead. . . . . I offered thy prayer to the Lord." (Tobias xii. 12.) . . . . "The four and twenty ancients fell down before the Lamb, having every one of them harps, and golden vials full of odors which are the prayers of the saints." (Apoc. v. 8.)

SHORT SKETCHES OF THE

APOSTLES AND EVANGELISTS,

TAKEN FROM ECCLESIASTICAL HISTORY.

ST. PETER.

After the apostolic labors recorded of St. Peter in Holy Scripture, he preached the gospel in Italy and other provinces of the west, and meeting St. Paul in Rome, whither he had returned after his first imprisonment, they both preached the faith in that city, and sealed it with their blood in the first general persecution raised by Nero. St. Peter was condemned to be crucified, at the place of execution, through a spirit of humility and compunction, and a desire of suffering for his Divine Master, he begged that it might be with his head downwards. The feast of St. Peter is kept on the 29th of June.

ST. PAUL.

St. Paul having been released from prison in Rome, where, as mentioned in the Acts, he was confined two years, went back to the East, and after many apostolic labors returned to Rome, where he and St. Peter used their united exertions in cultivating that portion of the vineyard, in which both suffered martyrdom, St. Peter being crucified as related above, and St. Paul beheaded. His head is kept in the church of St. John Lateran, but his body lies with St. Peter's, half in the Vatican, and half in his own church, on the Ostian road, near Rome. The feast of St. Paul is kept on the 30th of June.

ST. ANDREW.

St. Andrew, as mentioned in Holy Scripture, was brother of St. Peter, and, like him, a fisherman. He was a disciple of St. John the Baptist, but on hearing him point out our Blessed Saviour as the Lamb of God, he immediately followed him, and was the first called of the apostles. True charity being ever active, St. Andrew lost no time in bringing his brother, then called Simon, to our Lord, who at once admitted him, and gave him the name of Peter. After the descent of the Holy Ghost, St. Andrew preached the gospel in Scythia in Greece, and was crucified for the faith at Patræ, in Achaia; the general opinion is on a cross in the form of the letter X. The feast of St. Andrew is kept on the 30th of November.

ST. JAMES THE GREAT.

St. James, surnamed the Great, to distinguish him from the other St. James, called the Less, perhaps from his stature, was brother of St. John the Evangelist, and a fisherman. He and his brother John were called the same day, but he was considerably older. Our Blessed Lord gave them both the surname of Boanerges, or sons of thunder, probably to denote their great zeal. It is supposed that on the dispersion of the Christians, after the martyrdom of St. Stephen, St. James preached to the dispersed Jews, (the tribes scattered among the gentiles,) and also to the people of Spain. He returned to Jerusalem, after ten years apostolic labors, and was beheaded for the faith the year following, by Herod Agrippa: he was the first of the apostles who suffered martyrdom. His feast is kept on the 25th of July.

ST. JOHN.

St. John the Apostle and Evangelist, styled by excellence the beloved disciple, was brother of St. James the Great, and son of Zebedee and Salome. He was young when called by our Lord, and survived his Divine Master seventy years. To him our Lord committed the care of his blessed Mother, recommending her to him from the cross. Like the other saints who were present at our Lord's crucifixion, he did not actually end his life by martyrdom, but he is styled a martyr on account of his sufferings, and particularly from his having been carried to Rome and there thrown into a caldron of boiling oil in the second general persecution, under Domitian, from which he miraculously came out unhurt. He was then banished to the island of Patmos, where he was favored with the revelations he has left us. His exile did not last more than about a year, for on the death of Domitian all his edicts were reversed, and St. John resumed his apostolic labors with unabated charity and zeal, though then advanced in years. Finding on his return from banishment, that St. Timothy, Bishop of Ephesus, had been crowned with martyrdom some months before, he took on himself the government of that see, and there died in peace, never ceasing to his last breath to exhort his flock to mutual charity. His feast is kept on the 27th of December.

ST. PHILIP.

After the descent of the Holy Ghost, St. Philip went to Phrygia, where he preached the gospel. He lived to an advanced age, and died at Hieropolis, in Phrygia. His feast is kept on the 1st of May.

ST. BARTHOLOMEW.

St. Bartholomew is considered to be the same person as Nathaniel, a doctor of the Jewish law, who was brought to Christ by St. Philip, and chosen for an apostle. The ground of this opinion is, that whereas St. John never mentions Bartholomew among the apostles, the other three evangelists take no notice of the name of Nathaniel, and constantly put together Philip and Bartholomew, as St. John says, Philip and Nathaniel came together to Christ. After the descent of the Holy Ghost, St. Bartholomew travelled throughout the East, and preached the gospel in India. He returned again to the western part of Asia, and met St. Philip, at Hieropolis, in Phrygia; thence he went to Lycaonia, and after many labors reached a place in Armenia, where preaching to some obstinate idolators, he was crowned with martyrdom. Some historians say that he was crucified; others that he was flayed alive. His feast is kept on the 24th of August.

ST. THOMAS.

The call of St. Thomas, his devotedness to his Divine Master, his incredulity respecting the resurrection, with his admirable profession of faith, have been related in the early part of this book as taken from Holy Scripture. After the descent of the Holy Ghost, St. Thomas preached throughout Parthia. When he had converted many in that kingdom, he preached in other parts of the East, in Media, Persia, and, according to some, in India and Ethiopia. The modern Indians say that St. Thomas preached to the Brachmans, and to the Indians beyond the great island Taprobana, which some take to be Ceylon, others Sumatra. They add that he suffered martyrdom at Meliapor, or St. Thomas's, in the peninsula, this side of the Ganges, on the Coromandel coast, where his body was discovered with marks that he was slain with lances, and the tradition over the East is, that such was the manner of his death. His feast is kept on the 21st of December.

ST. MATTHEW, APOSTLE AND EVANGELIST.

St. Matthew first preached the gospel in Judea; afterwards in the East. He led a very austere life, ate no flesh, but supported nature with roots and herbs. His humility is conspicuous in his gospel, in which, though the other evangelists name him before St. Thomas, he gives that apostle precedence, and adds to his own name the epithet of the publican. He ended his course in Parthia, some say by martyrdom. His feast is kept on the 21st of September.

ST. JAMES THE LESS.

St. James, surnamed the Less, as some think from his stature, was son of Alpheus and Mary, the sister of the Blessed Virgin. After our Lord's Ascension he was appointed Bishop of Jerusalem which see he governed midst perpetual danger from the fury of the people, but with such eminent sanctity that it acquired for him the surname of the Just, and even the Jews reverenced him. He led a most austere life, and so frequent were his prostrations, that the skin of his knees and forehead became as hard as the hoofs of a camel. During a vacancy that occurred between the death of one Roman governor and the arrival of his successor, the High Priest Ananias, son of the famous Annas mentioned in the gospel, took on himself to assemble the Sanhedrim, before which council St. James was accused of violating the Mosaic law and condemned to be stoned, the Jewish manner of executing criminals. Some historians say that they took him up to the battlements of the Temple, and tried to make him renounce his faith; but he addressed the people in different language from what they wanted, publicly and solemnly declaring his faith in Jesus Christ, at which they cried out, "The just man also hath erred," and immediately threw him headlong to the ground. St. James, though much bruised, raised himself on his knees, and lifting up his eyes to heaven, begged of God to pardon his persecutors. The infuriate mob covered him with a shower of stones, and a fuller gave him a blow with his mallet on the head, of which he died. The feast of St. James is kept on the 1st of May.

ST. JUDE, SURNAMED THADDEUS.

St. Jude was brother to St. James the Less. After the descent of the Holy Ghost, he preached throughout Judea, Samaria, Idumea, and Syria, and returned from his missions to Jerusalem after the martyrdom of his brother in the year 52. Some historians say that St. Jude suffered martyrdom in Persia; others say at Ararat, in Armenia, being shot to death with arrows; others add, whilst on a cross. His feast is kept on the 28th of October.

ST. SIMON, SURNAMED THE ZEALOT.

St. Simon is surnamed Zelotes, or the Zealot, to distinguish him from St. Peter and St. Simeon, the brother of St. James the less. He is also called the Canaanean, whence he is supposed to have been born at Cana of Galilee. After his conversion he was exceedingly zealous for the honor of his Divine Master, and showed a pious indignation against those who dishonored their holy faith by the irregularity of their lives. No further mention appears of him in the gospel than that he was adopted by Christ into the college of the apostles, and with the rest received the miraculous gifts of the Holy Ghost. It is said that he preached in Egypt and other parts of Africa; and afterwards in the East, where it is supposed that he was crucified in Suanir, a city of Persia. His feast is kept on the 28th of October.

ST. MATTHIAS.

St. Matthias was elected as before-mentioned to succeed the unhappy Judas. After the descent of the Holy Ghost, he preached the faith in Cappadocia, and on the coasts of the Caspian Sea, residing chiefly near the port Issus. He was remarkable for his mortified austere life, and he must have undergone great hardships among the savage people, who formed the portion of the vineyard allotted to him. He received the crown of martyrdom in Colchis. His feast is kept on the 24th of February.

THE FOUR EVANGELISTS.

The account of two, SS. Matthew and John, has been already given among the apostles.

ST. MARK.

St. Mark was of Jewish extraction, and a disciple of St. Peter. Some historians think he was the John Mark, mentioned in the Acts, and styled by St. Peter his son. At the request of the Romans, he committed to writing what he had learned from the apostle respecting our Divine Lord, for it is asserted by some that he had never seen him. St. Peter revised the work, and approved it, which is probably the reason that St. Mark's gospel was by some attributed to St. Peter. In it the humility of both is conspicuous, inasmuch as neither the high commendation given by our Lord to St. Peter, nor his walking on the water are mentioned; but all the circumstances of his denying his Divine Master are recorded at full length. St. Mark was appointed by St. Peter to the see of Alexandria, where he made a great many converts, but had twice to withdraw from the fury of the populace. At length on the pagan feast of the idol Serapis, they found him offering to God the prayer of the Oblation or the Mass, and seizing him, they dragged him by the feet through the streets, and then cast him into prison. On the following day, the infidels dragged him as before, and while the streets were strewed with pieces of his mangled flesh, he ceased not praising and thanking God for his sufferings, until he happily expired under his torments. His feast is kept on the 25th of April.

ST. LUKE.

St. Luke was a native of Antioch, in Syria, but whether a convert from Judaism or paganism is uncertain. Historians are also divided as to whether he ever saw our Divine Lord or not. St. Luke received a liberal education, and was by profession a physician. He is said to have excelled also in painting, and to have drawn several pictures of Christ and the Blessed Virgin. He accompanied St. Paul in many of his journeys, and shared the labors, dangers, and sufferings of that great apostle who mentions him in his epistles, styling him, "Beloved physician," and "Fellow-laborer." St. Luke wrote his gospel, as he himself assures us, from the relations of those, "who from the beginning were eye-witnesses and ministers of the word." He lived to an advanced age, and according to some, closed his life by martyrdom. Others say, that though he endured many sufferings for the faith, he ended his life in peace. His feast is kept on the 18th of October.

CHRONOLOGICAL TABLE
Of the Principal Events in Sacred History.

FIRST AGE.

	A. C.
Creation of the world	4004
Able killed—aged 128 years	3876
Adam dies—aged 930 years	3074
Seth dies—aged 902 years	2962
Enos dies—aged 905 years	2664
Methusalem dies—aged 969 years	2348

SECOND AGE.

Universal	2348
Tower of Babel	2247
Noah dies—aged 950 years	1998
Abraham born	1996

THIRD AGE.

Call of Abraham	1921
Destruction of Sodom	1897
Birth of Isaac	1896
Birth of Jacob	1836
Joseph sold by his brethren	1729
Jacob goes into Egypt	1706
Birth of Moses	1571

FOURTH AGE.

Law of Moses given	1491
Passage of the Jordan	1451
Gedeon Judge	1245
Samson dies	1117
Samuel Judge	1116
Saul is anointed King	1095
David reigns	1054
Solomon succeeds David	1015

FIFTH AGE.

Temple of Solomon dedicated	1005
The Kingdom divided	980
Roboam, King of Juda	980
Jeroboam, King of Israel	980
The Prophet Elias taken up to Heaven	892
Isaias put to death by Manasse	715

APPENDIX.

	A. C.
The Prophet Jeremiah	629
Captivity of Babylon	608
End of the Kingdom of Juda	587
Daniel the Prophet	555

SIXTH AGE.

End of the Babylonian captivity	533
Dedication of the second Temple	516
Commencement of the seventy weeks	454
Rebuilding of the walls of Jerusalem	442
Alexander enters Jerusalem	322
Version of the Septuagint	281
Persecution at Alexandria	220
Heliodorus chastised for attempting to enter the Temple	176
Persecution of Antiochus	170
The martyrdom of the Machabees	168
Mathathias takes up arms	168
Judas Machabeus becomes leader of the Jews	166
He is victorious over the enemies of his country	162
Death of Antiochus	159
Judas Machabeus is killed in battle	158
Jonathan becomes the leader of the Jews	157
John Hyrcanus assumes the title of King	135
He is succeeded by Aristobulus I.	107
Alexander Janneris reigns	106
Alexander succeeds in	79
Hyrcanus II.	70
The crown usurped by Aristobulus II.	67
Hyrcanus re-established	63
Herod	40

Nativity of our Lord and the Christian era begins.

www.ingramcontent.com/pod-product-compliance
Lightning Source LLC
Chambersburg PA
CBHW030325240426
43673CB00040B/1272